FASCISM

FASCISM

The Career of a Concept

PAUL E. GOTTFRIED

NIU PRESS / *DeKalb*

Northern Illinois University Press, DeKalb 60115
© 2016 by Northern Illinois University Press
All rights reserved
Printed in the United States of America
25 24 23 22 21 20 19 18 17 16   2 3 4 5

978-0-87580-493-4 (cloth)
978-1-60909-183-5 (ebook)

Book and cover design by Shaun Allshouse

Cataloging-in-Publication Data is available online at http://catalog.loc.gov
Library of Congress Control Number: 2015951724

Contents

ACKNOWLEDGMENTS
vii

Introduction
1

Chapter One
Defining Fascism
16

Chapter Two
Totalitarianism and Fascism
42

Chapter Three
Fascism as the Unconquered Past
59

Chapter Four
Fascism as a Movement of the Left
87

Chapter Five
The Failure of Fascist Internationalism
105

Chapter Six
The Search for a Fascist Utopia
129

Chapter Seven
A Vanished Revolutionary Right
151

APPENDIX
Fascism and Modernization
159

A Final Loose End
163

NOTES
175

INDEX
209

Acknowledgments

Among those I would like to thank for reading all or part of this text while it was still in progress are Professors Lee Congdon, Stanley G. Payne, Jeffrey Taylor, Robert Weissberg, Mircea Platon, William B. Newsome, David S. Brown, and Boyd Cathey. All these attentive, knowledgeable readers provided useful suggestions for improving my manuscript, and I benefited from their advice enormously in doing revisions. I should also express gratitude to my wife, Mary, for saving me from the consequences of my computer ignorance. Each time I lost a draft of my evolving text, she managed to retrieve it from some mysterious computer wasteland. Without her kindly assistance, this book would not be at the point of being inflicted upon you, the reader. I would also like to acknowledge the help furnished by the efficient staff of Northern Illinois University Press in bringing my project to completion. Their cooperation and skills were evident throughout the production process.

Finally, I should mention an irritant without which this book would not have been conceived. While listening to TV and reading newspapers from both here and western Europe, I noticed that news reporter and news interpreter referred to what displeased them as "fascist" or "playing with fascism." Most of these references had nothing to do with the historic phenomenon known as fascism and were instead attempts to excite the audience by linking the speaker's or the writer's current peeve to some long-ago unpleasantness. This semantic abuse seemed to be so widespread that when a friend (who is now, unfortunately, deceased) suggested that I write about it, I proceeded to do exactly that. Although I doubt the appearance of this book will have any effect in lessening the abuse in question, my reaction to the misuse of the term *fascism* caused me to undertake an ambitious task that would not likely have been begun without the stimulant described.

Introduction

The Uses and Abuses of *Fascism*: The Career of a Concept

This study will examine the semantic twists and turns undergone by the word *fascism* since the 1930s. Like other terms that have changed their meaning, such as *conservatism* and *liberalism*, *fascism* has been applied so arbitrarily that it may be difficult to deduce what it means without knowing the mindset of the speaker. Fascism now stands for a host of iniquities that progressives, multiculturalists, and libertarians all oppose, even if they offer no single, coherent account of what they're condemning. Some intellectuals and publicists may be demonstratively antifascist but feel no obligation to provide a historically and conceptually delimited definition of their object of hate.

Certain factors have contributed to this imprecision, perhaps most of all the equation of all fascisms with Nazism and Adolf Hitler's efforts to exterminate European Jewry, subjugate Slavs, and conquer the Eurasian landmass. This equation has come from serious historians as well as partisan publicists. German intellectual and cultural historian Ernst Nolte famously characterized Nazism as "radical fascism" while insisting that German National Socialism resembled conceptually more generic forms of fascism. All fascisms, according to Nolte, have the same characteristics, which can be uncovered by selectively adapting the Marxist analysis of the revolutionary Right. Fascist movements were "counterrevolutionary imitations of leftist revolution" that developed as reactions to the danger of leftist upheavals.[1]

In the German case, this counterrevolutionary development became particularly nasty since it was a reaction to Stalinist communism that took over the murderous policies of its adversary. It was the physical proximity of the Soviet communist experiment, the detailed knowledge of Stalin's crimes in interwar Germany, and the disproportionate role of Jews in advancing the Soviet cause that contributed to the virulence of German "radical fascism."[2]

Nolte, however, became a moving target for the academic and journalistic establishment in Germany when he denied the "uniqueness" (*Einzigartigkeit*) of Nazi tyranny. In his writings he compared Hitlerism to other brutal anticommunist dictatorships. But this indiscretion had an unintended effect on Nolte, who served the cause of antifascist activists by making a linkage between fascism and Nazism.[3] The multicultural Left happily accepted this equation because it justified their attack on their opponents as Nazis and not simply generic fascists. Why restrict oneself to one accusation when it is possible to kill two birds with one stone?

A second factor that has contributed to muddying the concept of fascism is the rise of a post-Marxist Left. We are speaking here about a Left that is no longer guided by Marx's socioeconomic critique of capitalism but that expresses predominantly cultural opposition to bourgeois society and its Christian and/or national components. This latest outgrowth of the Left, which has replaced an older Left, has come to transform our politics and culture in the wake of the breakdown of the Soviet Empire, the disintegration of European communism, and the rise of movements devoted to expressive freedom and lifestyle liberation. The new liberation has carried a price, namely the construction of institutions designed to fight discrimination and eradicate opposition to what is seen as a privileged form of self-expression. Those who stand in the way of social change and whose "bigotry" must be addressed are conveniently dismissed in western Europe as "fascist," an epithet that has an added value because it is no longer associated with state corporatism and other now widely ignored but once-essential features of fascism. Calling someone a fascist today means that he or she is a Nazi.

A distinguished professor of sociology at Boston University has objected to my practice of putting quotation marks around *fascism* in my books and articles. Allegedly I sympathize with an inexpressibly evil movement but am trying to conceal this perverse taste. I may even resemble those academics who could never find a real communist anywhere, as opposed to agrarian reformers or impassioned civil rights activists who were mistakenly branded as communists. In a similarly evasive manner, I have refused to admit that some wayward dictator was a real fascist, as opposed to a well-meaning general seeking to maintain order.[4]

My actual motives are different. I am certainly no fan of a corporatist nationalist economy; nor do I yearn to see teenagers in black shirts saluting maximalist leaders with medal-covered chests. Rather, I think the term *fascist* has a specific historical meaning and should not be hurled at anyone who holds what are now unpopular opinions. As a historic phenomenon, fascism has nothing to do with advocating an isolationist foreign policy, trying to restrict Third World immigration, or favoring significant income redistribution in order to achieve greater social equality. I mention these associations because all of them are characteristic of recent, divergent attempts to identify fascism with whatever the speaker happens to dislike—and then belaboring his or her target with the accusation of sympathizing with Nazi atrocities. I also deny that I am trying to exculpate Muslim terrorists or European politicians who offend the media simply because I decline to call them fascists. Rather, I refuse to mislabel political actors as representing an ideology that has mostly come and gone.

Fortunately the abuse of the term *fascist* has not retarded scholarship on the real article. Since the 1960s, seminal works have appeared on various aspects of European fascism, such as Renzo De Felice's multi-volume study of the genesis and evolution of Italian fascism; Zeev Sternhell's investigation of the pre–World War I antecedents of French fascism; Ernst Nolte's *Der Faschismus in seiner Epoche* (misleadingly translated as *Three Faces of Fascism*); Pío Moa's, Stanley Payne's, and Arnaud Imatz's works on the Spanish Falange and the Spanish Civil War; and Eugen Weber's provocative analysis of the Iron Guard.[5]

One should also mention here the voluminous studies of such fascism scholars as Roger Griffith and A. James Gregor.[6] Both these historians have analyzed the modernizing aspects of fascist movements, and Gregor in particular has explored to what extent interwar Italian fascism provided a model of ruling that could be transferred to non-Western societies and later time periods. Such authors (and there are others) testify to the possibility of doing serious research on what has become in popular literature and newspaper editorials a free-floating accusation. Although work is still proceeding in fascist studies, this may become less and less the case if further politicization occurs. Examinations of fascism operate on two levels: a scholarly one that remains isolated from partisan causes, and a journalistic one that is less refined but may be gaining ground. Unfortunately, many of the best fascism interpreters are well on in years or no longer alive.

The Spanish historian Pío Moa was widely celebrated in the Spanish media and in academic circles when he was still a self-described Maoist. Moa, however, became a nonperson when he began writing studies that suggested that the Spanish Falange (and the rest of the Spanish Right) committed far fewer atrocities during the Spanish Civil War and in the period leading up to it than the anarchists and communists. Indeed, the worst orgies of violence during that strife—including the rape and murder of clergy and the desecration and dynamiting of churches and holy sites—came from the Spanish Left. Moreover, before the Spanish nationalists launched their uprising in July 1936, according to Moa, the Left had been on the point of overthrowing the republic three times after losing key elections.[7] Although Moa and Payne do not whitewash violent Spanish fascists, they do demonstrate, to the consternation of establishment historians throughout the West, that the revolutionary nationalists were less impulsive in their savagery than their enemies. Not all fascists were "radical fascists," if one might use Nolte's term, in the German mold.

This monograph will trace the evolution of fascism's polemical function within the context of our own ideological struggles. Although a development that was already underway during the Second World War, ideological antifascism gained momentum with the rise of the present, post-Marxist Left. Next to the present Left's manipulation of historical labels, the attempts made by Marxists in the past to arrive at an understanding of fascism look like rigorous analysis. We may credit Marxists in the interwar period for their often carefully researched explanation for fascism's emergence and development. Chapter 1 notes that it was the Marxist Left, far more than the pro-capitalist and European liberal side or the monarchist Right, that devised the first causal explanation for fascism in its time. The Marxists offered a socioeconomic explanation rather than a moral attack on fascist movements, particularly in central and eastern Europe. The task then fell to others to come up with plausible alternative explanations.

The focus of chapter 2 is treatments of fascism that were present in post–World War II discussions of totalitarianism. This framework of discussion was based on making a sharp distinction between the totalist and exterminatory character of the Nazi dictatorship in Germany and garden-variety fascisms, which have sometimes been categorized as "authoritarian regimes." The idea advanced here was that Nazi tyranny resembled Stalin's rule more than it did other anticommunist national revolutions, such as Benito Mussolini's prolonged, erratic rule. Certain political developments contributed to the rise of this perspective in the 1950s, such as the onset of the Cold War, the integration of the German Federal Republic into the Western alliance system, and widespread recognition of the murderous history of the Soviet regime that had been hidden or played down during the Second World War.

Although political factors contributed to the success of the totalitarian model, they were not the only reasons for its acceptance. This particular model of totalitarianism took into account the difference in destructive character between the Nazis and other less vicious, less anti-Christian fascist movements such as Austrian clerical fascism and the Spanish Falange. The exponents of the once-prevalent totalitarian model, such as the disillusioned communist Franz Borkenau and the German Jewish exile Hannah Arendt, focused on the striking overlaps between Nazi and Soviet rule. Decades before Ernst Nolte raised his comparison between the Soviets and the Nazis, former communists were stressing Hitler's repeated borrowing from the techniques of Stalin's reign of terror, including the creation of concentration camps.[8]

A final factor that may have contributed to the longtime success of identifying garden-variety fascism with authoritarian structures was the scholarly work that came out of this research. Here one might mention the former Yale Sterling Professor of Political Science Juan L. Linz, who, in *Totalitarian and Authoritarian Regimes*, distinguishes between what he deems as conventional personalist regimes and such grim governments as Hitler's and Stalin's. Linz views authoritarian regimes as transitional or temporary ones that are dependent on leader figures, the favor of the military, and obsolescing social classes.[9]

By contrast, totalitarian regimes do not recognize independent social space and established communities. Thus, explains Linz, Hitler decided against incorporating specific aspects of organic democracy, such as vocational councils or updated estates that exercised real power, which the traditional interwar Right was keen on, because it would have removed power from the *Führer* and his confidants. Although Linz misses no opportunity to affirm his liberal democratic missionary spirit, he does recognize that there are degrees of evil attached to regimes that he finds unacceptable. He underscores the "distinctiveness of totalitarianism" while describing "the whole range of non-democratic and anti-liberal regimes and the differences among them." Linz also quotes the warning of the Italian socialist political theorist Norberto Bobbio in 1996: "we cannot attribute the characterization of 'fascism' to whatever authoritarian regime. There are dictatorships of a military nature, which insofar as they are autocratic regimes are also opposed to democratic regimes, but they are not fascist."[10]

The focus of chapter 3 will be the fading of the totalitarian model under the assault of protest movements arising predominantly on the Left. German "antifascists," Cold War neutralists, communist apologists, and Jewish and Christian groups stressing the unique evil of the Nazi Holocaust objected to the likening of Nazi to Soviet tyranny and failed to recognize that fascism was more reprehensible than communism. Although one might criticize some aspects of the totalitarian model—for example, by noting that Nazism was at least as murderous as Soviet communism but not as economically and culturally controlling—such analytic criticisms were not primarily responsible for the paradigm change. The pressure of political and cultural opposition and the unexpected collapse of the Soviet Empire led to this interpretive shift. But even before Soviet rule came crashing down, the totalitarian model fell under attack for allegedly overestimating the enormity of Stalin's crimes and/or for understating Nazi evils. And even when there was recognition of Soviet enormities, these crimes were ascribed to Stalin's cult of personality but never allowed to cast doubt on the nobility of the communist experiment. Advocates of this position contrasted "Stalinist centralization and fascist oppression" with "democratic socialism." Generic fascism became identified with Stalin and Hitler while every new communist revolution was depicted as offering the hope of "democratic socialism."[11]

The focus of chapter 4 is on how the now-widespread view of fascism as a movement that embraces both Nazism and all "right wing" ideas has fallen out of favor. According to this interpretation, which has gained traction in Germany and western Europe, communism was always an ally in good standing in the struggle against the racist, anti-Semitic Right. Any expression of anticommunist sentiment among the German intelligentsia typically elicits charges of being sympathetic to fascism and refusing to acknowledge the extraordinary evils of the German past. Not surprisingly, Christian Democratic German Chancellor Angela Merkel traveled to Moscow several years ago on the occasion of a celebration of Russia's victory in the Second World War to thank the Red Army for "liberating my country from fascism."[12]

Although Merkel had supported the German Democratic Republic until shortly before its collapse, she later became the head of what is considered to be the center-right party in Germany. Her obeisance to East Germany's former Soviet masters caused her no noticeable problems in gaining control over her party and rising to the political top in the German Federal Republic. Merkel represents the now-dominant view in Germany that fascism equals Nazism and that Stalin "liberated" Germany in the Second World War. The mass rapes and murders committed by the Red Army and the subsequent despotism imposed on the eastern and central parts of Germany by the Soviets are no longer relevant. They have been airbrushed out of the antifascist account of modern history.

It would be impossible to truly understand this interpretation of fascism without taking into account the Frankfurt School. According to Critical Theorists who, in interwar Germany, set out to combine a Marxist revolutionary alternative to bourgeois capitalist culture with a Freudian understanding of sexual repression, fascism was the outgrowth of an unreconstructed repressive society based on "authoritarianism." In the anthology *The Authoritarian Personality* (1950), put together by two leading representatives of the Frankfurt School in exile in the United States, Theodor Adorno and Max Horkheimer, there is both a far-reaching commentary on American life and sweeping proposals for addressing the fascist peril.[13] It was not enough, according to these social theorists, to have parliamentary forms of government in order to avert psychic and political tyranny. It was also necessary to enact sweeping socioeconomic change, together with a reconstruction of family and gender relations, to stave off a fascist triumph. Wherever sexual repression, gender inequities, homophobia, and inequitable distribution of income are allowed to endure, there supposedly exists a fertile ground for fascism. This evil must be understood, or so the Frankfurt School argued, as a planned reaction to the Left's attempt to erect an erotically fulfilled, socialist society.

The Authoritarian Personality came out one year before another voluminous assessment of the recent past was published by a Jewish exile and member of the German Left, *Origins of Totalitarianism* by Hannah Arendt. Unlike Frankfurt School exiles, Arendt was not interested in fascism as such but rather was preoccupied with the peculiarities of German and Russian totalitarianism. When she defined Italian fascism, she treated it almost dismissively as "an ordinary nationalist dictatorship developed logically from a multiparty democracy."[14] In contradistinction to the Frankfurt School, Arendt never claimed to be discovering a fascist epidemic sweeping across the capitalist West. She focused instead on the related evils of Nazism and Soviet communism under Stalin.

The focus of chapter 4 will be definitions of fascism that have gained currency among its "democratic capitalist" foes. Although less popular than those that have issued from the antifascist Left, these generalizations may be just as ideologically driven. In the 1930s American critics of the New Deal drew comparisons between FDR's fashioning of an American welfare state and Italian fascism. A juxtaposing that surfaced in the censures of John T. Flynn, A. J. Nock, Friedrich Hayek, and other opponents of the new managerial state, it was not entirely without foundation. Roosevelt, his advisor Rexford Tugwell, those who wrote for the social democratic *New Republic,* and other advocates of centralized state power in the United States looked to Mussolini's Italy as a paradigm for reform.[15] They quoted freely from the Italian Fascist *Carta del Lavoro,* promulgated in 1927, which called for a corporate state in which managers were workers by another name.

The later friendship agreement between Hitler and Mussolini in 1936 and Mussolini's sending of troops to the Nationalist side in the Spanish Civil War caught his American admirers by surprise and led to a revision of their favorable opinion. Nonetheless, the pro–free enterprise American Right continued to see fascism, and to some extent Nazism, as a revolutionary leftist force; even the attempts made by the American government to aid the English side at the beginning of World War II were interpreted by its critics as bringing fascism to America.[16]

Far from Nazi sympathizers, many isolationists, including those who belonged to the anti–New Deal Right, were terrified of "fascism." They saw it as taking root in the United States in an activist, interventionist government, and they generally did not believe that fascism was a reactionary or counterrevolutionary force. These considerations are pertinent for explaining the recent sales success of Jonah Goldberg's *Liberal Fascism* (2009), a work that reprises some of the same assumptions about European politics that prevailed among anti–New Dealers eighty years ago.

A widely featured star of the Murdoch Media Empire and syndicated Republican columnist, Goldberg goes after Democratic politicians who, according to him, are pursuing economic and social policies similar to those of Mussolini and Hitler. Programs aimed at American youth are compared to Mussolini's *Balilla* and the *Hitlerjugend*, and American public works proposals are seen as derivative of or closely related to fascist and Nazi plans of the 1930s.[17] After hundreds of pages of these often strained comparisons between fascist and Democratic orators, it is hard to miss the point: if Democratic partisans in Hollywood have gone after Republicans as fascists, then the other party should be allowed to play the same game.

Goldberg's partisan attack is far from convincing. The early American critics who made the comparisons in question were looking at the way political actors defined themselves: American New Dealers and their social democratic allies were praising the Italian fascist model while establishing an American welfare state. One cannot recall the last time the Obama administration extolled either Mussolini or Hitler when trying to bail out the Obama administration's supporters. Goldberg's application of the fascist branding iron has its origin in intermural politics. It is part of a game in which the advocates of one party cast aspersions on those of the other. Modern industrial democracies have huge welfare states that the major parliamentary blocs (there are usually two) accept as a given. If we wish to condemn one of the two institutionalized parties as "fascist" for building and sustaining a large administrative state, then why not make the same judgment about the other? Nowhere does Goldberg suggest that he would rescind the "fascist" handiwork that he attributes to the Democrats before the election of Obama. And for a good reason! By now that handiwork belongs as much to his party as it does to the opposition.

The focus of chapter 5 will be the exploration of various efforts, which were particularly noticeable from the mid-1920s into the 1930s, to define fascism as an international movement. Although the decision of fascist Italy to invade Ethiopia in 1936 and then Mussolini's rallying to Nazi Germany weakened the internationalist tendency advanced by Italian fascist theorists and publicists, these developments did not stifle their initiative entirely. Fascist internationalists, like Asvero Gravelli, continued to play up the pan-European significance of the Italian fascist movement and make what became politically inexpedient distinctions between this original Latin fascist model and the degraded form that it took in Nazi Germany. Fascist internationalists also drew invidious distinctions (according to Mussolini) between fascism as a movement and the routinized governance (*tran tran*) into which the Italian fascist state had collapsed after Mussolini's consolidation of power. It was hoped that the transformation of Italian fascism into a vehicle for national revolution outside of Italy would lead to a reinvigoration of fascism as a "permanent revolution" at home.

The focus of chapter 5 will be an explanation of why these efforts at launching a fascist internationalism were doomed from the outset. In this chapter, I will look at explanations for this failure beyond those that have been typically stressed in the past, such as the disastrous results of fascist movements becoming associated with Nazi Germany and the cynical, inconsistent fashion in which Mussolini promoted the internationalist potential of Italian fascism. In chapter 5 I will also emphasize the peculiarly Latin Catholic character of generic fascism, which was an essential property despite the fact that the Catholic content was tainted by heresy. Generic fascism of the kind that Italian fascist internationalists were propagating traveled badly in Protestant countries with traditions of orderly constitutional government. The Italian import became a sideshow in England, despite the frenetic attempts made by a prominent political leader, Oswald Mosley, to promote it in his homeland. Finally, the fascists could not offer a credible internationalist doctrine because they were wedded to the idea of organic nationalism, which they placed in opposition to leftist internationalism. It was almost impossible for fascists to occupy these two divergent positions in a plausible manner. It was equally hard for them to present themselves as advocates of permanent revolution when much of their appeal beyond Italy was based on the view of them as the party of order.

In chapter 6 I will examine a question that is also taken up in chapter 7, which discusses fascism as a vanished revolutionary Right. In both chapters, I approach from different angles the question of whether fascism features a utopian vision that approximates that of the Left. This much-vexed historical problem has not yielded consensus among serious scholars. In the 1990s Ernst Nolte and François Furet debated the question of whether fascism presented its followers with a compelling picture of the future. Unlike Nolte, Furet insisted that fascism featured such a view, although it was strikingly different from the modified, messianic-age vision of the Left. It was based on the triumph of the most powerful nation in a struggle for world domination among rival peoples. And part of the attraction of this vision was that it stood in grim opposition to any vision that emanated from the revolutionary Left. Furet assumed a fierce, bloody competition among rival historical views in which each resonated with its respective adherents in interwar Europe.[18]

A more interesting understanding of a fascist utopianism springs from the work of the Italian philosopher Augusto Del Noce, who stresses the overlap between the Marxist and fascist historical visions. Del Noce maintains that the fascists were not only inspired by the revolutionary Left but took over the Left's concept of progress, with certain modifications. When Italian fascists spoke of building a new age of the world, commencing with Mussolini's March on Rome in 1922, they were not simply expressing nostalgia for past Latin glory: they believed themselves to be living in a modern society that looked forward to a new political order that was not parasitic on Roman symbols and Roman notions of authority. Fascists considered themselves the beneficiaries of the Italian democratic revolutionaries of the nineteenth century, and it was their destiny to erect a state-of-the-art regime that differed equally from old-fashioned Italian principalities and corrupt liberal parliamentary administrations.[19] They also incorporated the secularizing tendencies that had become decisive in the West starting with the Enlightenment, and fascists proposed, however tentatively, a post-Christian vision heavily shaped by science and religious skepticism. Like Marxism and scientific positivism, according to Del Noce, fascism was a contender in trying to establish a post-Christian faith shaped by the Enlightenment.

The polar opposite view was expressed by Nolte, namely, that fascists were "escaping transcendence" as the form of history preached by the Left. In place of this secularized millenarianism, fascists offered the prospect of struggle that would culminate in a hardened human type and, in the near term, the defeat of an internationalist leftist adversary.[20] Fascism proposed a naturalistic explanation of human nature and politics, which was dictated by the historical situation that the fascists faced.[21] They were opposing an ideology that was predicated on global transformation, and so fascists countered it with an anti-utopian anthropology that was intended to depict people as they actually were—that is, combative and in need of authority, as opposed to how the Left might have wished to see the human race. In contrast to their foes, fascists were focused on a mythic past in which they saw their mission prefigured.

This, however, did not prevent national movements from inclining toward fascism without necessarily embracing fascism's picture of the future. Not all fascist sympathizers shared the pessimistic perspective that Nolte ascribes to his subjects. Interwar nationalists may have been drawn to what they perceived as an alternative to leftist internationalism without giving any thought to "escaping transcendence" or privileging naturalistic interpretations of political struggles. It is also necessary, even while recognizing the essentially anti-utopian character of fascism, to notice its persistent exhortations to its adherents to work for a brighter future. Unrelievedly gloomy pictures of what was to come would not have excited its followers to heroic action, particularly if they thought that what awaited them was endless struggle. In any case a vigorous debate continues to unfold about how fascist theorists and the founders of fascist parties conceived of the future and their movement's role within it.

In chapter 8 I will also underline the relation between the fascist vision of history and what made the fascist movement essentially right wing. Although distinct from the traditional Right and far more prone to violence than European conservatism, fascism and an older Right shared overlapping characteristics. Both rejected the ideas that human nature could be changed through progressive government policies, that all human beings were capable of governing themselves and should possess the same human rights, and that the future would be characterized by a self-improved humanity. Fascists were not unique in holding these views, which were equally operative in traditional conservatism. What set fascism apart from the conservative tradition were two historical factors. Fascism arose after a traditional aristocratic society had either collapsed or was on its way out; therefore, it was necessary for the fascists to reconstruct a hierarchy and structure of authority in the absence or weakening of the kind of society that classical conservatism wanted to preserve.

Further, while conservatism sought to defend or bring back an order that was identified with an ideal past, fascists promoted a cult of the coup d'état. This went back partly to the immediate past and the poet-adventurer Gabriele D'Annunzio, whose attempted takeover of Fiume from Allied control in 1919 was sometimes regarded as a model for later fascist seizures of power.

Fascism would be unthinkable without its cult of violence, which drew on the reflections of the French anarchist Georges Sorel and on those who prefigured and helped plan Mussolini's March on Rome. In this respect the fascists were not only unlike traditional conservatives but also distinct from traditional men of the authoritarian Right such as Francisco Franco and Antonio Salazar. They belonged to a revolutionary Right in the sense that they planned to take power by force, and they viewed this exercise of force as a redemptive act. The violence that would lead to the anticipated fascist overthrow would precipitate a break from a decadent present, one marked by false internationalism and corrupt party rule. Although fascists may not have been true social revolutionaries, they nonetheless reveled in the prospect of overthrowing whatever political authority blocked their ascent. But this tendency could not be expressed equally by fascists everywhere. In England, for example, those in the local fascist movement accepted parliamentary elections as the path by which they would have to try to come to power.

Lest any confusion arise about what I am offering in this book, it may be appropriate to state at the beginning what I do not furnish. As the reader will soon discover, this work is not entirely sequential. Anyone looking for a step-by-step demonstration of a single thesis would do well to consult another source. What follows in this study is bounded by reference points but does not develop an argument by progressing from point A to point Z. Rather, what is herein presented proceeds as a collection of studies dealing with various interpretations of fascism from the time fascist movements became a historical force in the 1920s. It became obvious while writing this volume that my chapters could not be fitted into a tightly structured framework. There were too many loose ends left as I tried to configure this work, and in the end I decided to offer my chapters as discrete studies rather than as the demonstration of a premise that is steadily developed from beginning to end.

A source of thematic unity in this work that one may perceive in retrospect concerns the authors who are treated here. Among foremost interpreters of fascism and Nazism that I pay special attention to in this book are Stanley Payne, Renzo De Felice, Zeev Sternhell, Hannah Arendt, Rainer Zitelmann, and A. James Gregor. This study also deals to a lesser extent with such other worthies as Roger Griffin, Robert Paxton, Juan Linz, Arnaud Imatz, Emilio Gentile, Erik von Kuehnelt-Leddihn, Augusto Del Noce, and Bertrand de Jouvenel. Although these authors have all influenced my work, the historian who shaped my thinking on fascism the most decisively is Ernst Nolte. If Nolte's presence haunts these essays, the reason is not that I believe he is more learned or more diligent than other interpreters of fascism. Most of the other scholars herein discussed write more lucidly and have made fewer gaffes in defending their arguments. If I argue for Nolte more often than for Gregor, it is not because I think that Nolte does more scrupulous archival research or necessarily understands the details of Italian fascism better. Rather, I think he understands the big picture better than a more methodical researcher like Gregor. Nolte excels at what the Germans call *Anschauung*. His intuitive grasp of the nature of fascism is his strongest selling point.

I should note, however, that exploring historical problems is not the same as doing simple addition or subtraction. There are no definitive answers for historians beyond the acceptance of verified factual information; so even if some explanations seem more convincing than others, one may learn as much from those with whom one tentatively disagrees as from those whose conclusions one tentatively accepts. Equally important to note is the fact that people may agree on historical conclusions while arriving at them for entirely different reasons, not all of which are shaped by one's research data or by an equal openness to where a historical problem leads. Nolte and today's antifascist activists arrive at the same view about fascism being a disguised movement of the Right while Gregor and some contemporary political journalists, by contrast, assign fascism, together with Communism, to the Left. Not all of those who take one side or the other are equally scholarly or equally informative, and whether one accepts or rejects the conclusions of a particular interpreter should count for less than the quality of what that writer brings to his subject. It may therefore matter less in a study of this type that I lean toward the conclusions of Nolte than that I respect some of his critics equally.

Given the format of my text, I felt free to add a long appendix dealing with two interpretations of fascism that I examined after the others discussed in this volume. These interpretations seemed worth presenting because they offer original arguments, one about the literary and cultural preconditions of European fascism and the other about the revolutionary, modernizing thrust of Nazism. The two authors who are discussed in this final section, Rainer Zitelmann and Roger Griffin, view fascism as an interwar phenomenon. Neither would suggest that either the fascists or the Nazis still bestride the European political stage. Zitelmann contends that the Nazis achieved modernizing feats of such importance in the 1930s that they prepared Germany for the postwar age both economically and socially. Zitelmann deals only parenthetically with generic fascists but presumably regards them as less innovative, less socially radical, and certainly less murderous than their partial imitators in Germany. Griffin stresses the pervasive influence of modernism as an art form in the fashioning of a fascist world view. It was the combination of this artistic achievement with ultranationalist sentiments in interwar Europe that spawned fascist movements, most notably those that emerged in Latin cultures. Griffin's work highlights a fascist aesthetic in showing the interpenetration of art and politics in the attraction of fascism as a movement.

One perceptive reader of this text has noticed that my illustrations of fascism in political practice are extremely limited and center almost entirely on Mussolini's regime. This was not an oversight. There are just no other examples of generic fascism in practice that this author and other researchers on my subject have been able to come up with. If one discounts clerical fascist regimes, such as the ones briefly tried by Engelbert Dollfuss in Austria during the interwar years and Antonio Salazar's New Order in Portugal, which were essentially Catholic authoritarian governments, and the puppet governments imposed on conquered countries by Nazi Germany, it is hard to think of real examples of fascism in practice beyond interwar Italy.

The Nazis ran a highly eclectic totalitarian operation, which borrowed from fascism as well as Stalinism and, perhaps most of all, from Hitler's feverish imagination. Although experiments such as Juan Peron's rule in Argentina borrowed features of European fascist movements when fascism seemed in season, they also drew from other anti-American forces, often for decorative effect. Authoritarian military leaders like Francisco Franco and Ion Antonescu made expedient pacts with homegrown fascist movements but were delighted to dump these allies at the first opportunity. Nor should readers be swayed by efforts to tar governments that journalists disapprove of as "fascist." Although certain regimes may not enjoy media approval, this hardly attests to their fascist pedigree.

As a young, impressionable person, I was told by a family friend that an opera singer whose voice I greatly admired had become a "fascist." When I asked whether this singer was a devotee of Mussolini or José Antonio, I was told that the opera singer had recently converted to Catholicism. Our family friend, who was a militant atheist, equated a singer's religious conversion with an affirmation of the most extreme form of fascist enthusiasm. The same kind of rhetorical overkill is present in a dossier in the French news magazine *Courrier International* (December 2014), which offers this headline summary: "With his iron arm turned against the Western democracies, the master of the Kremlin preaches a model of society inherited in direct line from Germany and Italy in the 1930s."[22]

A scholar reading this news story would have trouble figuring out what it is exactly that makes Putin a "fascist" as opposed to a traditional Russian expansionist and defender of the Russian Orthodox faith. An apparently clinching proof, which turns out to be no proof at all, is that Marine LePen, who heads the rightist Front National, states that Putin is "conscious that we're defending the same values, which are the values of European civilization."[23] Other putative evidence for Putin's "fascism" is that he has cracked down on clandestine immigration and has openly scorned gay rights. Up until about thirty years ago, one could easily imagine Putin's "fascist" stands being taken by American leaders without an international news magazine feeling free to characterize them as "fascists." Fascism in practice is something other than failing to keep up with social changes introduced long after the Second World War.

Finally, I am not claiming that this book is based on new archival research. A mountain of monographs and published documents on the history of fascism and, in particular, European fascist movements already exists, and it would be difficult to come up with entirely original research in a field that has already been extensively and intensively investigated. What this work does offer inter alia is a classification and examination of already published studies. Further, the several chapters will attempt to contextualize interpretations of fascism that became popular at different times, often in response to changing political climates. This study will also attempt to judge relevant writers in terms of how well they have conducted their investigations. If the impression is thereby created that greater truth is not necessarily achieved the farther one moves from one's object of study, this impression is most definitely intended.

Contrary to an assumption that arose in the nineteenth century, objectivity is not necessarily more available to those who stand at a greater distance from the events and personalities they are treating. Certain historical events and movements (and there are many) become more controversial as they recede temporally because they engage partisan passions more intensely as we move away from them. This perception impressed itself on me with increasing force as I worked on this book. I noticed how comments about fascism dating from the 1940s and 1950s sometimes seemed more convincing than interpretations published at later times. For example, I discovered that Hannah Arendt's distinctions between Nazism and what is here described as "generic fascism" were perfectly plausible, although Arendt arrived at her conclusions in the 1940s, as someone who was personally and emotionally involved in the epoch under consideration. But there is no reason to believe that those authors who followed Arendt were more objective or less encumbered by political passions. History is of immediate practical interest to political partisans, and this affinity has allowed a contentious activity to be sometimes grossly abused. In the case of fascism, as a continuing epithet in journalism and political debate, this observation seems especially true.

CHAPTER ONE

Defining Fascism

Is There a Fascist Idea or System?

Certain conceptual problems inevitably arise for anyone trying to understand fascism. First, there is the question of fascism's essential character—that is, whether fascist movements and fascist programs exhibit a coherent, uniform content. Can one define fascism in any place and at any time in terms of a consistent body of ideas, as opposed to a mere reaction against movements or ideologies that the fascists were resisting? That is a question that has sometimes divided scholars and has been asked repeatedly ever since Mussolini's followers marched on Rome in October 1922, in order to force the Italian king to elevate their leader to the post of Italian premier. Except for its vague corporatist principles, rhetorical appeals to Italian national destiny, and the willingness to take up arms against the revolutionary Left, Mussolini's movement was at least initially a mystery to most observers. Since Mussolini and others in his movement had been formerly identified with the far Left, it was not clear that despite their battles with socialists and anarchists in northern Italy, fascists were of the Right.

The most prominent German historian of fascism, Ernst Nolte, has characterized the fascist movements of the interwar years as a "counterrevolutionary imitation of the revolutionary Left." Although not a Marxist, even if he leaned toward being one in his youth,[1] like the Marxists, Nolte treats fascism as a counterrevolutionary strategy that reacted to a leftist challenge.[2]

According to this view, fascism had no autonomous existence apart from the critical situation that gave rise to it. It was inseparably related to the interwar period and to the threat to the bourgeois order that then existed. That threat came from Italian socialists and Italian anarchists, whom the fascist *squadristi* were organized after the First World War to combat, or, in Germany, from the communists and their Jewish backers, whom the Nazis and their supporters claimed to be fighting.

According to Nolte, the fascists absorbed the disruptive tactics and revolutionary élan of their leftist enemies in order to vanquish them. Outside of interwar confrontations, moreover, it would be hard to understand the successes of European fascism. Although fascists could claim a multifarious genealogy going back to nineteenth-century counterrevolutionaries, critics of rationalism, and even Italian futurists, its ideology was contrived to lend credibility to a movement of resistance. Unlike Marxism and Christianity, fascism was an essentially reactive movement, and its oppositional nature could be grasped most clearly by looking at its "escape from transcendence."[3] Fascists rejected a *leitmotiv* that appeared in Christian theology and throughout the revolutionary Left, namely, that human beings could be morally transformed and raised above their natural condition to become more fully human or less beastlike. The fascists exalted what was primordially collectivist, or biologically rooted, and in the end pieced together a counter-vision to the teachings of their enemies.

In the 1990s, Nolte held conversations with French (and French Revolution) historian François Furet about whether fascism was, in Nolte's judgment, "a purely secondary phenomenon" relative to the Left. Furet dwelled on the distance between fascism and "the counterrevolutionary ideas of the nineteenth century," which pointed backward toward the prerevolutionary past. At an earlier time, according to Furet, fascism was "an idea of the future" that could inspire the young to action.

When Hitler entered Vienna in 1938 and Paris in June 1940, or when Mussolini's followers marched on Rome to inaugurate a national revolution, fascism gave the appearance of being a movement that looked toward a new age.[4] In December 1934 the Italian government sponsored a Fascist International Congress in Montreux, Switzerland, which focused on the "universality of the fascist idea." This week-long conference, which was partly a tribute to the creative genius of Benito Mussolini, drew participants from across Europe. Such enthusiasm, Furet says, could not have surged forth if fascism were a purely secondary, or "reactive," force. Those who rallied to the "fascist idea," however they defined it, saw themselves, no less than the Left, as being in the vanguard of history.[5]

By the mid-1930s millions of Europeans welcomed fascist movements extending across the continent, from the British Union of Fascists, founded by Sir Oswald Mosley in 1932, and the Irish Blueshirts to the Romanian Iron Guard, the Polish Falanga, and the Finnish Lapua. This is not even to count non-European groups that were brushed by fascist ideology, like Marcus Garvey's Back to Africa movement in the United States and the Zionist Betar, whose founder, Vladimir Jabotinsky, was a longtime admirer of Mussolini.[6] The onetime popularity of fascist thinking, whether inspired by the German or Italian example, suggests that it was something that could not be dismissed as a "secondary phenomenon" in the political culture of the interwar period.[7]

With due respect to both sides in this extended debate, it is entirely possible for a self-proclaimed reactive force to elicit mass enthusiasm and to be considered by its followers as speaking for the future. If one imagines that a leader or movement has saved one's country from a disastrous course, say, succumbing to Marxist internationalism, then one might applaud a person or group credited with that achievement, even if one's benefactor does not offer a rigorously worked-out picture of human history.

In *The Last European War: September 1939–December 1941*, John Lukacs evokes the often ecstatic enthusiasm that the Third Reich encountered as its armies rolled across western Europe. Although Lukacs may exaggerate the European-wide mass support that the Nazis enjoyed when they were still in the ascendance, quite possibly their well-wishers endorsed them for the reasons that Nolte gives in *Der europäische Bürgerkrieg* (*The European Civil War*): the fascists, including their more savage Nazi cousins, were perceived as the enemies of the Bolsheviks and the Jewish allies of international Marxism. They were thought to be standing with the good people in the battle between communism and anticommunism or between bourgeois Christian and socialist-atheist societies. It is certainly possible for movements that are reactive in nature to draw enthusiastic followings, often in proportion to the hostility felt for the forces that these movements are combating.[8]

Moreover, in his magnum opus *Der Faschismus in seiner Epoche*, Nolte treats fascism as something more than a secondary or derivative movement without positive content. He devotes almost four hundred pages to tracing the impressive pedigrees of three supposedly related fascist traditions, namely, the French reactionary, royalist Action Française, Italian Fascism, and German Nazism. Abstracting from certain methodological questions, for example, whether French monarchists should be bundled together with Italian nationalist revolutionaries or the Nazis, one finds in Nolte's work the fleshing out of a distinctly fascist world view.[9] His work confirms, albeit unwittingly, the judgment of America's outstanding scholar of Italian fascism, A. James Gregor, that there is a "fascist ideology." This ideology makes sense and was rationally defended by those who formulated it. Nor should readers assume, according to Gregor, that those who defended the fascist ideology were irrational or mentally disturbed. Its apologists supported fascism for many of the same reasons that the Left gives for upholding its revolutionary tradition. Fascists imagined their world view to be "just," factually defensible, and historically inevitable.[10]

Gregor's argument, however, clashes with Nolte's on several main points. Unlike his German contemporary, Gregor treats fascism as a persuasive revolutionary movement. Gregor began his lifelong study of this movement in the late 1960s because of what he perceived as the inadequacies of earlier research and because of the failure of historians to present fascism as a unified body of ideas. Gregor thought that fascism endangered liberal institutions precisely because it offered persuasive arguments about human nature, the economy, international relations, and the corruptness of parliamentary institutions.

A prolific historian of fascism, Gregor has been criticized by the Left because he makes fascists look more reasonable and more ethically motivated than most intellectuals would like to believe. Gregor attributes to the fascists a degree of intellectuality that some intellectuals would like to ascribe exclusively to the Left. But there are two elements of Gregor's argument that his critics would do well to note. One, like John Lukacs, he considers fascism to be a terrifying danger precisely because it makes sense at some level and in some situations—indeed, far more than Marxist internationalism, which appeals to a largely imaginary world proletariat. Two, unlike Lukacs, who identifies the fascist danger with the nationalist Right in both Europe and the United States, Gregor treats fascism as an infectious variation of Marxism. It is a revolutionary socialist movement in which the nation is substituted for the working class and in which socialist collectivism is preserved without the dream of an economically liberated humankind. According to Gregor, by the late 1920s Italian fascism was morphing into a leftist "totalitarian" movement decked out as romantic nationalism.[11]

Stanley Payne takes a middle ground between Nolte and Gregor when he examines fascism's ideological content. Essential to this movement's upsurge in whatever country it became a force was an already established opposition to institutions that the fascists condemned for undermining national traditions. The fascists' list of enemies was fairly constant and would have included parliamentarianism, left-wing socialism, internationalism (except in a form acceptable to the fascists), free market capitalism, Freemasons, and pacifists. Payne devotes considerable care to outlining these adversaries, because they determined what fascism advocated as well as what fascists urged others to combat. Payne assigns his subjects to the revolutionary Right and distinguishes between the traditional Right and authoritarian nationalist parties and what he presents as fascism's cobbled-together ideology.[12]

Payne makes distinctions that one encounters equally in the studies of Francophone Israeli historian Zeev Sternhell. In *Ni droite ni gauche* and *La droite révolutionnaire*, Sternhell deals with the sui generis character of the fascist Right, the origin of which he lays out for us. In France during the Third Republic, a new Right surfaced among those who rejected parliamentary institutions and capitalism that exhibited a strongly nationalist character. The French littérateur Maurice Barrès, who in the 1870s and 1880s coined the term "integral nationalism," and the French political group Cercle-Proudhon, which in the early twentieth century brought together dissident intellectuals from Right and Left, were, according to Sternhell (and Payne), precursors of interwar fascism.[13] It was Sternhell's signal accomplishment to have located in the French reaction to laicism and the human rights doctrine of the French Third Republic the seedbed of later fascist movements. France furnished the fascist counterrevolutionary as well as the revolutionary with ideas that took hold in the rest of Europe.

The Right that emerged during the French Third Republic stood in defiant opposition to parliamentarianism and internationalism, and it invoked a distinctive combination of ideas that became fundamental for fascism. Neither fascist partisans nor what they stood for—be it the theory of creative, redemptive violence taught by the French social theorist Georges Sorel, the vitalism of Nietzsche and Henri Bergson, or the proto-corporatism of Barrès—should be confused, however, with traditional European conservatives. Indeed, the fascists should not even be equated with any nationalist Right that saw fit to operate in a parliamentary context, which was a context that incipient fascists in France rejected.

Although Payne insists that fascists were theoretically resourceful, and, although his work on the Falange treats in detail their Spanish Catholic representatives of the 1930s, the movements that he depicts did not engage in systematic thinking about economic and social affairs. Payne reconstructs a fascist world view that looks like a grab bag of ideas borrowed from different sources. In *Fascism: Comparison and Definition,* the readers are given characteristics that Payne deemed common to fascist movements everywhere: they are all marked by a "permanent nationalistic one-party authoritarianism," "the search for a synthetic ethnicist ideology," a charismatic leader, a corporatist political economy, and "a philosophical principle of voluntarist activism unbounded by any philosophical determinism."[14]

Is There a Fascist Time and Space Horizon?

The most definitive comment on the limits of fascism's historical and cultural framework can be found in the conclusion to Nolte's *Faschismus, von Mussolini zu Hitler* (2002):

> The First World War was its nurturing soil and the Second World War was its most significant result: it recognized no higher court than that of war and the decision went against fascism. Historical circumstances gave fascists an opportunity that as late as 1918 would have seemed entirely unlikely, and after 1945 it became impossible for a European nation ever again to wage war in order to assert and secure its hegemony. This became clear even to the onetime devotees of fascism who now saw (in this changed situation) the critical weak point in their movement.[15]

Fascism, as Nolte defines it, was a purely interwar phenomenon encouraged by the continued rivalry of European nations, the threat of bolshevism, and the possibility that European countries could operate independently of a non-European superpower.

After 1945 Europe became tributary to powers that were committed to internationalist and antifascist world views, and in the case of Germany, even its continued existence as a political entity became linked to anti-Nazism and a very explicit antinationalism. Nolte suggests that the only Western country still capable of practicing "racial, continental fascism" after the fall of the Soviets is the American empire not only because of its periodic racial tensions but also because of the extent of American power. Unlike the currently pacified, weakened states of Europe, the United States still enjoys a freedom of action that European fascist powers claimed in the interwar period but that "resulted in conflicts they could not surmount when there was still time to do so."[16]

According to Nolte, European countries are no longer disposed or likely to return to their interwar fascist past. The "taboo-making of fascism" in the present European antifascist political culture has gone so far that "all conservative forces in Western countries" have frenetically distanced themselves from anything even vaguely associated with fascist movements. Even the supposedly fascist-looking National Democratic Party of Germany cannot in any sense be compared to the Nazis although NDP leaders have been accused of whitewashing Nazi crimes. Aside from the problem of attracting few votes by comparison to the explicitly antifascist parties on the German Left, even a triumphant NDP, according to Nolte, could not alter Germany's international status: "Any party that believes that through a declaration of Germany's atomic-free neutrality and the exploitation of anti-American resentment, it can reestablish not only the German Second Empire but also regain the Greater Germany lost by Hitler, is being deluded by dreams that cannot be described even as wishful thinking." The NDP offers at most a "new emphasis on the sovereignty of the German Federal Republic.[17] But nothing that this or any other German party could possibly do would move Germany even one micrometer closer to pre–World War II fascist practice, if for no other reason, than because Germany lacks the means of asserting itself."

Nolte denies that "military dictatorships" that have established themselves in Third World countries have been able to revive European fascist ideology. Unlike European movements in which one could perceive "the primacy of their epochal character," African dictatorships are impromptu robber states, merging anticolonial resentments with changing cults of personality. Throughout the Cold War, such governments practiced not "national socialism" but "national Marxism." They combined internal corruption with statements of friendship for the Soviets and other communist powers and "came to represent the very opposite of the typical fascist view of international relations between 1919 and 1945."[18]

Nolte does not consider the idea that fascism could and did become a Third World movement as carefully as he does the possibility that fascism might again dominate European politics. Gregor, by contrast, argues strenuously that fascism is alive and well in the Third World: "Anticolonialist movements in Africa and Asia have enjoyed special recruitment advantages," as they work toward building fascist, totalitarian structures of authority. These national liberation movements have appealed to "status-deprived people composed of a variety of classes, social strata and productive categories, aspiring to bridge the distance between themselves and their former superiors."[19] Further, their nationalist movements have replaced class struggle with "national solidarity." And since those "economic circumstances that prevailed in the countries of western Europe" do not really apply to Third World countries, Third World leaders feel free to abandon the "distributionist biases of classical Marxism" for the "avowedly productionist intentions of Fascism."[20]

Fascists already in the early 1920s, Gregor tells us, subordinated the removal of material disparities to the goal of national industrial development. Post–World War II African dictator Leopold Senghor in Senegal highlighted his country's "collective will for development," together with his own mystical notions of "Blackness, *négritude*." The depiction of liberated colonies as "proletarian nations," a description that was particularly dear to Guinean strongman Ahmed Sékou Touré and to Ghana's Kwame Nkrumah, was foreshadowed by fascist characterizations of an economically exploited Italy having to compete with its rich northern neighbors. Equally characteristic of fascist oratory and Third World nationalist movements have been the sneering references to "the plutocratic countries" that allegedly stand in the way of true revolutionary nations.

Gregor cites other shared characteristics of "liberated" Third World and European fascist governments. Chief among them was the predominance of counter elites who were preoccupied with taking power from those they hoped to displace, but they never quite arrived in permanent posts of authority (from whence comes the notion of a continuing, fluid revolution). Fascist practice was an unfinished national task led by "a minority movement of national insurgency" or "a declassed minority elite." The insurgents never saw themselves as becoming the ruling class, nor did they wish to define themselves as such. Equally important is the fact that neither the fascists nor Third World governments have held any brief for a pluralist society. Both have presented themselves as "creating a social and political order of solidarity in which all classes, strata, and categories would unite under the leadership of a single party."[21]

Although not as immediately threatening to the European bourgeoisie as it has been to the working class, fascism in practice would ultimately endanger all social groups equally. In neither Africa nor Europe were the national revolutionaries who took power fond of capitalists or respectful of the environment that the bourgeoisie needed to prosper. Like Third World nationalists, fascists "exploited what support they could attract from interest groups deployed in its political environment" but "did not represent the specific interest of any."[22]

A variant on Gregor's mutating fascism theme are the works that have been published on "antimodern modernism." These multiple studies treat fascism as an enduring model for antiliberal forms of modernization. Exponents of this interpretation, Jeffrey Herf and Roger Eatwell, have recognized what the Left has usually denied: that fascist movements have displayed considerable revolutionary energy.[23] Interwar fascism was a prototype for countries trying to catch up to the First World economically while preserving their distinctive Third World identities.

Here one might distinguish (for the first time in this text) between the generic fascism that flourished in Italy and (at least in theory) in Spain and France and the more dynamic Nazi totalitarian model. German historian Rainer Zitelmann, in a detailed biography of Hitler and in a subsequent study titled *Hitler: The Politics of Seduction*, explores the revolutionary side of the Nazi leader and his commitment to economic modernization.

Zitelmann argues that, in contrast to what Hitler viewed as a backward Latin version of his movement, Nazi Germany underwent a rapid transformation into an economically and socially modern country.[24] Whether mechanizing agriculture, working through his Labor Front minister Robert Ley toward the goal of full employment, bringing the lower orders into the officer corps and women into the workforce, Hitler, according to Zitelmann, viewed himself as a modernizer.

Even Hitler's "scientific racism" was totally modern and based on what he could grasp of anthropology or reconcile with his anti-Semitic world view. Zitelmann's compelling portrait of Hitler, including his depiction of this revolutionary's contempt for aristocracy and priests and his demonic attempts to justify his genocidal politics as a scientific procedure, commands our attention. What made Hitler "seductive," according to Zitelmann, and what distinguished him from generic fascists was not only his brutal ruthlessness but also his success in improving his subjects' living conditions. Of course, one should qualify this by adding that the improvements gained were followed by the horrors of catastrophic war.

The fascists as portrayed by Gregor were certainly less economically productive than the Nazi regime depicted in Zitelmann's work. But efficiency is not what Gregor is looking at. Despite their economic ineptitude, fascists, wherever they arose, offered a workable, dirigiste alternative to communism. This happened as Third World elites became concerned with industrial growth more than with the distribution of wealth and goods. The new fascist model also spilled over eventually into some self-identified communist countries. Anti-pluralism, appeals to national solidarity, and fascism's cult of the leader all resonated among communist elites as they moved away from a nineteenth-century picture of working-class revolution. In Gregor's view, intellectuals are so fixated on the presumed polarity between communism and fascism that they willfully ignore the revolutionary, modernizing qualities of what they condemn as reactionary.

Is Fascism of the Right or Left?

At least in the popular press and in conventional political discourse, the answer to this question may seem a no-brainer. The current equation of fascism with what is reactionary, atavistic, and ethnically exclusive would seem to answer this question even before it has been asked. The initial momentum for locating fascism on the counterrevolutionary Right came from Marxists, who focused on the struggle between fascists and the revolutionary Left and the willingness of the owners of forces of production to side with the fascists when faced by revolutionary threats. Sooner or later most of the bourgeoisie made their peace with fascist regimes. The reputation that fascists acquired in some countries, such as Italy and Austria, as a force of "order," confirmed the already established view of them as the shock troops of a threatened capitalist system.

Works equating "advanced capitalism" with fascism center on the intimate relations that existed between fascist governments and big business. One finds this pivotal connection being made in seminal studies produced in the 1930s by French Trotskyist Daniel Guérin and German revolutionary socialist Franz Neumann.[25] Such authors stress the role of fascist movements in protecting economic elites in the face of rising threats from the Left. According to Marxist theorists, the social organization that Italian fascism and, perhaps to a lesser extent, Nazism imposed had only minimal effect in redistributing earnings and resources. Further, the wars of aggression that fascist leaders initiated were intended to silence internal discord, jump-start slumping capitalist economies by building up arms industries, and open up foreign markets while subjugating foreign populations. All Marxist historians agreed that fascists were not truly revolutionary but seized on revolutionary themes and theatrical tricks in order to forestall social change that might have come from real revolutionaries.

Fascist milestones could be cited to prove fascism's connection to the European Right. In 1929 Mussolini's government concluded the Lateran Pacts with the papacy that ended the strife between the Italian monarchy and the Holy See, going back to the seizure of the Papal States, including Rome, during the period of Italian unification. In return for what turned out to be temporary peace with the Church, Mussolini and his education minister, the philosopher Giovanni Gentile, conceded to the Church broad powers over educational and civil affairs. The fascist state thereby ended the liberal or laic phase of the fascist regime, which started in 1923 and which radical fascists like Alfredo Rocco hoped to preserve.[26] After the outbreak of the Spanish Civil War in July 1936, fascist Italy and Nazi Germany both provided arms and military divisions to the right-wing nationalists against the leftist Republicans.

In November 1936 Nazi Germany and Imperial Japan signed the Anti-Comintern Pact, which named international communism as the shared enemy of the signatories. In November 1937 what became the anti-communist Axis was enlarged to include fascist Italy, which, in 1938, tried to catch up with its German ally by excluding Italian Jews from the Fascist Party, civil service, and professional posts. Before that time as many as ten thousand Italian Jews held *tessere del partito* not as communists but as fascists. Among prominent Italian Jewish fascists before Mussolini's anti-Semitic measures were Aldo Finzi, who had been head of the Fascist Grand Council, and Mussolini's lover and biographer, Margherita Sarfatti.[27]

Although some critics have taken aim at the reductionist character of Marxist interpretations of fascism, it is nonetheless possible to discern in them a springboard for original readings. The interpretations of fascism proposed by James Burnham, Ernst Nolte, and Rudolf Hilferding were all shaped to some extent by the Marxist or Marxist-Leninist world view that these thinkers had adopted earlier. It may therefore be hard to trace how these political analysts came to understand fascism without noting their prior Marxist frame of reference.[28]

In *The Managerial Revolution*, Burnham, who in 1940 was still a recovering Trotskyite, considered fascism, communism, and social democracy to be different forms of managerial rule in a post-bourgeois and soon-to-be post-capitalist society. Burnham's view of a managerial revolution as succeeding late capitalist society—and bringing about a transfer of power from the propertied bourgeoisie to an organizational class—went back to his youth as a socialist revolutionary. It was Trotsky's view of the post-Leninist Soviet Union as being a managerially derailed form of socialism that inspired Burnham's depiction of modern managerial society. The former Trotskyite studied the three faces of this political phenomenon in its fascist, communist, and social democratic manifestations. Rudolf Hilferding likewise took over Trotsky's critique of a derailed Soviet experiment but blamed the excesses of fascism and Soviet communism on a particularly virulent form of the modern state. As an Austrian socialist, Hilferding had produced what became the authoritative Marxist study of imperialism. But it later became clear to Hilferding that Marx had underestimated the energies of the political class, especially its ability to manipulate the populace in promoting its interests. Like Burnham, Hilferding re-centered his research on the self-aggrandizement of the modern state, which he thought took on monstrous proportions in Hitler's Germany and Stalin's Russia.[29]

Perhaps the most creative adaptation of the Marxist understanding of fascism can be found in Ernst Nolte's extensive study of fascism's genealogy and "epochal character." Such signature concepts as "the counterrevolutionary imitation of the Left" and "the European civil war" point back to the Marxist origins of Nolte's work. Nolte took conventional Marxist views of irreconcilable social conflict and the appeal of counterrevolutionary tactics to a threatened class and integrated them into a daring interpretive synthesis. Like conventional Marxist historians but with more conceptual inventiveness, Nolte treats the social strife in interwar Europe as the background for fascism's rise to power.

Readers should observe that Nolte's "contextualization" of the "European civil war" incorporates certain key Marxist assumptions, for example, that social contradictions cannot be assigned to ages and parts of the world that do not show the characteristic developments of advanced capitalist societies. The "civil war" in which the communists and fascists locked horns was specific to what was economically and socially the world's most developed region. This perspective went back to a firm Marxist belief about where a socialist revolution would first erupt, but this perspective was partly abandoned when the New Left came along and glorified what communist historian Eric Hobsbawm mocked as Third World "exotica." Suddenly in the 1960s underdeveloped parts of the world were given a face-lift from a distance by progressive intellectuals. Disappointed would-be revolutionaries looked beyond their own countries for an upheaval that did not materialize in the West.[30] Nolte, in a sense, is returning to a traditional Marxist view by focusing on, among other things, a social crisis that befell interwar Europe.

Gregor again sets himself in opposition to Nolte in the place he assigns to fascism on the ideological spectrum. He presents fascism as a "variant on Marxism" that took over Marxist collectivism but merged it with nationalist themes. Gregor also discerns in fascist theory a collectivist view of "mankind" that he finds foreshadowed in Marx's early writings. In these writings we are confronted with the absence of individual identity in prerevolutionary societies. The young socialist Mussolini, explains Gregor, may have espoused an anti-pluralist, antiliberal conception of social organization as a result of having been exposed to Marx's ideas about class solidarity. The later fascist leader adapted for his purposes the undifferentiated group identity that Marx ascribed to social actors before the advent of the proletariat revolution.[31] Fascists created their own variation of what Marx called "prehistory," which was imagined to define human existence up until the reconstruction of human beings under socialism. Marx's group identity of classes was now redefined as the group identity of organic nations.

Gregor cites the numerous references to economic collectivism in fascist documents of the 1920s, most importantly in the Carta del Lavoro issued by the fascist state in 1927. According to this formulation of fascist economic policy, "the Italian nation is an organism having ends, life, and means of action that are superior in power and continuity to those of the divided and organized individuals who compose it. It is a moral, political and economic unity, which realizes itself in the fascist state." In addition: "Work in all its organizational and executive forms is a social duty. For this reason it must be supervised by the state."[32] Although the Carta explains that "union and professional organizations are free," it also stipulates that "only those constructed under the aegis of the state will be able to represent legally all categories of the givers of work (the managers of industry) and the working class, to protect them in relation to the state and to represent their interests in dealing with other professional associations."[33]

Gregor enriches his picture of fascism as a leftist collectivist ideology by bringing in such key intellectual figures as Alfredo Rocco (1875–1935), Giuseppe Bottai (1895–1959), and the later leftist Ugo Spirito (1896–1979). These theorists, who were grouped around the journal *Critica Fascista* in the 1920s, defended the socially radical aspect of Italian fascist corporatism. Despite their fascist associations, one could possibly locate such figures—at least in the interwar period—somewhere on the left.[34] The hard-line fascists were anticlerical and opposed (with varying degrees of anger) the signing of the Lateran Pacts. They judged the Carta as being defective because of its tolerance of "private initiative," and they complained about *Il Duce*'s (the Leader's) unwillingness to subdue the owners and managers of heavy industry, who are euphemistically designated in the Carta as *datori del lavoro*. Bottai, who helped draft the original Carta that was later modified in an antisocialist direction, expressed unhappiness with Mussolini's reluctance to introduce a truly socialist society in line with fascist doctrine.[35] To whatever extent fascism was true to its essence, the ultra-corporatist Spirito was quick to point out, it must aim at integrating all occupations into an organic framework, one that subordinated the acquisitive individual to the social good. Like Bottai, Spirito was relentless in his attack on capitalist greed and in his call for collectivizing the economy.[36]

It is also a matter of record that many fascists, like Mussolini, were *transfuges* from the Left, and one can easily divide these deserters or converts into two categories: those who give the appearance of having undergone genuine changes of heart and those who became Nazi collaborators after the fall of France. There were also those who moved from one camp into the other as a kind of natural progression, seeing in fascism a collectivist project that they had already supported without calling it by its proper name. The organizer of the pro-fascist Parti Populaire Français (PPF) in 1936, Jacques Doriot (1898–1945), may have been an in-between case. Doriot started out politically as a communist and then broke from the party in 1935 for having failed to take a sufficiently strong stand against Nazi Germany.

In 1936, however, this flexible politician was excoriated as a veritable volte-face when he cofounded the PPF, which appealed to antiliberal intellectuals, including the future political theorist Bertrand de Jouvenel. Doriot's party looked to fascist Italy for a national corporatist model and sought to cultivate good relations with the homeland of European fascism. Even before the fall of France, Doriot laid the groundwork for the collaborationist camp and subsequently helped set up the pro-Axis Rassemblement National Populaire, an umbrella organization for political collaborators that lasted through the Vichy government. Doriot also helped organize the Parti Ouvrier et Paysan Français, which broke off from the Rassemblement and was partly composed of former communists who had shifted to the collaborationist side.

The shifting of former communists and socialists into the fascist or collaborationist camp was by no means an exceptional situation in the late 1930s. Such figures included, among many others, Sir Oswald Mosley (1896–1980), who founded the British Union of Fascists after organizing a radical faction of the Labour Party as Independent Labour in the late 1920s. Mosley moved toward English fascism because the Labour Party would not go far enough in promising to revamp British society.[37] The American fascist sympathizer Father Charles Edward Coughlin (1891–1979), who edited the journal *Social Justice* and founded the National Union for Social Justice in 1934, was certainly no apologist for American capitalism. Despite his over-the-top harangues against Jewish bankers and East Coast warmongers, Coughlin came out of the left wing of the New Deal Democratic Party and returned to his New Deal Democratic roots in the 1960s. Although terms like "ultraconservative" and "right wing" predictably show up on website biographies of him, Coughlin's anticapitalist credentials may have been beyond reproach. His plan for nationalizing the Federal Reserve (an institution that the pro-capitalist presidential candidate Ron Paul hoped to abolish) and for putting all banking under state control suggest that, in the economic sphere, this Catholic priest shared common ground with the radical Left.[38]

The co-organizer, with José Antonio Primo de Rivera, of the Falange, Ramiro Ledesma Ramos, whom the Spanish Republicans murdered in 1935, entered Spanish fascism by way of anticlerical national syndicalism. As a student at Heidelberg in 1930, Ramos had worked to synthesize nationalist and social revolutionary ideas, an enterprise that also attracted the left wing of German National Socialism.[39] A later German collaborator, Marcel Déat, was a cofounder of the Parti Socialiste de France; in 1936 Déat broke from Léon Blum and other supporters of the Popular Front as an antimilitarist who refused to pursue a collision course with Germany and Italy. Although opportunism may have driven Déat toward the Axis powers, it would be hard to imagine him leaning right before he declared his affinity for fascism.[40] Even more striking is the case of Belgian socialist Hendrik de Man (1885–1953) who, after spending decades as a leading Marxist theorist, went over to German National Socialism following the German occupation of his country. De Man and many of his followers drafted and signed the "Manifesto of the Members of the Belgian Labor Party" (1940), which presented National Socialism as an acceptable path to true socialism. This example may be particularly telling for those who wish to assign fascists to the Left.[41]

For many fascists, their engagement flowed from their perception of the historical situation. Spirito summed up his time-centered perspective in a lecture at the University of Pisa in 1932: "The corporatist regime, like the fascist revolution, is the fruit of an evolution of thought which ranges from the highest form of specialization to the minutest practical determination and which therefore represents one of the infinite forms of control that science is able to study; nonetheless, the fascist corporate state is the unique historical reality that has emerged from the most advanced stage of historical consciousness."[42] This form of organization that was supposed to be keyed to the historical moment became known in Vichy France as *planisme*.[43] Not surprisingly, soi-disant architects of an up-to-date social-political order moved toward fascism and then, in some cases, once fascism had failed, toward the socialist or communist Left. These sea changes were not always attributable to careerism. Aspiring state-planners were looking for chances to advance their plans and rallied to any regime that seemed open to their proposals.

Finally, one could cite John Diggins's *Mussolini and Fascism: The View from America* and Wolfgang Schivelbusch's *Entfernte Verwandtschaft* as two of the many studies that document the inspirational effect of Italian fascism on American progressives and socialists.[44] Despite dissenting newspapers like *Corriere degli Italiani,* run by exiles in Paris, the fascist government could usually count on a favorable press abroad. Indeed, Socialist Party leader Pietro Nenni complained from exile in 1927 that the Italian people sit idly by "while being stripped of all their rights and subordinated to a regime that treats them approximately the way civilized Europeans treat their colonies." Further: "Italians are being driven to compensate for the abolition of their political rights with the industrial development of their country, from whence they expect to see economic improvement for everybody."[45]

But it was precisely this political organization of the economy for the purpose of modernization that caused non-Italian progressives to marvel at Mussolini's "experiment." Support for the fascist experiment included the pro-socialist and at least mildly pro-Soviet *New Republic* and New Deal advisor Rexford Tugwell. FDR had kind words for Mussolini's organizational abilities and lavished praise on *Il Duce*, up until the time that the Italian leader strayed into an alliance with Hitler.[46] Strangely enough, the Italian fascist regime was able to preserve its popularity even after fascist toughs assassinated Socialist leader Giacomo Matteoti in June 1924 and even after Mussolini achieved a modus vivendi with the Church.

Progressive state planners had large enough imaginations to include more than one object of admiration, even if it meant making room for such diverse figures as Mussolini and Stalin, or Mussolini and Trotsky. Foreign admiration for the Italian national revolution reached a crescendo in the mid-1930s when Mussolini took center stage as the leader of the anti-Nazi Stresa Front. This united front under Italian initiative consisted of countries that opposed Nazi German belligerence, and it took shape after Hitler tried to topple the Austrian government in 1934 with internal assistance in Vienna. Mussolini also created a helpful anti-Nazi image for himself by publicly deploring Hitler's anti-Semitism. At the same time he offered asylum to German Jews and allowed the Revisionist Zionists, who were well disposed toward his rule, to train their forces on Italian soil.[47] The antagonism between Italy and Germany, for as long as it lasted, served to heighten a distinction between a civilized Latin fascism and a barbaric fascist movement that had reared itself north of the Alps.

The Nazis and Generic Fascists

Given the variety of interwar movements that have been classified as fascist, it may be useful to bring up both the common and distinctive features of these fascist organizations. At one end of our hypothetical spectrum can be found Austrian clerical fascism, the Spanish Falange, and perhaps the conservative Catholic regime of Antonio de Oliviera Salazar in Portugal. These partial or qualified forms of fascism blended a corporatist theory of the state, taken from such sources as Thomism and the encyclicals of Popes Leo XIII and Pius XI, with plans for a national authoritarian government. Neither a general racial theory nor racial anti-Semitism was foundational for these religiously shaped authoritarian ideologies. One clerical fascist, the Christian Social Chancellor of Austria Engelbert Dollfuss (1892–1934), proclaimed a Christian corporatist state in January 1934 but soon after fell to Nazi assassins.

This misfortune occurred after an attempted takeover of Austria by the Nazis, a plot that Dollfuss doggedly resisted before being murdered. Like the Falange and, to a lesser extent, Salazar's government, Austrian clerical fascists maintained friendly relations with fascist Italy and even imagined that the Italian corporatist state was an imperfect embodiment of a Catholic, anti-Marxist polity.[48] Although the Italian fascists in the 1930s harassed Catholic youth organizations, the fact that Mussolini reached an agreement with the papacy about the Church's sphere of influence won the approval of his clerical fascist admirers. Equally important is the fact that, up until the late 1930s, the Italian government was committed to protecting its Austrian allies against any attempt by the Nazis to seize control in their country.

At the other end of the spectrum stood the German Nazis and their vicious collaborators, like the Croatian Ustashi and the Hungarian Arrow Cross Party. These groups, which Nolte would classify as "radical fascists," were led by genocidal anti-Semites and tightly tied to Nazi Germany. Arrow Cross partisans under their chief Ferenc Szálasi (1897–1945) would never have achieved political dominance in their homeland without the German occupation of Hungary in October 1944.[49]

Like the Salò Republic set up after Mussolini was freed from captivity by a German agent in September 1943, and like German puppet regimes such as the Ustashi government in Croatia under Ante Pavelitsch (1889–1959), the Dutch followers of the Nationaal Socialistische Beweging under Anton Adriaan Mussert (1894–1946), and members of the Parti Rexiste in Belgium who remained faithful to Leon Dégrelle (1906–1994), the Arrow Cross and Szálazi achieved their programmatic goals through the imposition of foreign rule. "Radical fascists" were given a free hand under a German puppet state, but this only happened when the Germans occupiers had no other practical choices.

It is open to debate whether these collaborator movements illustrated characteristic fascist features. Perhaps it would be nearer the truth to describe them as anti-parliamentary national movements that combined anti-Semitism with anti-bolshevism. Their leaders welcomed the German occupation as the necessary step that would lead to their empowerment. This may have been especially true of the Norwegian collaborator Abraham Vidkun Quisling (1887–1945) who was an unsuccessful political adventurer before the German invaders allowed him to construct a "national regime" in February 1942. Quisling had been a war minister in 1932 under an earlier Norwegian government that included his Peasant Party. He then went on to found the Nasjonal Samling, which featured boilerplate corporatist planks but lacked any sharp fascist profile. It took nothing less than a foreign occupation to put Quisling and his party on the political map.[50]

Stanley Payne remarks that "Hitler found it more satisfactory to deal with conservative, right-wing authoritarians as satellites, for they were more compliant and less challenging."[51] Authoritarian governments that could be swayed to cooperate with Hitler were easier to deal with than the Arrow

Cross and Ustashi. The excesses of such movements made it hard for the Germans to control occupied countries. Some of the leaders of indigenous movements that welcomed the Nazi German occupation, like Mussert in Holland, did not enjoy any discretionary power under the occupation. In Holland the post of *Reichskommissar* was given to the Austrian Nazi leader Arthur Seyss-Inquart, whom Hitler found more trustworthy than the Germans' flighty Dutch collaborator Mussert. The Walloon collaborator Dégrelle was also denied a government post under the Germans. But as a meager compensation, he was allowed to volunteer for military service in an SS unit on the Russian front.[52]

In Hungary Hitler got rid of the authoritarian governing coalition of his erstwhile apparent ally, the Hungarian Regent Miklós Horthy. He may have taken this step reluctantly when it became apparent that the Hungarian regime was trying to negotiate peace with England. Payne and historians of Vichy France Michael Marus and Robert Paxton have all challenged the onetime received wisdom that Vichy France incarnated fascist principles. They view it as a mostly pliable satellite of Nazi Germany that was run by technocrats and flaunted Catholic social theory and nationalist rhetoric. The willingness of the Vichy regime to cooperate in rounding up foreign Jews and handing them over to the Nazis was morally reprehensible but did not reveal a "fascist" state. Although such collaborators as Doriot and Déat expounded fascist principles throughout the German occupation, Vichy's "stringency of police power" and "state economic controls" did not suffice, according to Payne, to prove its fascist bona fides.[53]

Two authoritarian military leaders whom Hitler hoped to rely on, Francisco Franco in Spain and Ion Antonescu in Romania, were able to incorporate fascist or *fascisant* movements into their ruling coalitions while reducing these forces to more or less window dressing. Franco, who led the Nationalists in the Spanish Civil War, had a certain freedom of action conferred on him by virtue of the fact that the Falange's founders were executed by their enemies at the beginning of the war. Taking advantage of this situation, Franco merged the Falange with the ultra-Catholic Carlist monarchists and other rightist allies in April 1937.[54] Out of this merger came the *partido único*, the coalition through which Franco ruled Spain for decades and in which the Falange initially provided an aesthetic dimension for a government of order. Thereafter exuberantly pro-Axis youth were sent off to die in the Blue Division fighting for the Third Reich in Russia; meanwhile, dissident Spanish fascists were jailed or encouraged to leave the country if they did not accept the increasingly technocratic regime of the victorious Caudillo.[55]

Antonescu's rule in Romania was more cynical and more brutal than Franco's in the way that it dealt with the local variant of a fascist movement. In Romania this role fell to the Legionnaires of the Archangel Michael, a group of militant nationalists organized in 1927 and renamed the Iron Guard in 1931. The Guard's cofounders, Corneliu Zelea Codreanu (1899–1938) and Ion Motza (1902–1937), were fiercely anti-Semitic Romanian nationalists. As an intended act of kindness, Motza provided his fellow citizens with a translation of a work that he had chanced upon as a student in Paris, *The Protocols of the Elders of Zion*. This depiction of a Jewish conspiracy contrived in Prague to take over and exploit Christian Europe traveled easily to Motza's Francophile Romania. The imported fanciful narrative was well-suited to an impoverished peasant country in which urban Jews contributed disproportionately to the shopkeeping and financial class. Three other elements went into the mix of positions that characterized the Iron Guard: Eastern Orthodox piety blended with Romanian nationalist passions, a fierce hatred of bolshevism, and a penchant for violence that expressed itself in the assassination of political opponents.

Some Guardists left their homeland to fight on the nationalist side in Spain; Motza died there in combat. Others stayed behind and were jailed. In 1938 Codreanu was conveniently shot while trying to escape his captors.[56] His movement suffered further setbacks. The Romanian King Carol II (1930–1940) spent his personal rule, from 1938 to 1940, combating the Guardists, often by violent means. After this struggle Antonescu's rightist dictatorship, which lasted until 1944, tried to mobilize the peasants around its own authoritarian nationalist movement. Antonescu's government turned to the corporatist ideas of a then-fashionable Romanian economist, Mihail Manoilescu, for its inspiration. From Manoilescu the Romanian military dictatorship drew a scheme for building a corporate state that would eventually achieve national self-sufficiency.

For several months after Antonescu took power in September 1940, he negotiated with the Guardists, who were then popular in Romanian universities. But when these militants launched an uprising in Bucharest in early 1941, the army proceeded to crush them. The German government backed this show of force unconditionally. Antonescu thereafter preserved some of the outward trappings of interwar fascism, supported the Axis against Soviet Russia, and made ritualistic noises about international Jewish capitalism. Despite this background music, Jews in anti-Semitic Romania were largely spared, because they were allowed to bribe the government into protecting them against deportation to concentration or extermination camps. It was only in Transnistria, on the Ukrainian border, that the Nazis were successful in getting Antonescu to turn over Jewish residents.[57]

Here there is a further complication in trying to narrow the definition of fascism, and it is one that Payne and other scholars have considered at length. Most European countries in the interwar period were under governments and/or parties that featured a "fascist style." Such appropriations could be compared to how post–World War II societies selectively incorporated fashionable aspects of the American or Soviet government and then labeled their local adaptations "democratic." This process resulted from the effects of a hegemonic power more than from any sweeping internal transformation of smaller, weaker states. A similar distinction may apply to countries that fell under German or Italian sway or which were trying to imitate fascist powers that seemed to be in the ascendant. How exactly do historians tell the real product from mere imitation?

Even more troubling (if it is worth the effort) is trying to include in the same category the government of Engelbert Dollfuss and those Nazi agents who killed him. Is there some feature shared by clerical fascists and Nazis that is more noteworthy than what distinguished them? One may of course try to limit the fascist club by excluding both Catholic authoritarians and Nazis. But are historians justified in ignoring certain overlaps that run across most of the fascist spectrum? For example, fascists (however typologically marginal some of them may have been) had a predilection for corporatist language and organic concepts of society and a dislike for multiparty systems and the socialist Left. One may supplement or replace this list by what Sternhell has described as the "fascist minimum"—"a combination of anti-rationalism, anti-materialism, anti-liberalism, anti-individualism."[58] But, on second thought, this "minimum" may seem too negative and abstract for present purposes.

One encounters at least some fascist characteristics in both Degrelle's Catholic followers and the neo-pagan, anti-Christian wing of Italian fascism. Corporatism was a persistent theme in the speeches and writings of all "generic fascists," together with a mystical concept of the Nation and an unmistakable contempt for parliamentary governments. But at this point there may be need for qualification. The agrarian parties in interwar Hungary and interwar Bulgaria stressed a corporatist economy but were emphatically anti-Nazi as well as anticommunist. Degrelle's party, the Parti Rexiste, was Catholic and corporatist, but only a minority followed Degrelle into the collaborationist camp. Most Rexistes took up arms against the German occupation.[59]

This leads readers back to the question of whether we can determine a fascist essence in interwar Europe. If there is such an essence, then neither racism nor anti-Semitism necessarily belonged to it. There were fascist movements in which these characteristics were secondary or nonexistent. Moreover, not all fascists were Christian traditionalists or neo-pagans or secularists. The same movements sometimes contained all three. Nor would it be correct to say that all fascist movements admired Hitler or that all governments that cooperated with Hitler fit the fascist grid. Payne defines "generic fascism" in terms of his own "fascist minimum."[60] Whereas the typology "would demarcate the kind of movement classified as fascist," we should not assume that "the generic typology could define all the most important feature[s] of any individual movement." Perhaps this generic typology may be compared to the "ideal type" employed in the sociology of Max Weber. The model can be recognized as typologically fascist, even if it does not fully describe a particular fascist state or movement.

At the very least two additional qualifications should be made. One, it is hard to treat Nazi Germany and its murderous collaborator regimes as being only northern European manifestations of the Falange, clerical fascism, or, before the late 1930s, Italian fascism. Whatever affinities may have existed between various forms of fascism and both the Nazi government and those who collaborated with Hitler, these shared features should not cause us to blur critical distinctions. With due respect to Nolte, what distinguishes generic fascism and Nazism are far more than degrees of concern about bolshevism or the seemingly incidental feature of genocide.

Two, it is useful to keep in mind Payne's distinction between traditional authoritarian and nationalist authoritarian governments and full-blown fascism. Unlike the conventional authoritarian Right, represented by Franco and Horthy, the fascists did not view themselves as running a caretaker government. Often they regarded themselves as "revolutionaries" who stood in the tradition of national democratic movements of the nineteenth century. Contrary to the idea that Italian fascists were merely imitating Catholic counterrevolutionaries like Joseph de Maistre, theorists like Gentile and Rocco glorified the democratic revolutionaries Garibaldi and Mazzini.[61] They considered the "Italian national revolution" to be the fitting culmination of popular national movements that originated in an earlier era. Clerical fascists may have thought they perceived a kinship between themselves and Italian national revolutionaries, but they clearly missed certain aspects of more mainstream fascists. Clerical fascists were Catholic authoritarians who embraced a corporatist idea that they shared with more normative fascists.

Finally, it is imperative that we stress the difficulty of characterizing fascism as a leftist movement—that is, as a "variant on Marxism." Such a view had its most unanimous support among members of the traditional Right. For example, Habsburg monarchist Erik von Kuehnelt-Leddihn viewed the Left as lurching from the French Revolution and Robespierre to Hitler and the Third Reich. According to Kuehnelt-Leddihn, modern democracy teems with totalitarian dangers, and only to the extent that we accept a traditional ruling order and nineteenth-century constitutional limits on popular rule can we avoid the Left's assault on authority.[62]

From this perspective all attacks on traditional authorities are necessarily leftist because the true Right is coterminous with responsible, hereditary sovereigns and a nineteenth-century parliamentary system. The scholar of international relations George F. Kennan made the same distinction and viewed revolutionary governments, no matter what they called themselves, as belonging on the Left. Like Kuehnelt-Leddihn, Kennan made exceptions for some leaders who were rightly or wrongly identified as fascists. He considered Dollfuss, Salazar, and Franco—but not Hitler and Mussolini—to be conservative authoritarians and, from his perspective, true men of the Right.[63]

Despite limited usefulness for understanding post–World War I politics, this traditional conservative interpretation is entirely consistent given its implicit assumptions about legitimate government and those who defend it. From the standpoint of the pre–World War I ruling class, Fascists, Nazis, Social Democrats, and Bolsheviks all came out of the Left. And so it once seemed. In the Austrian parliament of the 1880s, anti-Semitic nationalist Georg Ritter von Schönerer (1842–1921), whom Hitler celebrated as a precursor of the Third Reich, raged against the dynasty, the Catholic Church, and Jewish bankers. Schönerer called for universal manhood suffrage, providing tax relief for tradesmen (*Gewerbetreibende*), separating German Austria from the rest of the Empire, and strengthening workers' unions.[64]

From the early 1870s on, this déclassé nobleman, whose mother had been a stage actress, belonged to the radical wing of the Austrian Liberal Party, from whence he moved into becoming a prominent but eccentric figure among the German Nationalists (*Deutschnationale*). In the Austrian assembly Schönerer sat on the far left, along with the revolutionary socialists. In all probability the Emperor Franz Josef and his ministers viewed the Deutschnationale, like the Slavic separatists and Marxist socialists, as equally dangerous demagogues. All these subversives (*Wühler*) posed grave dangers to an already weakened imperial rule. The imperial family detested with particular intensity the German nationalist Schönerer, whom they regarded as a traitor to his class. The emperor was delighted when the courts stripped this figure of his noble patent after he vandalized the office of a newspaper that reported prematurely the death of the German emperor Wilhelm I. (The paper's inaccurate report supposedly betrayed insufficient regard for the true German government, which was in Berlin rather than in multinational Vienna.)[65]

From the perspective of interwar Europe, however, revolutionary nationalists who favored corporatist economies did not really belong to the Left. They occupied a different situation as enemies of the Left and particularly the Bolsheviks. Fascists rose to prominence and often power as the adversaries of leftist internationalism, equality, and any form of capitalism that worked against the organic unity of the nation. If fascists were against the free flow of capital and unregulated economic growth, they took these positions as anticapitalists of the Right. Not all opposition expressed to free market capitalism has come historically from the Left.

In the nineteenth and early part of twentieth century, romantic conservatives Adam Müller and Franz von Baader and Catholic corporatist theorists Karl von Vogelsang and Albert de Mun wrote critically about what came to be called "Manchestrian economics." Such critics decried the surrender of the working class to the vagaries of the free market. They championed the idea of workers' guilds, and from the encyclicals of Leo XIII and Pius XI, which warned against free market capitalism, Catholic conservatives extracted a neo-medieval critique of modern capitalist society.[66] It may be reasonable to view fascist and, particularly, clerical fascist complaints against predatory capitalists as being affected in varying degrees by Catholic social thinking. Although less characteristic of the anticlerical fascists, this anticapitalist mindset may apply to this group as well. Like clerical fascists, anticlerical fascists typically came out of Latin Catholic cultures.

The use of plebiscitary democracy by fascist or quasi-fascist leaders did not necessarily betoken leftist politics. Since the nineteenth century, when Louis Napoleon, Disraeli, and Bismarck instituted universal suffrage, voting has been a tool of the party of order as well as that of the party of revolution. The Catholic authoritarian Carl Schmitt considered democratic constitutions to "represent the dynamic emergence of political unity and the ever renewable development of this unity springing from an underlying source of energy. The state should be regarded not as something enduring or static but as an entity that remained in a situation of becoming. Out of conflicting interests, opinions, and aspiration, political unity must constitute itself daily."[67]

Schmitt's association of popular rule with "homogeneity" and a "unified will" is not a call for social engineering from the Left. It is a veiled plea for a plebiscitary reconstruction of an organic community led, preferably, by a dynamic executive embodying the will and energy of a unified people. Schmitt sets apart this regime from a monarchy, in which the popular will is incidental to rule, and from a "nineteenth century liberal order," in which legal norms, not cohesive peoples, hold sway. Schmitt, whose authoritarian ideas often leaned toward Latin fascism, regarded the continuity of national communities as the "existential ground" for democratic constitutions. This kind of state would not likely favor a free market economy or be primarily concerned with individual rights. But it would value service and solidarity and reflect an already formed nation, as opposed to an aggregation of individuals or the international proletariat.[68]

Equally relevant is the fact that the fascists did not carry out, or in most cases even try to incite, a socioeconomic revolution. In the case of the Nazis and their equally murderous collaborators, lots of killing and the expropriation of Jewish property took place. But despite these crimes, there was nothing like the wholesale nationalization and agricultural collectivization that accompanied communist takeovers. Italian fascists renamed economic actors in order to make them fit a corporatist model. They declared the state to be free to interfere in production, but the fascist state asserted this right in a limited way, though perhaps less often than "democratic capitalist" countries that are on the way to becoming social democracies.

To be sure, there were fascists on the Left, like Bottai and Spirito in Italy or the Black Front wing of the National Socialists, who in the early 1930s were led by two firebrands, Otto and Gregor Strasser. But such figures found no real acceptance for their ideas under fascist or Nazi rule. In Italy the radicals finally got their chance during the Salò Republic. Under what amounted to a German occupation in northern Italy, the socialist wing of Italian fascism was allowed to try out its reforms. Italian fascist socialists undertook their experimenting while Nazi collaborators were rounding up Jews and other designated enemies and desperate measures were being taken to hold off Allied advances.[69] Other radical fascists, led by Spirito, ran to embrace the Left after the war or, like Bottai, spent their golden years ineffectually trying to fuse leftist and rightist ideas. Unlike Mussolini, Hitler dealt harshly with the social radicals in his movement. Those who did not accept his measured reforms and agitated for more radical changes were summarily killed off. This was the fate of, among many others, Gregor Strasser, who fell in the Night of the Long Knives in May 1934. Needless to say, Hitler did not hesitate to imprison other recalcitrant nationalists, like the interwar founder of the German National Bolsheviks, Ernst Niekisch.[70]

Gregor's extended comparison of fascists to Marxist-Leninists is not entirely convincing from a social perspective. Looking at Mussolini's relations with what Renzo De Felice calls "ambienti industriali," namely the industrial elite in interwar Italy, one finds throughout the 1920s and well into the 1930s sustained support for the fascist government. Mussolini cultivated the friendship of the *datori del lavoro*, which is what he called the captains of heavy industry. The director of that massive business organization Confindustria and, incidentally, a Sephardic Jew, Gino Olivetti, remained on close personal terms with *Il Duce* until Mussolini's unexpected turn toward Nazi Germany.[71]

Although the Italian fascist government tried to curb crazed stock speculation in the 1920s and lavished inflated money on key industries during the Depression-ridden 1930s, it would be counterfactual to compare the fascist economy to a communist one. As Zitelmann shows, Hitler was a revolutionary modernizer, but it is significant that he appointed as his first economic minister the very pro-capitalist economist Hjalmar Schacht (1877–1970). Schacht warned against the policy of subsidizing farms and business enterprises that other countries hit by the Depression were pursuing. Because of Schacht's advice, the Nazi state eschewed the payment of such staples of the American New Deal as farm subsidies. Schacht, who mocked Nazi ideology and leaned heavily toward the free market, would have been inconceivable in Stalin's Russia.[72] The reason is certainly not that the Nazis were nice people. They were simply not as concerned as Stalin or Mao with collectivizing the economy and, although equally murderous, were less ideologically programmed.

Fascism as the Invented Right

What may render fascism a provocative object of study is its aspect of bricolage. It often seems to have been, because it so often was, a studied attempt to devise a counterrevolutionary imitation of the Left—that is, something that looked like the revolutionary Left but was not of the same genus. This may have been the case even when an undoubtedly great thinker, Gentile, furnished a theoretical defense of the fascist "system." Gentile's philosophy of the state (or what he presented as such as a fascist apologist) and the various adaptations of vitalism for fascist use may be viewed as afterthoughts for what started out as pure activism.

But this was not necessarily a hindrance to the movement's ascendancy. Fascism drew its strength from the attempt to oppose the Left while taking over some of its defining characteristics. This added to the difficulty of mobilizing against the Italian fascists and may explain why even the democratic Left sometimes and in some places celebrated Mussolini as a hero. But what must be factored in for understanding this phenomenon is a particular spatial and temporal context. Fascism and the revolutionary Left that it faced between the two wars are not eternally present forces but came to oppose each other in a particular time and place.

According to Nolte, this confrontation came out of the chaos engendered by the First World War and reflected the ideologies adopted and sustained by returning soldiers. This prerequisite must be kept in mind when looking at the attempt made by an eminent historian of fascism, Robert Paxton, to analyze the emotional components of fascist movements.[73] Although certain psychic characteristics may have contributed to a fascist predisposition in some countries, one may question how decisive they were in bringing about large fascist organizations. Brooding national resentment and a sense of national solidarity, which are two of Paxton's presuppositions for fascism, may characterize many societies, but minus a certain context, which interwar Europe provided, specifically fascist movements are not likely to emerge.

Treating any Right or any nationalism as identical to the one that engaged in the ideological battle of interwar Europe opens the door to methodological abuses. Among these abuses, and indeed the most conspicuous one, has been the supposed discovery of a ubiquitous fascist danger. Emotional predispositions are imagined to furnish a sufficient cause for why fascist movements arise and flourish. Once having reached this point, the interpreter does not merely exaggerate the applicability of his criteria of investigation. He may also succumb, more importantly, to the temptation of extravagant political rhetoric.

CHAPTER TWO

Totalitarianism and Fascism

Defining Totalitarianism

In *Interpretations of Fascism*, Renzo De Felice furnished a *vue d'ensemble* of the major works on fascism that have been published since the 1930s[1]. The views summarized by De Felice extend from the relevant writings of Catholic traditionalists, social psychologists, classical Marxist-Leninists, and analysts of national character to the author's voluminous study of Italian fascism. De Felice looked at, among other things, the backgrounds of those who chose to write about his field of study. He believed that it was hard to grasp the significance of these interpretations without paying attention to biographical details. Whether we are encountering Germans or Italians dealing with national traumas, conservative Christians lamenting the breakdown of religious institutions or their preemption by power-hungry governments, Frankfurt School Marxists exploring the "authoritarian personality," or communists analyzing capitalists who backed right-wing dictatorships, these distinctive interpretations arose out of different historical situations. Therefore, concluded De Felice, studying the backgrounds of interpreters of fascism has relevance for understanding the historiography they produced.

Focusing on the circumstances that shaped a particular interpretation does not detract from the value of its content. It permits us to understand more clearly the evolution of someone's standpoint. It also makes apparent the limits of a critical discussion, which may be necessary for a full evaluation of one's object of study. Like his older contemporary Augusto Del Noce and his student at the University of Rome, Emilio Gentile, De Felice set out to trace the "totalitarian" path taken by his country after it had become a parliamentary monarchy in the nineteenth century. De Felice undertook his research while still on the far Left. But his multi-volume work on Mussolini indicates that he departed from his youthful Marxism and his original view of the Italian fascist regime as "totalitarian" in practice. In *Mussolini il duce: Gli anni del consenso, 1929–1936*, he presents the fascist government as a conciliatory enterprise trying to balance divergent social interests. Mussolini and his advisors acted as political pragmatists when they worked to keep the socially anxious upper middle class allied with the petite bourgeoisie and those parts of the Italian working class that the fascists hoped to co-opt.[2]

Among those interpretations of fascism that found their way into post–World War II historiography, perhaps the most far-reaching view for several decades was the examination of "totalitarianism" as a peculiarly modern development. Identified most closely with Hannah Arendt in the late 1940s and 1950s, this interpretation rejects any approach to a "fascist enemy" that treats it as a unitary phenomenon. It assumes a distance in kind between the government of Nazi Germany and the Italian fascist state, particularly when the fascist regime was still in the process of organizing itself in the 1920s. This approach further rejects any effort to present Soviet Russia as it existed under Stalin as a qualitatively different tyranny from Nazi Germany and calls into question the indiscriminate equation of communists and communist sympathizers with "antifascists."

In *Totalitarianism, Origins of Totalitarianism*, and Hans Buchheim's *Totalitarian Rule: Its Nature and Characteristics*, "totalitarian dictatorship" is viewed as something distinct from authoritarian states and older forms of social and political organization.[3] Totalitarianism is defined as a twentieth-century problem that is illustrated most dramatically by Nazi Germany and Soviet Russia. It was radically antitraditional as well as antiliberal, and it presupposed for its ascendancy what Arendt calls "the breakdown of the class system." Further: "the fall of protecting class walls transformed the slumbering majorities behind all parties into one great unorganized, structureless mass of furious individuals who had nothing in common except their vague apprehension that the hopes of party members were doomed, that the most respected, articulate, and representative members of the community were fools and that all powers that be were not so much evil as they were equally stupid and fraudulent."[4]

Arendt's formulation stresses the breakdown of traditional authority as a precondition for the grim new order, which may have been the obvious impression of a German refugee who had witnessed the Nazis' ascent to power. In Friedrich's and Brzezinski's view, modern technology, political chaos, and the lack of a firm constitutional tradition were all critical factors for nurturing the kind of government that Stalin and Hitler created. Exponents of the post–World War II theory of totalitarianism perceived shared characteristics in the regimes that their country had been up against. These regimes devised elaborate ideologies that embraced every aspect of human existence and usually featured a future golden age, the realization of which was the goal of the subject population. These new forms of control were also marked by parties and dictators who surrounded themselves with cadres of true believers. The totalitarian regimes employed terror through the recruitment and deployment of secret police, for the purpose of instilling submission. This terrorist policy was aimed at dissenters or, less discriminatingly, at minorities who were condemned, often quite arbitrarily, as enemies of the regime.[5]

Declared enemies of the state were also designated, not incidentally, as opponents of the transformational experiment that totalitarian dictators claimed to be promoting. Getting rid of insidious, dangerous troublemakers en masse would supposedly help advance the common project imposed by the leader and bring about the desired end of history more quickly. Furthermore, the leader and his party exercised a monopoly over all forms of mass communication and were able to manipulate reality to serve political ends. The all-powerful leader disposed of all the weaponry and armed forces needed to carry out an aggressive foreign policy. All totalitarian states were by nature expansionist. Finally, centralized control was established over the economy and left in the hands of state servants. Formerly independent corporate-industrial units were thereby made subject to the head of the government and his inner circle. Even if some semblance of private ownership was allowed to persist, the state and its leader determined economic relations and who owned what.

This description captures in a nutshell what theorists considered the essential features of a totalitarian power structure. Such a structure of command is not the same as any "undemocratic" government or any state led by a single leader or a single mass party. It is also not interchangeable with any generic notion of fascism, and despite attempts during World War II to treat Hitler, Mussolini, and the Japanese militarists as ideologically equivalent, theorists of totalitarianism after 1945 and even earlier questioned this wartime demonology. Not all authoritarian or militaristic governments were totalitarian; the term was thought to cut across conventional right/left distinctions of the kind academics and journalists are still inclined to draw. Hitler and Stalin were not ideological opposites but similar dangers to human freedom who executed similarly oppressive, genocidal policies. Soviet and Nazi tyrannies were related to each other more than they were to other, less destructive forms of rule that were merely authoritarian or transitions to other types of rule.

This assumed linkage ruffled more than one group. If the pro-Soviet or the anticommunist Left and those who were especially fixated on Hitler's war against the Jews were unhappy with the extended comparison between Stalin's and Hitler's tyrannies, then Italian antifascists may have looked askance at studies of totalitarianism that appeared to trivialize their national trauma. In Italy a historiographical tradition reigns on the Left, but some Christian Democrats also treat Italian fascism as a model "totalitarian" movement. This view has been espoused by such leftist, antifascist historians as Gaetano Salvemini, Luigi Salvatorelli, and Herman Finer, as well as by Catholic traditionalists. The interpretation of fascism as a totalitarian movement also makes a brief appearance in De Felice's *Interpretations of Fascism*, which was published in 1969.[6]

A contemporary historian closely associated with this "totalitarian" reading of fascism, Emilio Gentile, has published multiple volumes on fascism as totalitarian politics and ersatz religion. Gentile has linked his subject to the concept of "political religion," which he drew from the German philosopher of history Eric Voegelin. Gentile views the tendency of interwar fascism to absorb and reprocess religious and salvific themes as perhaps its greatest danger. Fascists replaced Christian doctrines of redemption and cosmic reconciliation with God with beliefs in an earthly savior and in political redemption achieved through political practice.

It would take considerable space, perhaps more than this chapter could spare, to go over Gentile's elaborate arguments about political religion in fascist Italy and to provide an appropriately long critique. For the nonce, these critical observations may have to do. There are two ways in which Gentile fails to refute the more restrictive use of totalitarianism in Arendt's treatise. He does not prove that Mussolini's and Giovanni Gentile's advocacy of the "*stato totalitario*" resulted in an all-powerful regime. Looking at Italian fascist rhetoric and iconography may lead one to believe that these creations reveal the operation of "political religion." But these features of the fascist movement do not demonstrate that Mussolini controlled, or even tried to control, the lives and fortunes of his subjects to the same degree that Hitler and Stalin dominated their countries. Reading De Felice's description of the Italian fascist government leaves us with a distinctly different impression.

Another objection that might be raised to the attribution of totalitarianism to the Italian fascists concerns how fascist theorists such as Giovannii

Gentile laid out their proposed alternative to liberalism and Marxism. The *"totalizzazione"* that fascist architects praised was a process by which the state and members of the nation became fused in a common identity. But this was not to be achieved, as Erwin von Beckerath explains in his entry in the *Encyclopedia of the Social Sciences* (1937), through the imposition of an all-powerful structure of control. In both theory and practice, "the corporative state is still in a process of transformation." Indeed, as late as the 1930s, one could not "form an exact opinion as to how far the legal machinery set up for its realization has altered the actual features of the Italian economic system."[7] Beckerath stresses that in the corporative model, "the state administration allies itself with private enterprise and the preservation of the capitalistic order." Despite Italian fascism's supposed reorganization of political and economic functions and its insertion of overarching ministries and a national council of corporations into its governing blueprint, it would be hard to prove that commerce in fascist Italy changed significantly from the early 1920s onward. Any comparison between Stalin's economic policies and those introduced under Mussolini would uncover a veritable gulf between the two approaches to economic change.

As minister of education under Mussolini's regime, Giovanni Gentile was forced to put aside his anticlericalism and integrate Catholic instruction into the national education of his country.[8] If some fascists hoped they would be allowed to fashion political religion, they were sorely disappointed. Especially after the Lateran Pact in 1929, fascists were forced to share their social and educational space with the Church. Also unlike the Russian and German dictators, *Il Duce* was subject to higher political powers. On July 24, 1943, after the Allies landed in Sicily and began to move up the Italian boot, the Grand Council of Fascism dismissed Mussolini as head of state. On the following day the Italian monarch had his former prime minister arrested. Such actions would have been inconceivable in true totalitarian states such as the ones that existed in Germany and Russia.

It might also be that discussions of "political religion" are often overly selective in what they target. Emilio Gentile contrasts fascist political religion with the openness and non-ideological character of "liberal democracy," which he regards as having reached an awe-inspiring milestone with the election of the first Catholic president, John F. Kennedy. Although Gentile is entitled to his favorite president and favorite regime, a question (which I once posed to him in person) is: why are only fascism and communism to be regarded as "political religions"? Isn't traditional American civil religion—even before George W. Bush promoted American exceptionalism and tried to impose our human rights concepts on other societies—a form of political religion?[9] What renders "liberal democracy" resistant to the temptations to which liberal nationalists in Italy once yielded—namely, the impulse to idolize a particular form of the modern state? Canadian political thinker Grant Havers has asked why Americans have persisted in believing "that political religion happens only to undemocratic citizenries."[10] Havers quotes historian Michael Burleigh who locates political religion in, among other reference points, "the Christian world of representations that still informs much of our politics."[11] Gentile is describing not only a post-Christian tendency, which substitutes political ideology for religious doctrine, but a temptation that is inherent in Christian society.

There is therefore no sound reason to leap to the conclusion that political religion was a peculiar feature of Italian and German governments in the interwar period. Rather, we are dealing here with a more generalized feature of what Del Noce considered the "age of secularism." And even in this particular case, we should qualify this observation by noting that earlier Christian ages were never fully immune to what one of Gentile's favorite thinkers, Eric Voegelin, defined as the passion to "immanentize the Eschaton"—that is, believing that through radical political means one could construct Paradise on Earth. Voegelin cites multiple examples of these "derailments" in past Christian ages and ascribes them to the recurrent Christian heresy of "Gnosticism," which, in the modern age, has reemerged as political ideology.[12] The point is not whether this explanation accounts for periodic eruptions of apocalyptic politics in Christian societies (Havers and Burleigh believe that it does) but whether one can prove that Italian fascism, but not liberal democracies, fit the description of "political religion." One can easily find evidence to challenge this assumption (about the nature of liberal democracy).

Less problematic is the connection between theories of totalitarianism and the Cold War. The ascent in both the popular press and the popular imagination of the totalitarian model coincided with the postwar tensions between Stalin's regime and the Western "bourgeois" democracies under American leadership. The change in the world situation after World War II suggests why intellectual and political leaders embraced a distinction between "totalitarian and nontotalitarian" regimes that would have been harder to sell a few years earlier. That is to say, it would have been hard to win acceptance for this postwar view as long as America's Italian fascist enemy was being made to look more sinister than its Soviet allies.

An incisive article by two representatives of the New Left, Les K. Adler and T. G. Paterson, "Red Fascism: The Merger of Nazi Germany and Soviet Russia in the American Image of Totalitarianism (1930s to 1950s)," documents how the view of fascism established in the United States during the

Second World War was later transferred to the Soviets.[13] A preconstructed image of an anti-American, or anti-Western, adversary was made to apply to a former ally that, contrary to wartime propaganda, proved to be far less benevolent than the Western powers had once chosen to view it. Although Adler and Paterson may understate Soviet aggression in the post–World War II years, they correctly observe that labels originally designed for a fascist enemy were recycled during the Cold War.

The theory of totalitarianism accompanied the application of old negative descriptions to new enemies. It helped explain why the Western world was battling another menacing dictatorship so soon after it had dealt with the Nazis. We were being tested in a prolonged struggle against enemies who turned out to be more alike than different. It was all part of the struggle for freedom throughout the world. During the Cold War, the terms *totalitarian*, *Red fascism*, and *political religion* all gained currency, and whatever the conceptual differences among these concepts, they were all applied to the international scene and, more specifically, the confrontation between the West and the Soviet Empire.

What is sometimes missed in theories about totalitarianism is an accurate recognition of their point of origin. Contrary to a now widespread misconception, particularly in Germany, the view that there was a totalitarian commonality between the Soviets and the Nazis did not come primarily from the Right and least of all from apologists for Nazi or fascist regimes. This comparison came more typically from the Left or from that part of the Left that was shocked by the catastrophic Soviet experiment in socialism. Whether disappointed Trotskyists; anti-Stalinist socialists like Arendt, Franz Borkenau, and George Orwell; or mildly social democratic or pro-welfare state reformers like Juan Linz and Zbigniew Brzezinski, those who presented the theory of totalitarianism were certainly not, for the most part, embattled right wingers.[14] They were progressives who had been awakened to the evils of the Soviet regime and noticed its operational similarities with Nazi tyranny. Invariably the comparison went from Nazi horrors to Soviet evil, although in Nolte's work the opposite was argued—that the fascist, and preeminently the Nazi, experiment was an imitation of the Soviet government intended to counteract communist revolutionaries. (Nolte was still a figure of the Left when he was constructing this theory in the late 1950s.) It was the democratic and dissenting socialist Left that previewed the "Red fascism" perspective of Cold War liberalism but perhaps without intending to make it into a Cold War rhetorical fixture.

Soviet communism looked like Nazism in practice, and it consequently made sense to assume a family resemblance between the two. Big Brother's tyranny as depicted by the anti-Stalinist socialist George Orwell in *Nineteen Eighty-Four* gives evidence of Nazi as well as Stalinist features. The instrumental use by Big Brother of continuing war to unify his subjects points back to a fascist doctrine of perpetual struggle. At the same time, Big Brother's demonization of the obviously Jewish dissenter Goldstein points in a different direction, which is Stalin's vengeful pursuit of Trotsky. It is hard to read Orwell's allegory as an anticommunist work of art exclusively, considering the fact that there are leftist, and possibly even Trotskyist, fingerprints all over this literary creation.[15]

Anticommunists of the Right also noted a strong resemblance between Nazism and Soviet communism but stressed as a unifying factor something that the democratic Left chose not to emphasize. A characteristically conservative analysis of Soviet tyranny can be found in such figures as Augusto Del Noce, Gerhart Niemeyer, Aleksandr Sozhenitsyn, and various Catholic and Orthodox anticommunists. The antitotalitarian interpretation that proceeded from this school of thought accentuates the godlessness of modern political tyrants and the poisonous effects of materialist ideologies. Voegelin's disciple, the Anglo-Catholic priest Gerhart Niemeyer, devoted an entire work to exploring the "common feature" of all totalitarianism as a form of "ontological negation."[16] Overshadowing any distinction between "rightist" and "leftist" totalitarian regimes, says Niemeyer, is the shared desire among their defenders and builders to repudiate man's place in the chain of being. This, we are told, lies somewhere between animal life and the divine source of our existence. As a Christian, Niemeyer is struck by the hubristic claims of totalitarians in a world stripped of any divine reference point. Totalitarians, we are told, mistake their personal wills for the operation of an infinitely wiser being.

Another interpretation of totalitarianism focuses on its impersonal managerial features. Although developed by the former Trotskyite James Burnham in *The Managerial Revolution* and present in both Frankfurt School critiques of capitalist modernity and Hannah Arendt's picture of modern tyranny, the linkage between totalitarianism and managerial control comes up in other ideological settings. It has appealed to old-fashioned European liberals, who have given their own spin on the diagnosis of totalitarianism. Robert Nisbet in the United States, Herbert Butterfield and Michael Oakeshott in England, and Helmut Schelsky in Germany have all highlighted the potential for total control in the modern state and its hostility toward traditional communal and hierarchical associations.[17]

Although these critics have not regarded all managerial regimes as potentially murderous, they have seen in administrative control an intrinsic trait of modern despotism. Unlike the democratic Left, these antitotalitarian commentators question whether democracy and total government are incompatible concepts and whether totalitarianism is restricted to nondemocratic national cultures. The linking of "mass democracy" to "bureaucratic centralization" and Oakeshott's "enterprise association," an association designed to direct a common purpose from the top down, suggest that modern managerial regimes may be another road leading to totalitarian government.

Such critics have interpreted "soft despotism," in which state management is combined with public education and a media-shaped reality, as a means by which entire populations can have their brains laundered. This arrangement is conducive to a form of groupthink that effectively marginalizes significant opposition. Social engineering is seen as the path toward this strenuously managed society without the overt cruelty that was characteristic of interwar totalitarian leaders. We are therefore made to think that the Nazi and Soviet catastrophes were the cruder, more explosive forms of impersonal, bureaucratic rule, aiming at a kind of manipulation that modern democracies can achieve without violence. In short, interwar dictatorships were physically more destructive forms of what is a characteristically modern process of change.[18]

A variation on this theme of totalitarianism as managerial tyranny turned up in the postwar years among conservative German opponents of the Nazi regime. It is a view that was popularized by Arendt, who observed certain dislocations that she later listed in her magnum opus even before her flight from the Nazis. According to Arendt, totalitarian "movements" and their "leader principle" were engaged in "an invasion" of the state by alien, outside forces. Hans Buchheim quotes the aristocratic anti-Nazi Ulrich von Hassell who complained in the 1930s about the intellectual crudeness of the Nazis: "These people don't have the slightest idea what the state is."[19]

Another critic of the radical revolutionary regime who had been a government administrator, Werner Bergengruen, recorded in his memoirs that old-fashioned state servants were "totally isolated" under the new order. "At times it seemed that party loyalists and their organizations were members of an invading army that could barely speak the language of the conquered country and whose soldiers knew little about the speaking and thought patterns of the natives."[20] Common to these observers is a view of the inherited German order of things as a "state under law," one in which state servants, and particularly judges, were intended to apply established legal codes. The mobilization of government agencies and the judiciary for the purpose of advancing party goals struck these observers as a disruptive process that sometimes resembled an "invasion force."

Despite their differing points of attack, descriptions of totalitarian rule reveal remarkable overlap. All of them stress the modernity of their subject and treat totalitarianism as a danger characteristic of the modern age. The exponents of this interpretation plot the development of totalitarian regimes along a different axis from the left-right spectrum that has marked most traditional Western forms of government since the nineteenth century. To call Hitler a "conservative" and Stalin a "revolutionary leftist" would be to miss the main point about each one. What unites their regimes is exactly what should attract our attention. Arendt was particularly diligent in documenting how totalitarian leaders borrowed from each other. Hitler took his terrorist and genocidal politics from an already existing Soviet model, and after the Second World War, as Arendt notes, an already triumphant Stalin gave government sanction to anti-Semitism in Russia and throughout the Soviet bloc as a means of isolating a new public enemy.

By no means offended by this "mainstay of Nazi ideology," according to Arendt, Stalin ran to embrace it once his Nazi competitor was gone. Like Hitler he knew that anti-Jewish prejudice had "obvious propaganda value in Russia and in all the satellite countries, where anti-Jewish feeling was widespread." And by playing up anti-Semitic themes in Russia and the Soviet satellites toward the end of his life, Stalin was simply expanding his propagandistic repertoire. A Jewish world conspiracy provided a "more suitable background for ideological claims to world rule than Wall Street capitalism and imperialism."[21] Arendt observes that Hitler and Stalin abolished the class system that they had inherited. In each case, classes were replaced by a mob presided over by the leader and his single party base. This was more critical for understanding the Nazi and Soviet regimes than the fact that one talked about racial superiority and the other about social equality.

Although it is possible to criticize her digressive, Germanic style and labored search for the roots of Nazism in the Dreyfus Affair and other early manifestations of the "mob," Arendt's work fully deserves its place as one of the "most important" books of the twentieth century. It is also perhaps the most consistently insightful study of "totalitarianism," and any comparison between this monument of thought and painful human experience and the work of Brzezinski must definitely favor the German exile. Brzezinski treats Italian fascism as full-blown totalitarianism, relying for his picture on the time-bound work of Herman Finer. Most of his treatment of Soviet tyranny is based on recent studies by Sovietologists and seems designed to make Stalin's government fit into a certain World War II pattern of denunciation.[22] The intended impression is that America's recent enemies have all looked alike and should be seen as offering a continuing threat to Western democracy. This monochromatic depiction lends substance to the complaint about a contrived "Red fascist" enemy that issued from the New Left in the 1960s and 1970s. Brzezinski and his later collaborator, the legal scholar Carl Friedrich, were extending wartime conceptions of the fascist enemy to the postwar Soviet foe.

Perhaps Arendt's most original perception, beyond her description of how totalitarian states function, is found in her comments about how totalitarians approach "science" and "factualness." They feel no compunctions about distorting reality, because making their subjects believe in what is patently false increases the state's power. The Nazi and Soviet governments cynically presented lies as scholarship, and they mixed partial truths with glaring falsehoods (about class enemies or about those who were racially compatible or incompatible) in order to establish total power over their subjects' minds. Here all ideological distinctions broke down before the exercise of might and terror without regard for truth or traditional authority.[23]

In no sense was Arendt trying to make her work fit any specific American foreign policy.[24] She wrote to explain to herself and others the horrors of the lived past, and she defined totalitarian in such a way as to stress that it was a break from previous ages. It was radically antitraditional, thrived by unleashing terror, and exercised a distinctly modern form of control. Although some current governments may deserve to be pushed into oblivion, we need not assume that their mode of operation corresponds to Arendt's detailed description of totalitarian governments. She also strongly suggests in her first edition of *Origins of Totalitarianism* in 1951 that the terrorist regimes under examination do not reform themselves. They have to be overthrown from within or without.

The Limits of the Totalitarian Model

This brings us to the limits of the totalitarian model, which are already revealed in Arendt's work and duly noted in the third edition of *Origins of Totalitarianism* in 1966. In the introduction to what for the author was the last edition, she comments on the "detotalitarization process" that took place in Russia after Stalin's death in 1953. Although it was not clear that "this process is final and irreversible," by the 1960s it seemed that what changed "can no longer be called temporary or provisional." The Soviet army had become a key player in the post-Stalinist regime, and when Nikita Krushchev took power in the mid-1950s he "used the support of Marshal Zhukov and the army exactly the same way Stalin had used his relationship to the secret police in the succession struggle of thirty years ago."²⁵ Although Krushchev later removed Zhukov from the party's Central Committee, he never entirely freed himself from his dependence on the military. He required regular army units to crush the Hungarian uprising in 1965 since he no longer had at his disposal a vast secret police network to deal with his enemies. Although Hungarian dissenters were imprisoned and in some cases executed, no "typical Stalinist solution" that requires the "wholesale deportation of people" took place.²⁶

Krushchev openly denounced Stalin's "cult of personality" in a famous speech before the Twentieth Party Congress in which he no longer hid the crimes of his predecessor, much to the consternation of Communist Party members abroad. This would not likely have happened when Stalin was alive. Again unlike Stalin, Krushchev did not secretly execute those whom he regarded as his opponents. He tried his critics openly, rather than having them summarily killed. Dissenters were then imprisoned or treated as psychologically troubled individuals. Arendt here was not praising the changed Soviet regime for being relatively less ruthless than it had been in the past, but she does insist that it mellowed after Stalin's death.

Discussions of a "thaw" in the Soviet system could also be found in the work of Brzezinski, who, while writing on Soviet totalitarianism, began to see changes in his object of study. Like Arendt he regarded the Soviet government once Stalin was gone as being more open to modifications than it had been before. But the notion of totalitarianism was open to question from another direction, namely in the depiction of Nazi Germany as a totally closed, terrorist society. People sometimes equate the ghastly mass murders and territorial aggressiveness of the Nazi regime with a high degree of internal control. But the two conditions did not necessarily go together. Hitler killed tens of millions of people and overran other countries, but internally his government was nowhere as controlling as Stalin's Russia. Up until World War II, Germans, including German Jews, were allowed to leave the Third Reich. The economy, if we exclude such crimes as the confiscation of Jewish property and property and assets belonging to opponents of the Nazi state, was far more open than the economy in Soviet Russia. Equally noteworthy is that the Nazi government became increasingly indifferent to what went on in German universities.²⁷ The earlier enthusiasm displayed by Nazi officials who were hoping to make academic centers into showcases of party propaganda eventually fizzled out.

Although the number of Nazi critics who stayed behind may have been opportunistically exaggerated later, there were non-Nazi and even anti-Nazi scholars who remained in German academic posts during the war. Friedrich

Meinecke, Karl Jaspers, and Hans-Georg Gadamer were far from being the only members of this group. Ernst Jünger, the distinguished man of letters and a figure identified with the revolutionary Right before the Nazi ascent to power, openly ridiculed the Nazis but survived Hitler's regime.[28] It is unthinkable that such critics and skeptics would have escaped punishment in Stalin's Russia. Composers and poets in styles that displeased the Soviet dictator or those who did not parrot his political opinions were killed or placed in a Gulag.

Hitler may have been the more savage murderer, but he was not as obsessed as his Soviet counterpart with ideological conformity. For all his manipulations of Marxist-Leninism, Stalin may have been serious about fashioning a new society on the basis of a transformative blueprint: Stalin insisted on the collectivization of agriculture, a brutal experiment that it is hard to imagine the obsessively anti-Semitic and anti-Slavic but in other ways less programmed Hitler would have undertaken. On the other hand, such differences do not show that Hitler's regime would have unraveled the way the Soviet system began to do after Stalin's death. Hitler's aggressiveness caused the Third Reich to fall in a devastating war before it could be tested to see whether it was capable of self-correction.

This raises a further point about treating totalitarian regimes as forms of rule in which ideological identities are of secondary importance. Is this not the way others perceived and still perceive these regimes? Despite its instructional value, Arendt's work does not provide an adequate explanation as to why Stalin's Russia had far greater appeal than fascism or Nazism among intellectuals and artists. Admittedly, some intellectuals did cooperate with the Third Reich, especially during its heyday. But one can hardly compare this degree of popularity to the acclamation enjoyed by the Soviets over several generations as the champion of Marxist-Leninism. Nazi collaborators and fascist enthusiasts among the intelligentsia lagged in number and prestige well behind those who rallied to communism and the Soviets. It may be no more than a fraction of this noteworthy company that Paul Hollander discusses in his Baedeker of communist fellow travelers *Political Pilgrims* (1973).[29]

Observing this tendency is not to endorse Hollander's subjects, who fronted for nasty regimes. But certain realities must be registered if we wish to grasp how sides were taken in the interwar period. The loyalties in question were not reducible to the fact that certain ethnic groups, because of who threatened them more, would have inclined toward one tyranny or the other. There was also an ideological civil war, roughly of the kind Nolte evokes, that must be taken into account. Intellectual partisans were clustered around two conflicting poles, but by far the larger number stood with the Left.

Although this observation does not exclude noticing the similarities between totalitarian governments, for those who judged them and for those who still write about them, certain theoretical and moral differences have remained paramount. In the autumn of 1997 a political controversy broke out in France following the publication of the *The Black Book of Communism: Crimes, Terror, Repression* by Stéphane Courtois, a work that details the mass murders committed by communist regimes in the twentieth century.[30] This *livre de scandale* occasioned not only spirited defenses of Stalin's "antifascism" by, among others, Socialist Premier Lionel Jospin, but it also gave rise to exuberant invectives in the French national press against anyone who would be insensitive enough to compare communist victims to fascist ones. French journalist Roland LeRoy may have put the case best for his side in *Le Journal du Dimanche*: "At the heart of Communism is love of humanity; at the heart of Nazism is hatred of the human race."[31]

Similar sentiments surface in the comments made to Romanian President Iliescu in 2003 by Vladimir Tismaneanu, a onetime opponent of the communist Ceacescu regime who is now a political theorist at the University of Maryland:

> At least one aspect emerges clearly from the international debate on communism and fascism: if we can talk about communism with a human face it is almost impossible to talk about fascism or Nazism with a human face. Communism allowed at least the illusion of humanism and in the Communist tradition, maybe in Marxism in the Marxist anthropological tradition we can find a humanist tradition completely rejected by fascism. As you said earlier, and I believe that is important, I believe that at the origins of Marxism stood a sort of democratic aspiration.[32]

Even if Hitler's Germany and Stalin's Russia look in some ways remarkably similar, historians should not overlook the moral difference that intellectuals make between them. This widespread distinction may explain why glowing references to Stalin or his henchmen here and in western Europe evoke so little reaction while anything linked, however arbitrarily, to the Third Reich or fascism unleashes public outrage. Let us note an astute observation made by the cultural anthropologist Mircea Eliade: the one inestimable advantage that Marxists and communists enjoy in relation to fascists and other anti-egalitarians is their recycling of certain primal myths that are woven into Christianity about the "ultimate victory of the suffering Just." According to Eliade, these myths are so deeply embedded in our minds that political positions that seem to reflect them resonate with intellectuals no matter how disastrously they may turn out in practice.[33]

An attempt at a balanced assessment of the totalitarian concept, *Totalitarianism* has come from the English Soviet analyst Leonard Shapiro.[34] After summing up the "six point syndrome" that was developed mostly by Brzezinski, Shapiro asks whether the concept of totalitarianism continues to be "useful." It may be a mistake, he says, to treat governments that illustrate this syndrome as unchanging. In the Soviet case, the degree of tyrannical control had certainly diminished since Stalin's death, and clearly the system that had been put in place in Russia and its empire was being "breached through outside pressure." Still, what was breached was qualitatively different from a mere authoritarian regime. Characteristic of totalitarian states was "a superior power which can override all ostensible institutions, the subjugation of the legal order, and the lack of discrete and separate organs of power, in short omnipresent total control over the individual."[35]

Fascist Antimodernism

In recent years authoritarianism has emerged for political analysts as both a theoretical problem and a continuing nuisance. This refers to governments that are neither liberal nor democratic but reformable and not systematically oppressive. Distinguished scholars have analyzed authoritarian rather than totalitarian rule and have stressed the predemocratic character of authoritarianism.[36] Authoritarian states are not so much vicious as reactionary and resistant to political modernization. They function through an alliance of the military with landowners or an anxious bourgeoisie or tribal heads, all of whom are driven by fear of revolutionary upheaval. Because of their foot-dragging and occasionally resorting to violence, authoritarian regimes are mostly unstable. Liberal internationalists therefore conclude that it may be necessary to push them out of existence, lest they become a bigger source of worry for those in the "democratic West."

This liberal internationalist perspective has become most explicit in the neoconservative thinking that has intermittently dominated American foreign policy since the 1980s. Liberal internationalists and particularly neoconservatives, who are working toward a "global democratic revolution," regard "dictatorships" as backward states that require "regime change."[37] This view clearly clashes with the idea that fascist regimes embody their own form of organizational modernity. Still, from the liberal internationalist standpoint, this academic question is less relevant than whether we are dealing with good or bad regimes. All dictatorships represent a deviation from Western parliamentary systems and the ideology of human rights—that is, from what is now called "liberal democracy." This means that the rejected regime belongs to an oppressive past or else to a historical misstep. But "fascist" does have taxonomic value within this crusading doctrine. It survives as a rhetorical tool for denoting governments that are particularly offensive to Western political elites.

The identification of fascism with what is antimodern or defectively modern does carry with it certain definite implications. From this perspective, the enemy on the Right is not so much revolutionary as intolerably reactionary. Already in the 1960s De Felice lamented the unwillingness of those who were writing on fascism to recognize this movement's radical, dynamic side.[38] They treated it as arrested political development and attacked its leaders for holding back a desirable social future.

In other recent formulations fascism has been presented as a form of "antimodern" or "reactionary" modernism.[39] It illustrates a form of modernity that has been turned against itself and one that is believed to have existed in nuce in such aberrant modernizing societies as the German Second Empire or Imperial Japan. Although there are certain continuities or predispositions in particular societies that may prepare the way for later developments, the concept of a necessary path leading to modernization is not particularly instructive. As an implicit moral judgment, it leads to exaggerating the inevitableness of later problems in certain societies by reducing their supposed defects to time bombs waiting to go off.

What we are being told is that because things turned out as they did, they could only have gone in the direction they took. But even more questionably, these critics of *passéisme* plot a modernization process that reflects a selective view of what happened in their preferred Western countries in the modern period. We are thereby confronted with the secular progressive equivalent of medieval redemptive doctrine. There is supposedly no salvation for anyone who fails to follow those changes predicated on a Western Whig theory of history. Those who fail to imitate us are doomed to become destructive reactionaries and all the more so as they modernize without our present political values.[40] Also left out of consideration is that identifiably Western values continue to succeed each other as modernity continues to unfold. In advanced welfare state societies, for example, social equality has become a more prized value than individual initiative or free communal associations. Why should we consider the now more fashionable value as less modern than the one we prefer? It may be argued that all stages of modernization lead beyond themselves.

Another popular view of fascism is that it's an evil that springs out of antiprogressive forces lurking within us. German intellectuals seem particularly enthralled by this idea of fascism as "operating stealthily" among their fascist-prone nation, although rarely within their own morally intact interiors.[41] As seen from this angle, fascism is a kind of original sin that, unless continuously monitored, may rise to the surface with catastrophic consequences. Among these consequences is that fascism represses or checks what is good for humanity. It became particularly destructive in the interwar period, as it resorted to murderous measures to achieve its predestined end.

At least at the journalistic and hortatory level, fascism is further defined with reference to its most vicious (but not particularly mainstream) manifestation. All fascism is now habitually explained with reference to its Nazi embodiment, which combined mass murder with ethnic cleansing and a stubborn resistance to human progress. This identification of all varieties of fascism and, finally, all rightist or non-leftist authoritarian governments with Nazism came less from critical assessments than from other, less scholarly considerations. As the political culture began to change drastically in the 1960s, older interpretive perspectives were replaced by an approach to the recent past that focused exclusively on victims of the Right.

This sea change was aided by the rise of the New Left, which interpreted fascism as anything that opposed social transformation. The New Left drew support from another development that was occurring simultaneously—the elevation of the Holocaust to the most decisive event in all of Jewish history. The memory of Nazi persecution served to unify Jews at a time when their religious cohesion was eroding. Although those who expressed this overriding concern with fascism both past and present might not have agreed on other issues, e.g., Middle Eastern politics, they did share an interest in combating fascism, which became, in their minds, indistinguishable from Nazi atrocities and the fear that such outrages could be repeated.

It was thereafter widely assumed that fascism, however one might define it, was a far worse threat to humanity than communism, and certain changes on the international scene hastened the acceptance of this belief. Soviet tyranny had already begun to thaw, and although there were other communist regimes that were engaging in mass murder, they were mostly in the Third World. The failings of these oppressive governments were blamed either on the birth pangs of postcolonial governments trying to shake off the effects of Western imperialism or else on supposedly right wing American administrations that pursued a neocolonial war in what had been Indochina. The birthing hour had struck for a new form of antifascism, and the largely post-Marxist Left from whence this antifascism came was correct about one critical detail: historical fascism was indeed a creation of the Right, although, contrary to what the New Left believed, a Right that had once existed but which now only survived in vestigial form.

CHAPTER THREE

Fascism as the Unconquered Past

A Psychic Presence

Although others have contributed to the belief that fascism is a psychic condition that poisons our politics and culture, no circle of intellectuals has molded such thinking more definitively than the Frankfurt School. First organized in Frankfurt in 1924 around social thinkers Theodor Adorno, Max Horkheimer, Felix Weil, Herbert Marcuse, Erich Fromm, Leo Löwenthal, Otto Kirchheimer, and Friedrich Pollock, this school of thought worked to construct a Critical Theory focused on the defects of nonsocialist Western societies. The targeted structure of human relations was seen as emotionally and socially oppressive, and those who identified themselves with critical theory produced analytic commentaries exposing the inhumanity of late capitalist society and suggesting possible alternatives. Although some founding members rubbed shoulders with the German Communist Party, the Frankfurt School was at least mildly skeptical of the communist experiment initiated in Russia with the Bolshevik Revolution. The prevalent view among its members was that Marxist-Leninism, as put into practice in Communist Russia, represented only a truncated version of Marx's vision of the socialist future.[1]

In search of a fuller understanding of Marx's hope for "freedom from alienation," the Frankfurt School incorporated Freudian psychology into their analytic perspective. But their integration of Freudian ideas was pushed in a visionary direction that Freud himself would have never recognized. Rather than following Freud by acknowledging that the repression and redirection of primal urges was necessary for human civilization, some members of the Frankfurt School, most famously Theodor Adorno (1903–1969), Herbert Marcuse (1898–1979), and Erich Fromm (1900–1980), imagined that there could be a future in which sexual fantasies and social needs were both satisfied. This erotically and materially satisfying world could only be achieved, however, by putting an end to advanced capitalism. According to the Frankfurt School, this "irrational" economy perpetuated unfair human inequalities and forced its victims to repress and pervert their natural desires in order to survive in a system of domination over which they had no control.[2]

Members of the Frankfurt School have sometimes been described dismissively as "cultural Marxists" because they present cultural analysis as social criticism. For example, Adorno's longtime preoccupation with twelve-tone music and his war on what was merely "beautiful" reflected his quest for art forms that nurtured the revolutionary spirit. Adorno regarded culture as an instrument for radical change, and those antiquarian forms of it that soothed or carried snob value he judged to be, in the customary Marxist phrase, objectively reactionary. Adorno, who founded the original Frankfurt School with his lifetime collaborator Max Horkheimer (1895–1973), not only commented on music from his iconoclastic stance but also produced what he deemed suitably atonal compositions for piano.

He and his associates also advocated a "negative dialectic" by which existing social and cultural institutions were exposed to critical assault. In *Minima Moralia* (1951) and *Negative Dialektik* (1966), Adorno's approach to the "merely existent" as opposed to a non-actualized society often involved the assumption of a negative attitude toward everything that stood in the way of the envisaged transformation. Such speculative exercises recall the explication of the unfolding dialectic in Hegel's logic and epistemology. Although definitely a starting point for the "negative dialectic" and the subject of Herbert Marcuse's *Reason and Revolution: Hegel and the Rise of Social Theory* (1941), the Hegelian understanding of the contradictory nature of apparent reality, like Freud's psychology, is absorbed quite selectively into critical theory.[3] The negative dialectic leads not to an absolute mind or to an ultimate point in consciousness but to a demonstration of the absurdity of the conventional and antirevolutionary. This negative dialectical thinking may produce in the reader a sense of futility as well as an appreciation of the author's playfulness.

What gave the Frankfurt School special importance and explains its preoccupation with the "authoritarian personality" and the omnipresent danger of fascism was, above all, the experience of exile. When the Nazis took power in

Germany in 1933, the Frankfurt School was closed as a research center, and its preponderantly Jewish adherents were driven into exile. Despite initial attempts to relocate in Geneva and Paris, the group soon landed in New York where they became attached to Columbia University as the Institute for Social Research. Several of the members worked intermittently during the war for the CIA's predecessor, the Office of Strategic Services. In this advisory capacity they investigated the psychic origins of fascism and proposed far-reaching plans for curing the Germans of their aggressive political culture. This exploration of the social and psychological preconditions for a fascist society culminated in the publication of *The Authoritarian Society* (1950), a compilation of essays that fit into a series of commentaries titled *Studies in Prejudice*, which was financed and published by the American Jewish Committee. Horkheimer became a coeditor for the entire series, which dealt with the psychic and social causes of anti-Semitism. He later assigned the organization of the most famous anthology in the series, *TAP*, to his alter ego, Adorno.[4]

The editors prepared their monumental study of "prejudice" for the benefit of the American intelligentsia. Adorno explained that the "military defeat" of Germany should not be imagined to have ended the fascist threat. The Western victors were "advanced capitalist" countries that were vulnerable to authoritarian dictatorship, just as Germany was before the war. With the onset of the anticommunist Cold War, the struggle against fascism had been brought to a premature halt. Now the United States was drifting away from socialism, a path that Americans had been tentatively taking during the New Deal but from which they were now retreating.

TAP was aimed at an American society that was believed to be suffering from a democracy deficit. Just a few years after the United States' victory over Nazism, complained Frankfurt School emigrants, the American populace was falling for anticommunist demagogues and railing against modernism in art. Adorno announced in his English-language correspondence that "paradoxical as it sounds, the Germans were more willing to fight Hitler's battles than to join and listen to the music of his lackeys. In the United States, by contrast, the populace embraces folk ideas that are even more distant from the life of the people than the most esoteric products of expressionism and surrealism."[5]

Even more to the point, as Adorno's longtime collaborator Herbert Marcuse pointed out in February 1947 in response to a plan for reviving the Institute's periodical, the world was now divided between two powers, the very imperfectly Marxist Soviet Union and a "neofascist" West under American leadership: "The states in which the old ruling class survived the war politically and economically would soon become fascist; the other side stood in the Soviet camp." Further: "The neofascist and Soviet societies are economically and in terms of class structure enemies and a war between them is inevitable. Both however are in their forms of domination antirevolutionary and opposed to socialist development. In this situation only one path is open for revolutionary theory: relentlessly and without any pretense to resist both systems and to represent orthodox Marxist teachings without compromise."[6]

Allowances must be made here for what Marcuse, who was inspired by Freudianism and a vision of erotic gratification, understood as "orthodox Marxist teachings." He and his colleagues at the Institute espoused the following assumptions: fascism and its derivatives were products of the failure to move from capitalism into socialism. This failure was already apparent in Western countries that had defeated Nazi Germany but had not overthrown its ruling class and were now being diverted from social change through the Cold War. Even more ominously, the "cultural industry" in capitalist countries blinded the masses to the effects of living in a society in which production did not meet actual human needs.

Those who were poor, particularly marginal groups (*Randgruppen*), were having their minds numbed by kitschy art and foolish entertainment. Even more sadly, these hapless people were internalizing their alienation from irrational economic conditions due to their emotional and aesthetic deprivation. The "authoritarian personality" was the product of an alienated self, and fascism resulted not only from reactionary "forms of domination" (*Herrschaftsformen*) but from the psychic harm that accompanied a dangerous system of control.[7]

The very blunt Marcuse could not understand why his colleagues, although German Jews like himself, were so fixated on studying anti-Semitism. From his point of view, this was a bourgeois diversion from the grim revolutionary task of fighting two reactionary blocs, the neofascists who ran the United States and the Soviet corrupters of "orthodox Marxism."[8] Although some members of the Frankfurt School, like Eric Fromm, were preoccupied with both their Jewishness and Christian anti-Semitism, this would not have been true for Horkheimer or the half-Jewish Adorno, who had been raised Catholic. In any case the leaders of the Frankfurt School found the American Jewish Committee (AJC) hobbyhorse useful for their purpose, namely for underscoring the fascist, capitalist threat that was overwhelming postwar America. Horkheimer left his adopted country in 1950, even before *TAP* was distributed, and returned to Frankfurt to teach at Goethe University. Adorno, who once observed that Germany was now safer from the fascist threat than McCarthy's America, joined him at the university soon after.

The guiding themes of *TAP* were previewed in essays dealing with sadomasochistic "authority" in an anthology titled *Studien über Autorität und Familie*, which the exiled Institute put out in New York. The contributions to this earlier volume, directed by Horkheimer, Fromm, and Marcuse, stress the psychic displacements that accompanied the "crisis of bourgeois society." Here the authors dwell on the need of the emotionally distressed individual to find emotional satisfaction in "self-subordination." This behavioral and psychic pattern is repeatedly traced back to the turmoil of displaced emotions. The subjects of authoritarian societies identify themselves with the powerful while venting anger at their loss of self on those who are below them. The family suffers grievously from the resulting social and mental deterioration, as women and children are rendered subservient to the male heads of the household. Critical theorists, and particularly Horkheimer, Fromm, and Adorno, assume the development of later societies out of a primitive matriarchy. They build on an assumption allegedly confirmed by Johann Jakob Bachofen (1815–1887) who, in his early nineteenth-century anthropological work *Mutterrecht*, maintains that patriarchal cultures arose more recently than those happier societies that were matriarchal. Contrary to the views of Friedrich Engels and the Frankfurt School, the Swiss patrician Bachofen had viewed matriarchal societies as primitive relics and saw their supersession by patriarchy as a moral and social improvement that permitted his own aristocratic world to come into existence.[9] Ironically, an archconservative Swiss anthropologist would be cited by mid-twentieth-century social radicals as grist for their mills.

Fromm added to his attack on the psychic evils of late capitalism and patriarchal oppression expressions of his loathing for Calvinism as the religion of authoritarian wealth seekers. From his tract *Die Entwicklung des Christusdogma*, published in 1931, through his post–World War II English-language books on loving, psychoanalysis, and emotional sanity, Fromm decried Calvinism as a human catastrophe. He accused Calvinism of bringing together the multiple evils of an authoritarian deity, an ethic of capitalist accumulation, and a predisposition toward fascism.[10]

Since there is no demonstrable correlation between Calvinism and fascism but an oft-remarked connection between Calvinism and constitutional republicanism, Fromm's demonization is far from convincing. But it may indicate how far he strayed, even while thinking of himself as a Marxist, in the direction of a decidedly non-Marxist interpretation of the spirit of capitalism. Although Fromm viewed Protestantism's contribution to capitalism far more negatively than Max Weber did, he nonetheless drew from Weber's classic more conceptually than he did from Marx's materialist analysis. A task that would confront analysts of the critical theorists was determining to what extent their subjects were real Marxists (if one may make a German distinction, *Vollblutmarxisten* rather than *Edelmarxisten*). According to their orthodox Marxist critics, Frankfurt School theorists were falsely claiming a Marxist pedigree. They were dilettantes who were trying to make their ideas fashionable to progressive intellectuals who craved the Marxist label.

Save for Maria Herz Levinson's concluding study on the "potential fascism" of psychiatric clinic patients and her statistically laden judgments scattered throughout the volume, there is little in *TAP* that had not appeared in earlier Frankfurt School publications. Clearly the contributors took from their accumulated responses more than would have seemed justified to an objective interviewer. Adorno and his companions were searching desperately for politically useful correlations, for example, between those who did not share their socialist sentiments and those who wished to destroy Jews or degrade women or blacks. Levinson's attempts to identify these "fascist predispositions" with such emotional disorders as hysteria in women or antisocial traits in men seem to be ideologically driven (and are made even less digestible owing to the tedious prose).[11]

Adorno labels those who hold insufficiently progressive views as "pseudo-democrats" and emotional cripples. Here we face a nonfalsifiable position since it is hard to believe that Adorno and other contributors would acknowledge that someone could disagree with them on political and social questions without exhibiting a "fascist-authoritarian syndrome." Could one be seen as mentally healthy who did not share the contributors' values and sentiments? There is no reason to assume that they would have accepted this possibility, given the judgments in their book.

The citing of interviews and surveys as a cloak for the author's political inclinations and conversionary agenda runs throughout *TAP*. And this practice would go on and on. Adorno's self-proclaimed German disciple Jürgen Habermas would acquire academic respectability and a widespread reputation as an antifascist, which he has kept intact over the decades, by publishing a collection of interviews with German students, together with his own comments, in 1961. In this examination of "political consciousness" that drew on students' responses, Habermas claimed to be able to discern the right wing mindset of students who were thought to be apolitical to the point of total apathy. Behind what was widely seen as a "skeptical generation" of postwar German youth, Habermas found evidence of insufficient "democratic education."[12]

Opinion statements tricked out as "sociological research" can also be located in *TAP*, especially in its contributors' claim to be unmasking fascists and authoritarians. Their approach to silencing unwanted views illustrates their repeated practice of "pathologizing dissent." In one notably egregious reading of an interview with a "semifascist parole officer" who is cited as an example of "pseudoconservatism," the only proof of extremism adduced by Adorno is that the interviewee "agrees with the anti–New Deal Democrats and Wilkie-type Republicans and disagrees with the New Deal Democrats and traditional Republicans." On the question of whether the government should socialize medicine, the "semifascist" respondent expressed the unsettling (for Adorno) opinion: "I like the collectiveness of it but believe private business could do it better than the government."[13] Although Adorno is entitled to hold socialist views on economic issues, one might ask why a liberal Republican in 1940 should be regarded as a "semifascist" or "pseudoconservative" for holding political opinions that differed from those of Adorno. Even more inexplicable is the use of the term "pseudoconservative." Is one to assume that although Adorno rejects false conservatives, he respects authentic ones? Unfortunately for this contention, Adorno never offers an example of a "conservative" who is worthy of his admiration. He creates the impression that those who think differently from him and his fellow contributors are mentally deranged.

Two observations may be in order in evaluating *TAP*'s interpretation of fascism as a grave psychic disorder. Some defenders of the Frankfurt School have contended that it's unfair to judge their accomplishments by looking at the grotesque generalizations and tendentious statements in a work that otherwise substantial thinkers produced in exile for badly needed money. This author concedes part of this justification. Adorno and Horkheimer wrote another work in exile, The *Dialectic of the Enlightenment*, which is flawed but worthy of their critical intelligence. Even more relevant, Horkheimer moved away from Adorno's cultural radicalism in the 1950s and, in his later writings, shows a profoundly reactionary side to the point of defending Schopenhauer's pessimistic philosophy. Already in his contribution to the *Studien*, Horkheimer stands out by painting a generally favorable picture of the traditional *Bürgerstand*. He views the predatory nature of late capitalism, which the old bourgeoisie could no longer control, as a force that undermined bourgeois authority. In any case it is hard to read the *Studien* without noticing that not all its contributors speak with the same voice.[14]

Despite these caveats, it may be appropriate to bring up certain countervailing facts. The arguments in *TAP* are hardly original and can be traced back to Adorno's correspondence and writings long before 1950. What he and other critical theorists had expressed at an earlier point as intuitions or anxieties were recycled after the war as inferences based on interviews and tables of measurements. For better or worse, *TAP* is the magnum opus that one most easily associates with the Frankfurt School. Most of the group's multiple German texts, which are enumerated at the back of Rolf Wiggershaus's massive, sympathetic study, would not likely be known to anyone except for a critical theory researcher.[15]

Furthermore, as Christopher Lasch has persuasively argued, those who were attracted to this massive work were not necessarily revolutionary socialists or cultural radicals. The American Jewish Committee, made up mostly of Truman Democrats and the Cold War liberal S. M. Lipset, who was certainly no friend of Stalin's Russia, exuded praise for *TAP*. Lipset's only complaint was that the work failed to extend its study of undemocratic ideologies resulting from psychic problems to Soviet communism and communist sympathizers.[16] Presumably the work's approach was impeccably scientific and could be applied with equal force to other un-American or anti-American groups. But such endorsements, which Lasch quotes in abundance, are suspect. Lipset and his fellow academics who extolled the work were too well educated in research techniques not to be aware of its forced arguments.

The antifascism expounded by Adorno et al. pointed in more than one direction. Lasch is correct that in the United States Adorno's findings or opinions were not necessarily considered antipatriotic—this despite Adorno's concern about being dragged before the House Un-American Activities Committee for his attacks on American participation in the Cold War and his close relations with Communist Party members.[17] Progressive patriots viewed the United States as a self-perfecting pluralistic society, and the warnings in *TAP* against prejudice and the outbursts of the authoritarian personality were regarded as essential for building on America's success in fighting European fascism. The next desired phase in America's evolution would be to apply government power and educational institutions to eradicate "prejudice" and "discrimination" at home. In this bold undertaking those of good will were expected to welcome the scholarship provided by the American Jewish Committee, particularly its revelations about the persistence of anti-Semitism that had resulted in the murder of millions of European Jews.

As early as 1947 Adorno and his colleagues produced the California Test for examining where the test takers stood on the F-scale.[18] The devisers of this test claimed to be performing a socially useful task by measuring scientifically one's susceptibility to "right-wing authoritarian" ideas. The California Test reflected the thinking and proposals found in the final section of *The Authoritarian Personality*, and its application was not confined to inner circles of believers but became a tool in both police work and the psychological assessment of public school students. Although it was discovered that Adorno's F-scale did not allow for the fact that some respondents were groping vainly for answers to perplexing questions, the underlying correlation was never questioned by those who administered the test.

Those professionals who engaged in this enterprise never seemed to wonder whether lack of agreement between Adorno's political sentiments and those of the respondent indicated psychopathology. Widely read professional publications like *Journal of Abnormal and Social Psychology* treated F-scale testing as a serious scientific advance that would help free people from "prejudice."[19] Early in the 1980s Canadian professor of psychology Bob Altemeyer constructed a putatively better model for determining "right-wing authoritarian" personalities."[20] Note that such social engineering initiatives were not exotic influences that were thrust on American elites against their wills. They entered the land they supposedly converted with little resistance and became cultural and educational fixtures among educators and state administrators.

The main ideas of *TAP* had an equally dramatic effect on Germans, who were then being reeducated by their conquerors. In postwar Germany a linkage between antifascism and antinationalism would be established that endures down to the present. The recently elected leader of the German Green Party, Jürgen Trittin, has deplored German national sentiments and expressed the hope that his country, given its almost uniformly evil past, will soon be dissolved into a world political organization. This is hardly an isolated view in today's Germany. Gerhard Schröder, the former head of the German Social Democrats, expressed total agreement with Trittin's antinational, antifascist statements.[21] Nor would one likely hear dissent from the chancellor and head of the centrist Christian Democratic–Christian Social Union (CDU-CSU) party coalition, who like the leaders of the other parties on the left has spent millions of Euros on a "Battle against the Right." This battle consists of investigating all advocates of "German national" positions, including those in Merkel's centrist party, as purveyors of "right-wing extremism" and "threats to democratic freedom."[22]

This German preoccupation with ridding society of the historic Right, compounded with the need to apologize for the German past, including phases of that past going back well before the Nazi takeover, testifies to the success story of postwar German reeducation. In the Allied occupation zones, particularly in the American and British ones, persistent, organized efforts were made to identify not only hard-core Nazis and Nazi collaborators but those who were thought to be predisposed to fascist thinking.

Germans were required to answer detailed questionnaires (*Fragebogen*) in order to determine not only their possible association with the defeated regime but their social and political attitudes.[23] Licenses to publish newspapers and books were issued on the basis of the same considerations, and those who were suspected of being anticommunist or harboring nationalist sentiments usually had their requests summarily turned down. The Allied authorities heavily censored teaching materials and scheduled public lessons about the evils of the recent German past. Thus the Nuremberg Trials of Nazi war criminals were staged to advance public reeducation inside and outside of Germany. This process of changing German minds through foreign control went on longer than is usually recognized. Although the non–Soviet-controlled parts of what remained of Germany were allowed to form a constitutional state under Allied supervision by 1949, the Allied High Commission oversaw the Germans until 1955.[24] And even after this point, full sovereignty was not internationally recognized until after the unification of Germany in 1991.

Beginning with the occupation and with increasing diligence since the late 1960s, an extensive plan has been put into effect in Germany for helping its population "overcome their past." This process of *Vergangenheitsbewältigung* has assumed different forms, from critically reassessing German national heroes and cultural achievements to finding Hitler's tyranny and murders foreshadowed in the national past. Integral to this ritualized self-examination has been a concern with the psychic aspects of fascism and any disposition that might betray a fascist mentality.

Social psychologists entered wartime discussions by explaining how Germans and others could be relieved of their fascist psychic burden. The father of Gestalt psychology, Kurt Lewin, who came to the United States as a Jewish refugee, went about lecturing on how the Germans had to be psychically recoded in order to overcome their fascist-prone dispositions. In 1943 New York psychology professor Richard Brickner published a best-selling book introduced by anthropologist Margaret Mead in response to the question "Can the Germans be cured?" If healing was possible, Brickner told his readers, it would take massive effort on the part of the eventually victorious democratic side to make it happen.[25] The political activist and poet Archibald MacLeish prevailed on the Organization of Strategic Services (OSS), then still in its early stages, to allow him and a team of experts that MacLeish had assembled to come up with a plan to reeducate the Germans once the Allies won the war.[26]

The ones who came to lead this psychic crusade against fascism were the Frankfurt School exiles who were already in the United States. In May

1944 the American Jewish Committee organized a conference chaired by Max Horkheimer in New York City to lay the groundwork for what became *Studies in Prejudice*. At this early date a two-pronged strategy was planned: exposing the mental and emotional roots of "prejudice," the fruits of which were seen in fascist intolerance, and applying the projected study to fighting right-wing mental disorder in the United States while rooting out this problem in postwar Germany. The exiles who promoted these agendas had a chance to do both, and their presence on the German scene would have long-lasting effects. As advisors to the military command and the later occupational administration and as distinguished academics returned from forced exile, critical theorists exerted continuing influence over postwar German political and educational culture. From sociology departments in universities, which the occupation government favored as a vehicle of German reeducation, to journalism and the arts, one could find their disciples busily at work molding a new "democratic" consciousness.

A widely distributed manifesto issued in 1959 by the followers and doctoral candidates of Adorno, Horkheimer, and other senior members of the Institute for Social Research at Frankfurt offers an alarmist picture of fascist revival. According to this lament, "The Federal Republic is on the way to becoming an authoritarian society. Among the leaders of the major party, not a single one can be found whose thinking would contradict this development. If the permanent regime is prolonged, then the fate of the German Second Republic is sealed."[27] One perceptive commentator has noted: "The difference for this group between non-democracy and democracy comes down to whether one is ruled by authoritarian or liberal democratic men."[28] One gathers that the Institute thought its members should be the ones who decided the ideological makeup of democratic government.

By the 1960s the critical theorists had put their "antifascist" followers into German public administration, and even the moderately right-of-center Christian Democrats who governed the provincial government of Hessen permitted Frankfurt School theorists to reform their primary and secondary school curricula. University sociology departments throughout Germany were saturated with exponents of critical theory, and by the 1970s a major tension in these bastions of the antinational Left would be between orthodox Marxists and the disciples of Adorno. One could discern a similar doctrinal tension among radical university student groups, although by the 1970s the opposing sides were united by their hatred of "American capitalist imperialism" and by their noisy enthusiasm for the Vietcong, Maoism, and Castro.

A slightly different approach to antifascism would be represented by Habermas and Walter Jens, both second-generation critical theorists who emphasized the need for German atonement and abandoning any traditional German national identity. Although these emphases did not entirely please Horkheimer, who by then was in political transition, they suited German elites who were concerned with expiating the German past. Habermas pushed back the suspect past to a point well before Hitler came to power. He and a younger generation of German historians would find signs of the "authoritarian personality" in larger and larger swathes of German culture and history. According to this optic, 1945 was not only the "the zero hour" for Germany's justified total defeat but a moment of liberation from the German authoritarian past, a condition that had brought untold suffering to Europe and the world for generations.

An obvious feature of the second generation, perhaps best illustrated by Habermas, is a certain flattening of the cultural horizons of critical theory plus a fixation on overcoming the specifically national character of the German past. Unlike Horkheimer and Adorno, who came from educated, wealthy German Jewish homes and passed on the broad humanistic perspective of the German *Bildungsbürger*, critical theorists in the generation that followed combined a perceptible North German pietistic righteousness (Habermas was the son of a local Chamber of Commerce official in the Westphalian hamlet of Gummersbach) with little interest in German cultural achievements.

Despite their radicalism, members of the first generation could write knowledgeably and often appreciatively about Goethe, Beethoven, Hegel, and other German luminaries. Their attitude toward the German past was rarely as negative as that of their disciples, and the fact that they were driven into exile while Habermas, Jens, and other second-generation critical theorists had been members of the *Hitlerjugend* saved the returning émigrés from having to deal with any personal burden of guilt. Unlike many of their apostles who were preoccupied with proving or asserting collective German culpability, the first generation of critical theorists were mostly willing to let this hobbyhorse drop once they came back to Germany.[29] Their antifascism was more systematically grounded and in some ways less personal than the antifascism of those who came after them.

As an interpreter of German history, Habermas has stressed what is "pedagogically helpful" in enabling Germans to reconstruct their society. He is less concerned with the factual content of what should be studied than with providing moral edification. It was in this spirit that Habermas approached his widely publicized dispute with Nolte in the late 1980s about "comparing the unique evil of [the] Nazi regime" to Stalin's tyranny.[30] Habermas's assault on Nolte and his later unwillingness to debate his opponent underscored his single-minded dedication to "democratic instruction." Germany's self-appointed preceptor was indignant that Nolte was ignoring "democratic" concerns by placing recent German history in a broader European context. In his rejoinder to Nolte, Habermas deals only peripherally with the factual or structural validity of his adversary's comparisons. For him and other Germans who share his outlook, history is a behavioral tool—and only secondarily about trying to understand the past objectively.

Habermas has also undertaken to arrange for "nonhegemonic" discourse around rules that he provides without reference to a German, Christian, or classical cultural inheritance. In this discourse the best argument is supposed to win, and all participants should be given an equal chance to test their assertions. According to one canny German commentator, however, "the leftist reality in Habermas's real world turns out to be exactly the opposite. Nowhere as under the current German Left is an open discussion so severely hindered. Particularly through censorship that rages in leftist forums. Dissenting opinions and those who hold them are excoriated with charges of racism and fascism at the drop of a hat. Participants are allowed into the arranged discourse only if they hold the right opinion. Any heretic is unceremoniously banned."[31]

These charges are true, and in the collective assault on classical liberal freedoms, in which the government and its agencies have been called on to suppress "fascist" dissent, Habermas has rarely stood with the champions of "nonhegemonic discourse." The reason may have less to do with planned mind control than with a quality that Horkheimer (although not Adorno) noticed in their German epigones, a crude didacticism that critics of German antifascism have described as "the tyranny of the Good." Those who fit this description are seen as moral zealots who are driven by a sense of righteousness. Their conduct may also indicate the loss of a civilization of manners and a prideful scorn for what Germans once valued as *Kultur*. This moralizing intolerance, which has political and academic implications, may be among the long-range consequences of the Nazi accession to power.

Neofascism versus Neo-Marxism

In *The Eighteenth Brumaire of Louis Napoleon,* Marx observed how the nephew of Napoleon Bonaparte patterned his seizure of political power in France in 1851 on the steps taken by his uncle in overturning the French revolutionary government in 1799. In a mot that may have risen to the status of an eternal verity, Marx explained: "Hegel remarks somewhere that History occurs through the work of great figures and significant events. He failed to add: the first time as drama and the second time as farce." This may sum up the confrontation that has arisen since the late 1960s between neo-Marxists and those whom they depict as "neofascists." This battle is intended to bear a family resemblance to the prolonged crisis that Ernst Nolte characterizes as the "European civil war of the interwar years." To whatever extent this struggle actually occurred, it took place between, on the one side, the communists and their allies and, on the other, a supposedly unified fascist-Nazi opposition.[32]

This has become the paradigm, give or take some variation, for present ideological confrontations as conceived by the cultural-social Left. The antifascists, who regard the communists as distant cousins out of the past, are still combating fascism or Hitlerism without making sufficient distinctions between interwar movements and their present *bête noire*. For the antifascists in western Europe, the term "Marxist" still has cachet, although exactly in what way these antifascists preserve a genuine Marxist legacy is open to question. For about the last forty years, the descriptive category "neo-Marxist" has existed on the European Left, but as the Germanophone Greek sociologist Michael Kelpanides has exhaustively demonstrated in an underappreciated study, neo-Marxists have distinguished themselves mostly by academic snobbery and their resistance to empirical research.[33]

This school of thought went to bizarre lengths in defending the East German communist "experiment," and even when the Deutsche Demokratische Republik (DDR) was crumbling, its academic apologists pretended to be dealing with a viable, humane regime. Kelpanides's German neo-Marxists, by labeling themselves "Marxists," are employing a code word for "antifascist." They are taking a moral stance more than a research perspective or an economically deterministic world view. Neo-Marxists seem to be taking a page from Habermas's book when they give the impression that the Left has now gone beyond the need to prove Marx's view of historical causation. Although these embattled radicals may pay lip service to Marxist positions, their main interest lies elsewhere, namely in resisting the "authoritarian" social patterns that late capitalism created that have been presumably perpetuated after the apparent fall of fascism. One does not have to look far to discern here the shadow of the Frankfurt School.

According to their critics, the neo-Marxists expend considerable energy in Germany, England, France, and other Western countries grinding out convoluted studies, usually for each other, about the contradictions of capitalism, the immiseration of the working class, and the false consciousness of their opponents. The capitalist foe is often linked to a frozen picture of the market system, one that may have existed when Marx wrote *Das Kapital* in the 1850s but that now looks outdated. Sometimes the neo-Marxist critics address a global economy, but this complication is described in terms of corporate capitalists who are laboring to hold off an international workers' revolution. The studies criticized by Kelpanides do not typically draw on a wide data base, and the factual proofs offered come from those who reside in the same academic hothouse. Kelpanides is not a flaming anti-Marxist but seems to be a moderate social democrat impressed by the wonders of welfare-state democracy. He is not even hostile to those he criticizes but is irked by their imperviousness to reality.[34]

Kelpanides traces the rise of neo-Marxism to specifically German social developments. These include the expansion of the university system, particularly since the 1960s, which has entailed far more than the selection of university sites and the construction of buildings. Newer German universities, like Bielefeld in Hessen, have become magnets for socially radical academics, and the students they attract are especially open to their guidance. The young here typically come from the first generation in their families to benefit from higher education, and they gravitate toward those who shower them with neo-Marxist teachings. Kelpanides and, before him, Jost Bauch, and, long before them, German social theorist Helmut Schelsky (1912–1984) and social systems analyst Niklas Luhmann (1927–1988), have observed that sociology is the favored vehicle for neo-Marxist teachings in German universities.[35] As in other Western countries, the predominance of university majors in the "soft sciences" in Germany has provided impetus for radical leftist ideas and attitudes.

The trends that its German critics have discerned in neo-Marxism can also be located in other Western countries that have undergone comparable expansions and radicalizations of higher education. What Kelpanides fails to observe, however, are the continued effects of the reeducation that was imposed on Germans after World War II. Well-funded sociology departments in German universities were seen as tools for combating the reactionary tendencies of an older German society that had supposedly contributed to the Nazi disaster. A study by German historian Stefan Scheil documents the extent to which this development came out of the recommendations of refugee advisors who were attached to the American military command and, later, to the Allied High Commission.

The reestablishment of the Institute for Social Research in Frankfurt in 1950 was not an isolated happening, as Scheil proves. It fit into a plan for German reeducation that was vigorously promoted by the American occupation, which privileged a particular concept of sociology.[36] A concerted effort was made to redefine the discipline, which had once been dominated in Germany by conservative nationalists like Hans Freyer or by Austrian defender of organic social relations Othmar Spann. The Allied occupational forces planned to place sociology into the hands of those who shared their goal of social transformation.[37]

One more qualification should be made. Neo-Marxists in Germany are only one among other groups that have tried to resuscitate Marxist theory. There are also Analytic Marxists in England, like Jon Elster and Steven Lukes, who apply theoretical Marxism to their philosophical investigations. If there is ample reason to notice faulty economics among this school, as David Gordon does in a study of Analytic Marxists, it is nonetheless important to distinguish their enterprise from that of German neo-Marxists.[38] The same would be true of the various projects for world socialist revolution that have appeared in book form in the last few decades. Whether one is looking at the comparative economic studies of Immanuel Wallerstein or the best-selling picture of the future victory of the have-not peoples who are going to occupy the industrialized West according to Michael Hardt's and Antonio Negri's onetime best seller *Empire*, one thing is certain:[39] these forms of Marxism have a different focus from the radicalized sociology that Kelpanides and other critics have analyzed.

Other variations on Marxism do not stress the need to break from an evil national past to the same degree as German neo-Marxism. Neo-Marxists elsewhere are not as preoccupied as their German counterparts with fighting "authoritarianism" and are far less obsessed with an omnipresent fascist danger. These features, however, are not entirely missing from other self-described Marxists; they are just not as basic and persistent elsewhere as they are in Germany. Neo-Marxism, as a counterpoint to neofascism, carries a distinctly Teutonic flavor. It received a considerable boost from those who came as conquerors to reeducate Hitler's former supporters and subjects. This antifascist reeducation strongly shaped the thinking of the generation that took over German politics and culture after 1968.

The crusade against fascism developed over time into a call for vigilance against "neofascism," a specter that for German and other Western radicals became synonymous with American influence during the Cold War. The Red Brigades in Germany, which unleashed a wave of assassinations against pro-American politicians and corporate executives in the 1970s, was by no means explicitly anti-German. German radicals were not as hostile to the East German government as they were to the Federal Republic, and the reason they opposed the Federal Republic with such ferocity had more to do with their war against American capitalist imperialism than it did with disliking their nation. One need not fully accept the picture of anti-American radicalism from such onetime devotees as Bernd Rabehl and Günter Maschke, who later became German nationalists, to recognize the truth in their accounts.[40] At least some of those who joined the pro-Maoist, anticapitalist Left in Germany in the 1960s and 1970s were both anti-American and infused with German national feelings. Unlike a later or different Left, these radicals pitied their country for having been colonized by its American conquerors.

Although their Soviet occupiers had treated their German countrymen even more brutally, the Sixty-Eighters did not take the enemy to the east as seriously as they did the American colossus. A similar attitude characterized old-fashioned German conservatives after the war who disliked American reeducators (*Umerzieher*) more than what they considered a primitive Soviet dictatorship. The decision by the ruling Christian Democrats to allow the installation of medium-range American Pershing missiles on German soil in the 1970s brought together an oppositional force consisting of the far Left and an element of the national Right.[41]

There was also an explicitly antinational Left in Germany that was less violent than these anti-American activists. This group included an antinational school of historical writing centered in Bielefeld that was also active in other German universities. Postwar German historians were preoccupied with critically reassessing the Second Empire and other phases of the German "authoritarian" past viewed as a prelude to Hitlerism.[42] They worked to use historical studies the way sociologists did with studies of social attitudes in order to effect a total break from the national past other than recognition of the uniquely wicked legacy that Germans were expected to expiate. Academic antinationalists in Germany have reflected on but also played on feelings aroused by "the historic image of the Nuremberg Trials"—that is, the remorse about the German past that the trials of Nazi leaders after the war were designed to awaken.[43] Kelpanides' neo-Marxists generally fall into the same groove as other German antifascists in their war against national identity. For the neo-Marxists, the struggle against the remnants of a bourgeois society belongs to the same crusade as the discrediting of the German past, both of which are believed to have culminated in fascism and neofascism.

The struggle against a presumed fascist threat gained ground not only in Germany but throughout western Europe in the last quarter of the twentieth century. It correlated with the erosion of the large communist parties in France and Italy—that is, with the weakening or vanishing of what had been a major channel for leftist orientations and passions as well as centers for working-class planning and agitation. Communist parties after the Second World War had been able to attract over a quarter of the electorate in France and Italy, but by the 1980s they were hemorrhaging votes. By the 1990s the communists were reduced to junior partners in leftist coalitions while the Soviet regime they had backed collapsed, bringing down with it the Soviet Empire in eastern Europe.

The old communist theme of fighting fascism remained popular but was given a non-socialist focus sometime in the 1970s. Even in socialist coalitions, the socialist war against fascist-prone capitalists came to center less on nationalizing productive forces than on fighting prejudice and welcoming Third World populations into Europe. Prepared in the United States by Adorno and Horkheimer, *Studies in Prejudice* provided the guidelines for an updated form of antifascism that was increasingly divorced from Marxist historical materialism. At the same time certain old habits continued to manifest themselves in European leftist movements and parties, for example, identifying anticommunism with right-wing extremism and paying homage to the shades of the communist past.

The heart of this ascending ideology was an impassioned rejection of all forms of Western or European identitarian politics, be it national, ethnic, or religious, and an expression of solidarity with an idealized world community. The social base of antifascism now comprises the historic working class less and less as it has come to embrace intellectuals, public-sector employees, and Third World resident communities in Europe. Although often mocked as yuppie radicalism, this antifascist *Ideengestalt* and the following it has drawn have proved remarkably durable. All parties of the Left and most of those in the center in western and central Europe (outside of the former Soviet bloc) have been touched in varying degrees by the antifascist crusade.

The enemy this multicultural Left now has in its sights is "neofascism." This particular term has explosive power for those who wield it, and what renders it particularly useful is that it doesn't call for definitional precision. Whether we are speaking about the Austrian Freedom Party (especially under its now-deceased leader Jörg Haider), the already splintered National Front in France, the Lombard separatists in the Lega Nord, the Jobbik Party (*Jobbik Magyarorzagert Mozgalom*) in Hungary, or Romanian nationalists in the Greater Romania Party (*Partidu Romania Mare*) under Corneliu Vadim Tudor, journalists are free to describe the other side as fascism redivivus. But most of these supposed throwbacks show no real resemblance to Nazism and only a limited affinity with generic fascism. Like the Lega Nord, the Austrian Freedom Party, or the present National Front, groups on the European right stand out by virtue of rattling intellectuals and journalists. These groups uniformly oppose immigration from the Third World and praise the historic identity of those nations that they view themselves as being linked to. These aggregations of European nationalists also hold no brief for gay lifestyles and see themselves as following in the critical stance of both biblical Christian and traditional bourgeois norms.[44]

The Nationaldemokratische Partei Deutschlands, the Austrian Freedom Party under Haider in the 1990s, and the old National Front under Jean-Marie Le Pen fall into a second, even more suspicious, category, which is being insufficiently sensitive to Nazi crimes and, in Le Pen's case, trying to provoke, often quite tastelessly, the antifascist French Left. While one may be justified in calling attention to these improprieties, as well as to the failure of much of the European Left to acknowledge Stalin's mass murders, such indiscretions do not signify an upsurge of Hitlerism.

Le Pen was no more of a Nazi for characterizing the killing or deporting of Jews in France during the German occupation as "a detail" of the war than Lionel Jospin was a Stalinist for refusing to acknowledge Stalin's crime in the French Assembly when asked about them there in November 1998. Indeed, Le Pen never denied the Nazi genocide but tried to minimize its importance for French history. As even his journalistic adversaries admit, this eighty-five-year-old senior citizen who is perpetually trying to grab headlines in retirement after handing over his party to his daughter, Marine, has no documentable Nazi past. His family supported the Resistance, and until the general's abandonment of the Algerian French, Le Pen was an admirer of de Gaulle.[45]

A worthwhile anthology of essays on neofascism edited by Angelica Fenner and Eric D. Weitz includes an informative appraisal of the French situation by Michel Wieviorka. According to Wieviorka, although "racism and the rise of extreme right behaviors in France or elsewhere" are possible developments, we should not try to fit them into a pattern "of reproduction."[46] Attitudes that were once present in some groups, for example anti-Semitism among French nationalists, may surface in a later generation but among a very different group, for example, North African Muslims. Wieviorka also notes the evolution of the right-wing Front National from "prewar themes" as it went from being a relatively isolated pressure group to a national force in the 1980s.

Wieviorka's study of the Front concludes that "this party is characterized by significant ideological innovations, in contrast with the initiatives of smaller groups that bear greater similarities to prewar thought."[47] The changes that Wieviorka investigates suggest that the social and economic base of prewar fascist movements has been altered decisively since the 1930s. In the intervening years France has gone from being a predominantly rural society to a mostly postindustrial one that is dependent on a global economy.

Another relevant perception offered by anthology-contributor Richard Golsan is that the French Left's continuing tirade against "neofascism" leads the other side into bringing up communist atrocities that the Left denies or tries to sweep under the rug.[48] The two sides eagerly play off each other. In 1992 the French Left, with the help of the dwindling Communist Party, got the French Assembly to pass the *Loi Gayssot*, named for Guy Gayssot, a Jewish communist deputy who reinvented himself as a standard antifascist. The new law made it a criminal offense for anyone to deny publicly or in print the verdict pronounced by the Nuremberg Court in 1947 concerning Nazi mass murder and, more specifically, the details of the Holocaust.[49] But the law also defined "crimes against humanity" broadly enough, as Golsan points out, to allow those wishing to call attention to Soviet and other communist crimes to bring up a subject that the French Left wished to avoid.

The publication of the *The Black Book of Communism* in 1997 by Stéphan Courtois was a well-calculated attempt to call the Left's bluff. This exposé made it appear that it was the Left that suffered from amnesia about genocide if the crimes in question were committed by Marxist-Leninists. Indeed the "war against fascism" was a diversion from the Left's unwillingness to "overcome its past" as apologists for Stalin, Mao, and other murderous dictators. This challenge set off a row, but given the greater firepower of the antifascist Left, the outcome may have been foreordained. The offensive against neofascism would continue to advance.

The already fading German NDP, which the German left-center spectrum treats as a neo-Nazi pariah, may be in the same category of disdaining conventional political rhetoric but posing no threat to the existing constitutional order. There is nothing that the NDP advocates that seems aimed at overthrowing the German government. Most of its criticism of the regime is directed against the curtailing of liberal freedoms guaranteed under Germany's Basic Law, a repressive policy that is justified as a way of marginalizing the nationalist Right. More suspect by far is the generally revisionist picture of the Third Reich that the NDP transmits in political speeches. This effort at whitewashing may be intended to counteract the prescribed antifascist teachings of the German government—or, more precisely, the ceaseless sermonizing of a state-financed and journalistically incited "Revolt against the Right."

The NDP's understating of Nazi atrocities understandably offends those who were the victims of Nazi tyranny (my own family included). And this practice has reinforced the party's negative image while turning off potential voters. But measured analysis is different from antifascist grandstanding. Despite the harping of the German press and the official German parties on the dangers posed by the NDP, the party's rhetorical disasters should not be equated with an attempt to resurrect the Third Reich.[50] Nolte was right when he underlined the absurdity of comparing a party that is trying to rid Germany of American military bases and limit immigration to the aggressively expansionist, genocidal politics of the Third Reich.[51]

One would have to place the Jobbiks and the Greater Romania Party, which are at loggerheads given their diametrically opposed positions about who should own and inhabit Transylvania, in a more extreme nationalist camp. The Greater Romania Party does not shun comparisons with the Iron Guard[52] while members of Jobbik, which is the third largest party in Hungary, have scolded Jews for their disproportionately large membership in the Communist Party.

But other facts are needed for a balanced picture of the Romanian and Hungarian far Right. The Greater Romania Party does not advocate a repetition of the violence unleashed by the Iron Guard. It is a minor political party rather than an immense paramilitary force like the Legion of the Archangel Michael. Moreover, the Jobbik is tightly ensconced in the now ruling coalition of the Hungarian national right under Victor Orban.[53] Even more importantly, the anti-Jewish remarks of some of its politicians have been repudiated by other Jobbik politicians as well as by the Orban regime. The surfacing of anti-Jewish attitudes in an isolated faction of a far-right Hungarian party is certainly disturbing to those whose families suffered in the Nazi Holocaust. But it hardly proves that Hungary is on the verge of being taken over by neo-Nazis.

Needless to say, the continuing efforts of the European Union and the Western press to isolate conservative nationalist governments, such as the present Orban Administration in Hungary and Jörg Haider's Austrian Freedom Party in 1999 for Haider's unwillingness to express sufficient regret over the Nazi past, suggests a very different political climate from the one that existed in interwar Europe. Western and central European governments that deviate from the prescribed progressive pattern set by the European Union and, at least from behind the scenes, the United States, must deal with economic pressure and political marginalization.[54] These considerations should be kept in mind in looking at what, according to the press, may be the closest approximation to a "neo-Nazi party" in contemporary Europe, the Golden Dawn in Greece. The party head, Nikos Michaloliakas, collects Nazi memorabilia, and an EU deputy elected from his party, Ilias Panagiotaros, praises Hitler's leadership for lifting Germany out of the Depression.[55] Golden Dawn also organizes anti-immigration demonstrations, opposes gay rights, and resists the attempts made by foreign powers to rein in the Greek economy.[56]

What we are dealing with in this case, however, is widely described as a "protest party," which alternates with the far-left Syriza Party in appealing to victims of a mismanaged national economy. Although the Golden Dawn won almost 10 percent of the Greek vote in the EU elections in May 2012, it is hard to imagine it ever coming to power. The vast majority of Greek voters continue to favor center-right and center-left parties, and besides the efforts of party leaders to rattle the chains of their antifascist critics, it is hard to find much in the way of interwar fascist, let alone Nazi content, in what the Golden Dawn is offering. The international hysteria generated by the votes that the party is presently attracting may cause one to speculate about what would happen if this politically incorrect party ever gained control of the Greek government.

A comparison that may be enlightening (even if it represents a digression) would be between Jobbik and a Hungarian nationalist politician of the interwar period, Julius Gombos (1886–1936). A leader of the nationalist Right, Gombos was allowed to assume the prime minister's post in 1932. But the regent who appointed him, Miklos Horthy, required Gombos to foreswear his earlier anti-Jewish statements.[57] Gombos's anti-Jewish views seem to have been based largely on his reaction to the predominantly Jewish leadership in the communist takeover of Hungary in 1919. A member of the gentry, he participated in the counterrevolutionary government that was formed under Horthy in Szeged, in southern Hungary, against the revolutionaries in Budapest. Gombos was effusive in his praise of both Dollfuss and Mussolini, and despite his quintessentially Protestant background, seems to have been attracted to a Hungarian new order that would incorporate a Catholic-looking corporatist state.

Despite his rants against Jewish communists, Gombos never called for more exclusionary measures than the demand that Jewish quotas be applied to universities and the professions. If Jobbik did take over the Hungarian government, which is highly improbable, there is nothing to suggest that it would do even as much as Gombos advocated but later disavowed in trying to exclude Jews. Needless to say, the corporatist notions that Gombos attached to his politics are now totally antiquated. They belong to an interwar political culture. And there is another fact that must be kept in mind: not all generic fascists were concerned with a Jewish problem. The followers of José Antonio Prima de Rivera and the organizers of Mussolini's March on Rome did not rage against a Jewish danger. Indeed, prominent early fascists were Italian Jews.

The End of the Crusade against Totalitarianism

The crusade against neofascism and other manifestations of the European nationalist Right has led to the replacement of a totalitarian enemy by a struggle against "right-wing extremism." Three critical factors have led to this unfolding campaign. One has been the absorption of what were once large communist movements in France and Italy and an entire communist administration in East Germany into democratic parties of the Left. The effect has been to import a long-standing communist "antifascist" demonology into whatever parties former communists have entered or formed alliances with. This has led to a crucial change in the mindset of noncommunist socialist parties that once supported the anti-Soviet side in the Cold War.

A second factor in the rejection of the totalitarian model was its inevitable identification with American power during the Cold War. Although anti-Americanism was most noticeable in western Europe and Germany on the communist and procommunist Left, it arose for reasons other than keeping faith with the communist past. Anti-Americanism has had long-standing traction in European society and appealed to the traditional Right even before it became a staple of far Left propaganda. The German case may be particularly instructive. The postwar Christian Democrats, who were an exuberantly pro-American German national party, were committed to the proposition that communism and Nazism were twin totalitarian movements and had to be opposed by all freedom-loving countries. Those intellectuals who were showcased by the CDU, such as Joachim Ritter, Gerhard Ritter, Heinz Gollwitzer, Helmut Schelsky, Michael Stürmer, and Günter Rohrmoser, fully accepted and stated their opposition to totalitarian governments and ideologies.

This, however, was not necessarily evidence of a right-wing or nationalist position. Those who took this stand were staunchly pro-American and pro-NATO who shared the generally negative view of the German political past that had been instilled by the Western victors during the German Occupation. None of these figures expressed nostalgia for a past German government, except perhaps for isolated phases of the Second Empire and the Weimar Republic.[58] The charge later raised by the antinational Left against CDU-sponsored intellectuals—that they were unreasonably devoted to some pre–World War II German state—was patently untrue. The intellectuals favored by the CDU lavished praise on the liberal democracy that their American conquerors bestowed or imposed on them. And, to the horror of some German intellectuals, they sided with the pro-American West (*die Westbindung*) in its struggle against the communist East.

This position was unsettling for what remained of a real German Right, which was typified by Carl Schmitt and the Protestant nationalist Hans Zehrer. Both of these figures hated the Americans for imposing their will upon a prostrate Europe and allegedly vulgarizing German society.[59]

Although Zehrer, a onetime publicist of the interwar nationalist Right but a firm anti-Nazi, was a senior editor of a leading German newspaper, *Die Welt*, he eventually fell out of favor with its publisher and his onetime ardent disciple, Axel Springer. Unlike Zehrer and other predominantly Protestant German nationalists, Springer became a fervent supporter of the American-led alliance against the Soviets. This required a juggling act, particularly when other German nationalists were calling for a less pro-American foreign policy and playing off the Americans against the Soviets.

The famed legal theorist Carl Schmitt also stressed the advantage to the Germans and other Europeans of maintaining the Soviet-American "bipolarity" for as long as possible. Schmitt underlined the danger to a weakened Europe posed by American hegemony, and he lost no opportunity to point out the imperialist nature of American claims to represent "democratic ideas" throughout the world.[60] Anti-Americanism was once more common within the postwar European Right than is now generally believed. It contributed to a growing skepticism about the concept of totalitarianism, which was seen as justifying an unwanted American military presence in Europe.

On the Left, however, there was also a third and even more compelling reason to reject the moral equation of Nazi and Soviet tyrannies. Already in the 1970s one found what Helmut Schelsky characterized as "the politics of moral indignation." In his critical responses to Habermas as a social philosopher, Schelsky underscored the danger of privileging subjective conscience. It would lead to academic and constitutional suicide, according to Schelsky, if Habermas's selective anger against thinking what he considered potentially fascistic or insufficiently critical of the German past were allowed to "didactically" shape our concepts of legality and social scientific inquiry.[61]

What Schelsky feared eventually came to pass, but the antifascism that dominated German political culture was based on guilt as well as moral anger. A work that drew on both emotions in its diagnosis of a collective German mental disorder was *Die Unfähigkeit zu trauern: Grundlagen kollektiven Verhaltens* (1967) by two German psychologists, Alexander and Margarete Mitscherlich. The coauthors taught at the University of Frankfurt and shared the concern voiced by their close friend Theodor Adorno about the unconquered psychic causes of Nazism and its culmination in the Holocaust. According to the Mitscherlichs, the German people remained prone to right-wing hysteria as long as they failed to "mourn" their collective past. The incubus of fascism could only be exorcised if Germans confronted what German reeducation had not sufficiently emphasized, which was the extent of the wrongdoing that Germans had to atone for in order to become psychologically healed.[62]

The German word "*trauern*" is given a strange twist here: what that term means in the context of Mitscherlichs's work is "*tief bedauern*" (deeply regretting), as opposed to truly mourning. Having been present at the Nuremberg Trials, the authors were permanently marked by this experience and devoted much of the remainder of their lives to combating the unresolved fascistic pathology that they ascribed to their people. Alexander would rage at any mention of the fate of those ethnic Germans who had been brutally expelled from eastern Europe after the war. Although the number of these refugees may have numbered as many as fifteen million, the Mitscherlichs deemed it "obscene" and "morally perverted" to bring up their ordeal.[63]

Even without quoting the remark attributed to Adorno that "writing poetry after the Holocaust is barbaric," it is clear that both the fury directed against neofascism and the benign neglect of communist atrocities have some connection to the murder of approximately six million Jews by the Nazi regime. This is not even to take into account the slaying of Polish and Russian prisoners and other victims of the Third Reich, atrocities that have often been neglected in order to focus on Hitler's "war against the Jews." All these crimes are real enough but do not obviate the need to raise certain questions, which antifascists willfully ignore. Do Nazi crimes make any less real the crimes committed by other totalitarian regimes, say Stalin's Russia and Mao's China? Why are Germans not allowed to "mourn" their co-ethnics who were murdered or brutalized by postwar communist regimes or indiscriminately vengeful eastern Europeans?[64] Is it reprehensible for Germans to notice the firebombing of German civilian targets and the laying waste of entire inner cities by the Royal Air Force during the last year of World War II, when close to 600,000 mostly defenseless German civilians were incinerated?[65]

German antifascists and kindred spirits in neighboring countries do not wish to call attention to such atrocities primarily for two reasons: they divert attention from German responsibility for the Holocaust, and even noticing inhumanities that should be overlooked, according to the arbiters of political culture, betokens "moral perversion." It is therefore essential for analytic purposes to look at the Holocaust less as a grim historical event (although it was that) than as a flexible ideological symbol.[66]

An insightful analyst of this subject, Peter Novick, dwells on the changing perception of the Holocaust among American Jews and American Christians in *The Holocaust in American Life*.[67] After the Second World War, American Jews found no reason to dwell on Hitler's genocidal policies. Those who had suffered under the Nazis generally avoided discussing their agonizing experiences, and Jewish nationalists were generally ashamed that Hitler's victims had not resisted their enemies more forcefully. By the 1960s, however, interest in the Holocaust was growing perceptibly among both Jews and Christians. Jews began looking at their suffering as a kind of cement that could be used to hold together their already assimilating community. Zionists treated the Holocaust as a justification of Israel's existence and a bitter memory of persecution that might solidify support for Israel among American Jews. Moreover, while most historians previously (and rightly) viewed the Nazis as anti-Christian as well as anti-Jewish, since the 1960s the public has been awash in polemics blaming Christianity for the Holocaust.

One particularly severe commentator, Daniel Goldhagen, has moved in two successive books from characterizing all Germans as "Hitler's willing executioners" to shifting the blame for the Holocaust to historic Christianity.[68] Presumably there is enough blame to be spread around and more than enough Christians, as Novick proves, who are willing to accept it. Clearly it is not just Jews but also Christians who have blamed the Christian tradition for the anti-Semitism that issued forth in Hitler's Final Solution. Whereas in the older account proper recognition was given to the fact that Hitler and other key Nazis loathed Christianity and hoped to replace it, in the revised version all possible evidence of Christian anti-Semitism since the first century is brought up to explain Nazi crimes. This may tell us more about contemporary Christians than it does about what caused the Holocaust.

There are two attitudes that this changed reaction to the Holocaust has nurtured, beyond fear of repeating Hitler's misdeeds: "solidarity in guilt," to cite the opening paragraph of the Stuttgart Confession of Guilt issued by leaders of the German Evangelical Church on October 19, 1945;[69] and the belief that any rejection of the antifascist consensus indicates mental illness. The two often go together—that is, by highlighting the historic guilt of one's nation for Nazi crimes, one exhibits mental and emotional well-being. Mounting *plaques commémoratives* on buildings in Paris, from whence Jews were rounded up under the Vichy regime, is seen to serve two purposes: making French mindful of a past that should not be psychologically repressed while highlighting the still polluting guilt of the historic French people for being entangled in Nazi misdeeds.[70] On July 12, 2012, soon after arriving in the French presidency, François Hollande declared the need to acknowledge "all the crimes committed by the French in France." By this point, the French president was trying to include all those groups in France that had been granted "days of reconciliation," which is a code word for official state recognition for having been oppressed by the French nation.[71] The entry point for this culture of victimization, as Alain Besancon has devoted a considerable literature to showing, was the focus on French crimes (mostly of omission) committed against those deported under the Vichy government.[72]

The same antifascist concerns operate in what Germans call their *"Erinnerungskultur"* (culture of remembering), which entails the visual and verbal publicizing of Nazi crimes as a means of making the public mindful of their sinful national past. This moral imperative was brought home dramatically in a speech given on May 8, 1945 by German federal president Richard von Weiszäcker, who regarded the German defeat in the Second World War "as a day of liberation from the inhuman system of Nazi tyranny." Weiszäcker, whose father had been a high-ranking diplomat under the Third Reich, called on his nation to deal with a "difficult legacy."

Critics have suggested that the German president may have been shoving the truly reprehensible behavior of his own family onto his entire people.[73] In view of the extensive Nazi ties that Richard's father, Ernst, had sedulously cultivated, this observation may be apt. But the federal president was also previewing the position popularized by longtime leftist revolutionary and former German Foreign Minister Joschka Fischer that "Auschwitz is the founding myth of the German Federal Republic." Fischer was making a statement that German leaders have repeatedly affirmed since it was first spoken in 1999.[74]

Despite the long-standing linkage between antifascism and the Holocaust, antifascists have also shifted the burden of fascist guilt from the persecution of Jews under the Third Reich to more up-to-date causes. Both the despisers and representatives of Muslim culture have been denounced as fascists, depending on the accuser's purpose. Both Zionists and anti-Zionists have readily accused their antagonists of reviving Nazi programs and Nazi tactics in order to destroy newer and newer stand-ins for Hitler's victims. In such exchanges for propagandistic effect, older distinctions and analyses have been thrown to the wind. Terms like "totalitarianism" and "fascism," for example, have no meaning at the political and journalistic level. They function as charges rather than as attempts to make sense of the history of Europe in the twentieth century.

In this widening crusade against neofascism, all "insensitive" or unprogressive positions have been indiscriminately branded as fascist. Be it opposition to Third World immigration, complaints about the high rate of crime among Muslim residents in European cities, or the drawing of cognitive distinctions among ethnic or social groups, anything deemed as politically offensive indicates a fascist recrudescence. One striking example of this now ingrained practice can be found in protest letters sent to *Le Monde* after it was proposed in June 2000 that the remains of French composer Hector

Berlioz be transferred to the Paris Panthéon. Among opponents of this proposal were renowned music scholar Joël-Marie Fauquet, journalists Jean Kahn and Philippe Olivier, and the great grandson of Richard Wagner, a headline-grabbing antifascist from a family that has much to hide, Gottfried Wagner (1947–).[75]

Fauquet was particularly exercised that Berlioz had dared to take a stipend in the 1840s from the French monarch Louis Philippe. Gottfried Wagner and the other Berlioz critics were inflamed by Berlioz's production of the opera *Les Troyens*, which is based on Virgil's Latin epic *The Aeneid*. It seems this opera, which celebrates the sojourn in Carthage of Rome's legendary founder Aeneas, may have tempted Mussolini into launching a war of expansion in North Africa. The plan for Mussolini's Ethiopian campaign was supposedly implicit in both Virgil's epic poem and the musical work of its French admirer, Berlioz. One wonders whether *The Aeneid* will have to be stricken from curricula lest it lead to new fascist outbursts or Italian invasions of North Africa.

Gottfried Wagner insisted that the French would be sending the wrong signals by honoring someone whose music was so full of "fascist residues." It is hard to see how someone who was composing music in the 1840s was already filling his music anachronistically with "residues" of what didn't yet exist at the time. As a historical detail, the executive who patronized Berlioz was the most liberal monarch in French history, a patron of the arts and academic learning, and a zealous guardian of religious freedom. Would that French antifascist critics showed even a fraction of the tolerance for a monarch they are now intent on discrediting!

CHAPTER FOUR

Fascism as a Movement of the Left

Different Schools of Thought

The view that fascism was a movement of the Left came out of different sources, and it may be useful to classify these sources and the schools of thought they represent. The first school, viewed chronologically and in terms of the march of modern ideologies, was classical conservatives, some of whom were Catholic traditionalists. From this perspective, all movements that challenged "legitimate" authority were seen as coming from the Left, and more specifically from ideas associated with the French Revolution. The title of a tract by Erik von Kuehnelt-Leddihn, *The Left: From de Sade and Marx to Hitler and Marcuse*, exemplifies this classical conservative understanding of modern radical movements.[1] The unraveling of the ordered past is thought to have gone from the rebellion against throne and altar erupting in the French Revolution to the tyrannies of Stalin and Hitler.

A second, better documented interpretation of fascism as a leftist movement has come from archival scholars, most especially A. James Gregor. According to these interpreters, there are leftist or radical properties abundantly present in Italian fascism, e.g., in its welfare state measures, in its insistence that the means of production should serve the common good, and in the "revolutionary" implications of the national revolution proclaimed by fascist governments. Those who take this view can point back to De Felice's penetrating observation that the intellectual Left has routinely ignored what was dynamic and innovative in Italian fascism.

Ideological blinders have kept conventional leftist historians from appreciating how heavily the fascists borrowed from their side. And there are cases in which engaged leftist historians have behaved in a way that confirms De Felice's judgment.[2] Although the charge of neglecting the leftist elements in fascism can be raised against the arguments in this book as well as against those of others, this position in this book is not intended to protect the Left's honor. Rather, it is being argued that the programs and organizational techniques that fascism borrowed from the Left are not of primary importance for understanding its historic function.

A third group that has considered fascism to be a movement of the Left consists of American journalists who have fought the creation or expansion of the welfare state. Critics of this sort have been active ever since FDR unveiled his New Deal, and they have dwelled on the similarities between the evolving American welfare state and what looked like a command economy under Italian fascism. Although these critical observations are not always convincing, they seem more understandable and less driven by partisanship the further one moves back in time.

In the 1930s real cross-fertilization took place when New Dealers made Italian fascism into one of their models for reform, a process documented by German historian Wolfgang Schivelbusch in his study *Entfernte Verwandtschaften*.[3] Moreover, as John P. Diggins demonstrates, the editors of the progressive *New Republic* once regarded fascist Italy, as well as the Soviet Union, as an experimental socialist state that had much to teach American reformers.[4] This opinion became less and less acceptable the closer Mussolini moved toward an alliance with Nazi Germany and his invasion of Ethiopia. By now any comparison between advocates of social entitlements and interwar fascists has become a largely partisan gesture. Polemicists who engage in this comparison overlook the fact that all modern democracies, including the "conservative" opposition, accept extensive welfare states. This was hardly a unique feature of fascism. The construction of welfare states is a democratic characteristic that fascist states, to whatever extent they acted like popular governments, took over. Eighty years ago this trend and its accompanying internal dynamics were, however, less obvious in Western countries.

The Classical Conservative Attack on Fascism

Although too ideologically mercurial to be classified as representative of the classical Right, French political theorist Bertrand de Jouvenel in *Du Pouvoir* (*Of Power*) offers the following penetrating conservative critique of modern democracy: "The history of the democratic doctrine furnishes a striking example of the intellectual system blown about by the social wind. Conceived as the foundation of liberty, modern democracy paves the way for tyranny. Born for the purpose of standing as a bulwark against Power, it ends by providing Power with the finest soil it has ever had in which to spread itself over the social field."[5]

Viewed from this perspective, fascism was or is not an aberration from "democratic" government but one of several directions in which an inherently labile "system" could be "blown about by the social wind." Jouvenel does concede that more stable democracies create "makeweights" to prevent popular tyranny from prevailing in the short or even middle term. But Jouvenel, a member (on his father's side) of the French nobility, did not believe that constitutional restraints and decentralizing mechanisms could hold sway permanently in modern democratic government. Sooner or later these hindrances to popular rule are likely to be overwhelmed by those who speak for "the people." Although fascism is not the only direction in which democratic regimes, once freed of their inherited cultural baggage, could move, it was, for Jouvenel, together with Marxist-Leninism and egalitarian social policies, a truly democratic option.[6] All variations on modern democratic rule are departures from older forms of government, which limited power along the lines of class and tradition. Fascism should be regarded as the kind of democracy that had appeal in certain parts of interwar Europe.

It should be observed that Jouvenel is among the most persuasive of all those who treat fascism as a democratic ill. He is not necessarily looking back to a golden age or urging obedience to a religious authority. He is underscoring the problem of democracy as popular government that has lost any "makeweight" and which takes "direct action" while seeking to gratify "the people." Jouvenel most definitely does not argue that there is a good, stable type of democracy that is universally applicable and never turns despotic. Like ancient philosophers, he believes democracy must sooner or later end in tyranny, and he considers fascism to be one of several faces that democratic tyranny may eventually assume.

A less cogent case for the leftist origin of fascism is addressed in the work of Erik Kuehnelt-Leddihn, who maintained that liberty in its changing historical forms was the guiding principle for most predemocratic Western societies. Although the application of liberty did not guarantee its equal use for all social classes, the principle of liberty operated in such a way as to distribute power and prevent its monopoly by a central government. This was as true for medieval states as nineteenth-century constitutional monarchies; the simultaneous exercise of authority by the Church, burghers, guilds, regional nobility, and other social centers made it hard for monarchs or other sovereigns to oppress their subjects for more than brief periods of time.

Kuehnelt-Leddihn recounts all the steps taken by centralized power to subdue localized authorities and suppress historic liberties: from power grabs accompanying the Protestant Reformation on the part of secular princes, through the movement toward unified sovereignty in nation-states, down to an imperialistic democratic government committed to universal rights born of the French Revolution. All these developments, according to Kuehnelt-Leddihn, worked ultimately against freedom and traditional authorities. Especially ominous was the French Revolution, which, in the name of democratic equality, unleashed bloodbaths at home and abroad. The Revolution was the Pandora's box from whence all future political troubles sprang. In his most widely read polemic, *The Left: From Robespierre to Hitler,* or, as it was later titled, *The Left: From Robespierre to Hitler and Marcuse,* Kuehnelt-Leddihn assaults the Revolution's democratic centralism and its propensities for leveling social differences, both tendencies that culminated in the ascent of the Jacobins.

Kuehnelt-Leddihn, who was once sympathetic to Austrian clerical fascism, also displayed his traditionalist views by effusively supporting the Habsburg monarchy and its recently passed claimant to the throne, Archduke Otto. But he also remained a lifelong advocate of limited, decentralized government. And he desisted from criticizing democratic regimes, whatever he chose to call them, that maintained systems of divided power and allowed for inherited communal and social arrangements.

This Austrian *Freiherr* also insisted, however, that one knew most democracies by the bitter fruits they could yield. State worship, administrative control of society, and the bludgeoning use of central power were, in his eyes, the marks of this "deviant form of government" (to apply the Aristotelian term). From his standpoint, fascism and even Nazism were radical forms of democracy untethered from any principle of legitimacy other than the will of the leader. Without the example of the French Revolution, Kuehnelt-Leddihn explains, democratic tyranny would not have become such a huge modern problem. The Revolution's attempt to sweep away political and social institutions and reconstruct them in the name of a fictitious "people" as a homogeneous whole did not stop in the 1790s. It went on inspiring other upheavals including the Bolshevik Revolution and the "national revolutions" proclaimed by fascist dictators.

Another cognate view of fascism as an essentially leftist movement comes from the Catholic historian Augusto Del Noce, who is best known for his study of contemporary history titled *L'epoca della secolarizzazione*.[7] Del

Noce was a critic of the post-Christian, secular age in which he found himself unhappily situated, and he treated fascism as a post-Christian ideology that revealed affinities with other contemporary political trends. Del Noce accentuates the revolutionary character of the fascist movement, the devotees of which characterized themselves as radicals. He mentions fascism's willingness to borrow from the Church certain concepts, especially corporatism, but also notes its rejection of the core doctrines of the faith. Finally, he attaches to fascism a myth of progress, going from the nation's journey through the parliamentary chaos and economic exploitation of nineteenth-century bourgeois societies to the fascist "national revolution" of the early twentieth century.[8]

The career and thought of Giovanni Gentile, perhaps the prime architect of fascist theory, are cited to substantiate Del Noce's picture of fascism as a progressive, secular movement. An anticlerical of the heart and an admirer of Italy's democratic national leaders of the nineteenth century, Gentile would seem to have been a curious reactionary.[9] And other prominent fascists, like Giovanni Bottai, were heavily marked by bolshevism, even if they raged against its internationalist aspect. During the German Occupation in 1944, Italian fascists who remained loyal to the Salò Republic worked to impose true socialism on their short-lived political enterprise.

Traditional conservative and Catholic critics who accentuate fascism's leftist elements are usually not at home in our democratic late modernity, and, not surprisingly, they make their definitions fit their larger complaint against the historical tide. In this book, the author does not wish to slight these critics in light of their valuable insights. Still, these authors ignore certain crucial distinctions. Not all "democracies" have been the same throughout human history. In the ancient world and as late as two centuries ago, the operation of popular government was filtered through ethnic and social qualifications. In today's Western world, by contrast, democracies tend to be multicultural and feature extensive welfare states. They typically emphasize, both rhetorically and legislatively, the values of equality and universalism.

Some democratic governments, for example, in eastern Europe and Israel, still appeal, perhaps anachronistically, to national solidarity and national homogeneity, and democracies in transition from nineteenth-century bourgeois states incorporate, for at least a few generations, traditional liberal, capitalist features. But no democracy today would chose to call itself "fascist" although fascist governments in interwar Europe exalted the popular will and claimed a revolutionary democratic pedigree. Western states, which now regard themselves as embodying the only legitimate form of popular governments, have no trouble recognizing their family members.

Significantly, they would never accept into their family or club those regimes they consider "fascist" or those governments that remind them, however vaguely, of interwar fascist governments.

There is consensus among those regarded as democracies that fascism is alien and evil. Onetime communists are treated far more sympathetically in today's democratic sphere than any leader or government identified with any past Right. That is because Democrats perceive a moral and political overlap between their values and those of the Marxist Left. Former real or imagined fascists are treated with far less understanding. Although not intended as a justification for this double standard, this explanation is an attempt to understand why not everything that has called itself democratic over the past century is now accepted as such. Traditionalist critics of fascism should recognize that there are differing forms of democratic modernity, not all of which are considered by Democrats to be equally clubbable.

There are other explanations as to why anything associated with fascism is kept out of the democracy club. Fascists of all stripes are associated with the brutal crimes of the Nazi period and, together with the Nazis, went down to defeat in the Second World War. But communists may have killed even more people than Nazis, and certainly more than generic fascists, and yet this fact has not prevented former servants of and apologists for communist regimes from being admitted into democratic governments and wined and dined in our universities. The reason for these differing receptions should again be obvious. Unlike the revolutionary Right, politicians and publicists of the Left conspicuously uphold democratic ideals. Unlike the fascists, they claim (and are largely taken at their word) to embrace egalitarian, universal principles.

Other Scholarly Treatments of Fascism as a Movement of the Left

Despite this pan-democratic ban, well-credentialed historians still insist that fascists were so heavily influenced by the interwar Left that readers ignore essential aspects of their thinking and practices by ignoring their borrowing. Whether it was their invectives against the *borghesia vigliarda* (cowardly burghers), repugnance for moneyed interests, or propensity for state economic planning, fascists should remind us of the revolutionary Left. Although not alone in making this point, A. James Gregor has done so perhaps more systematically than anyone else by going though the major documents of the Italian fascist movement and pointing out their affirmation of collectivism and statism. Gregor has also tried to prove a structural and attitudinal continuity between Mussolini's movement and various Third World dictatorships that have combined centralized economic control with a cult of the leader and ethnic self-assertion. Like Italian fascist propagandists of the 1930s, their non-Western imitators invoke the struggle against affluent, plutocratic societies and call for "national unity" as a way of overcoming a legacy of exploitation.[10]

According to Gregor, the self-image of Third World dictatorships as "proletariat nations" could be drawn just as easily from fascist rhetoric as communist slogans.[11] Fascist concepts may be even more adaptable than Marxist ones to the needs of Third World despots since they justify a form of collectivism that does not have to bring equality but can be defended as ethnically authentic. Anticolonial ideologues, like the Baathists in the Middle East, banked on fascist ideas when they built national revolutionary movements. Gregor cites such facts to prove that fascism provided the paradigm for a form of radical politics aiming at both national solidarity and economic modernization.

One might, however, raise two questions about Gregor's contentions. First, how much did fascism make transferable politics available to Third World dictatorships? Different societies throughout the world may borrow programs and symbols from each other, just as, during the Meiji Restoration, the Japanese adopted certain features of English and German institutional life to advance their selective modernization. But are the borrowers so transformed by what they borrow that they come to resemble those whose institutions and habits they are borrowing?

This hypothetical connection becomes even more problematic when one seeks to determine the direct influence of Italian fascism on Third World countries. Here we are speaking about what is not even explicit borrowing but the absence of what Gregor would consider to be liberal or democratic features in the modern Western sense. Why should we assume that those who try or pretend to be trying to modernize under a corrupt tribal dictatorship are really practicing "radical politics" in the fascist vein? These leaders may be building states and economies under less than optimal conditions and looking for labels with which to adorn their limited achievements.

Another question that might occur to someone reading Gregor's exposition concerns the character of radical politics. Why was fascist Italy as a practicing regime more "radical" than post–World War II England, which drastically overhauled its economic structure, seizing control of key industries, while undertaking drastic income redistribution? Why are modern democracies that strip their monarchs and the upper houses of their national legislatures of previously established constitutional power or expel religious orders and nationalize church property not behaving in a radical manner? Through most of the fascist experience in Italy, economic relations were hardly touched, in comparison to the construction of social democratic states in post–World War II Europe. Although the Italian fascist regime surely had its oppressive and silly aspects, Mussolini's government in 1926 looked rather different from Castro's dictatorship or those African kleptocracies that Gregor treats as updated Mussolinian regimes.

With due respect to Gregor, solidarity as opposed to individualism is not necessarily a radical position, except among American libertarians. The entire European Right in the interwar period valued collectivism and organicism more than individualistically based political creeds. Gregor also neglects to focus on the counterrevolutionary manner in which fascist movements evolved and, in Italy, came to power as a force against the revolutionary Left. The competitors of leftist revolutionaries in Italy, Austria, or Hungary after the First World War were not nineteenth-century English Tories or English liberals. It was preeminently the revolutionary Right that performed this oppositional function. Moreover, the fascists did not operate as merely partisan opposition, like Republicans in the United States or the Conservative Party in England. They represented the "political" in the sense in which Carl Schmitt applied that term, namely as an adversary in a life-and-death confrontation between sides that did not view themselves as debating teams on a TV news program.[12]

Stanley Payne may come closest to grasping the rightism of fascism when he painstakingly differentiates it from other interwar European rightist movements. Fascists were different from the "new conservative authoritarian right," which was generally "more moderate and more conservative on every issue than the fascists."[13] The revolutionary Right also differed from the radical right, which was more rightist than the fascists, in the sense that these other rightists were "tied more to the existing elites and structure for support, however demagogic its propaganda may have sounded." The radical but not revolutionary Right was also "unwilling to accept fully the cross-cultural mass mobilization and implied social, economic, and cultural changes demanded by fascism."[14] All the same, fascists could cooperate with the counterrevolutionary Right, no matter what they may have borrowed from the Left. They coexisted with authoritarian nationalist Right in the same coalitions, for example, in Hungary in the late 1930s.

What may be confusing about locating fascism on a traditional right-left spectrum is the poor fit between fascists and the traditional Right. Fascist movements arose and flourished in what was becoming a postconservative culture. These fascist movements were a response to the revolutionary Left that, organizationally and rhetorically, was as radical as what it was mobilized to resist. Fascism also lacked the ideational coherence not only of Marxism but of the counterrevolutionaries of the early nineteenth century, the political principles of which Karl Mannheim examines in his study "Conservatism."[15]

It may bear witness to the diffuseness and purple prose of fascist theorists that efforts to create a European "fascist international" in 1934 broke down at least partly because the participants couldn't agree on what they were supposed to believe.[16] Neither the Austro-fascists nor the German Nazis bothered to attend the Fascist International Congress in Montreux in 1934 since neither considered its proceedings to be relevant to their ideas and programs. Moreover, while the Romanian fascists at Montreux wished to elevate anti-Semitism to a paramount international theme, other attendees were totally unconcerned with a Jewish threat. Like Italian fascist government as depicted by De Felice, logrolling went on at the conference. The delegates sought a compromise solution when they denied the racial aspect of the Jewish problem but expressed concern about a disproportionate Jewish influence in European politics.

One need not go as far as John Lukacs, who categorically rejects the concept of generic fascism, to notice the diversity within interwar fascist movements.[17] Equally striking, however, is that the Austrian clericalists and the German Nazis regarded themselves in 1934 as outliers in terms of their relation to mainstream fascists. The Romanians stood out as being more obsessively anti-Semitic than were fascist members and sympathizers from other countries, e.g., Quisling's party in Norway and the Irish Blueshirts. But the majority of those who attended at Montreux can be said to have combined a counterrevolutionary stance with a willingness to borrow ideas and slogans from the radical Left.

Once in power, fascist leaders had to decide how much of its radical program would be implemented. In fascist Italy, according to De Felice, this policy was shaped by a practical consideration: how well fascist leaders could hold together the lower- and upper-middle classes and at least some of the working class by appealing to all of them. But these efforts should not cause the reader to confound fascism's point of origin with its path to the top. Negotiating this tortuous path required a distancing of the movement from the socialist and revolutionary Left and dithering parliamentary liberals. Fascist propagandists also had to persuade their possible bourgeois followers that parliamentary politics could not meet the challenge of the hour by restoring order.

Anti–New Deal Journalists and Fascist Collectivism

Attacks on fascism as a collectivist threat to American freedom began in the 1930s, as proponents and critics of the New Deal assailed each other in print. Before the mid-1930s Italian fascism appealed strongly to American socialists as much as it did to Catholics, who commended Mussolini for the Lateran Pacts. Well into the 1930s, despite the adversarial press erected by Mussolini's predominantly leftist opposition in exile mostly in Paris, the Italian fascist government enjoyed some appeal across the American political spectrum. The lyric from the Cole Porter musical "Anything Goes," as rewritten for the London production by P. G. Wodehouse in 1935, celebrates Mussolini as the 'top.' This reference was dropped in later productions but suggests the enthusiasm once felt in the English-speaking world for a man "who made the trains run on time" in a longtime chaotic country.

The New Republic abounded with tips for how America might learn from the Italian experiment, and such socialist reformers as Horace Kallen, George Soule, and Stuart Chase rushed to recommend the fascist notion of autarchy and having the state protect corporate structures in a way that would benefit the working class. Although some New Dealers like Rexford Tugwell saw features of Soviet Russia that likewise attracted them, fascism seemed to offer a promising halfway point between bolshevism and capitalism.

According to New Deal critic John T. Flynn, an apparent moderateness rendered the Italian model even more insidious: "A man could support publicly and with vehemence this system of the Planned Economy without incurring the odium of being too much of a radical for polite and practical society."[18] In addition, Mussolini and, later, even more decisively, Hitler put the nails in the coffin of the true liberal tradition by constructing the "Planned Capitalist State." The "direct opposite of liberalism," fascism was "an attempt, somewhere between Communism and capitalism, to organize a stable society and to do it by setting up a state equipped with massive powers over the lives and fortunes of the citizens."[19]

Flynn's observations, which libertarian publicists of his acquaintance shared, would have made it hard for him and others of his persuasion to treat fascism as a strictly leftist movement: "This may be a wise dispensation, but it is the negation of liberal philosophy which for decades has been fighting to emancipate the people from the tyranny of all-powerful states." A preference for liberty over any kind of order, including traditional order, characterizes the minimal government rhetoric of American libertarians in the 1930s and 1940s, and it can be discovered in such representative works as Friedrich von Hayek's *Road to Serfdom* (1944) and Flynn's *As We Go Marching* (1945).[20] Here one finds articulated the thoughts of anti-collectivists who were at war with America's emerging welfare state. The ideological dividing line for them was not between a traditional Right and a traditional Left or between a revolutionary Right and a revolutionary Left but between collectivist and individualist conceptions of society.[21]

Libertarians Flynn, Albert J. Nock, Garet Garrett, and Frank Chodorov, all of whom were active in the 1930s or 1940s, viewed fascists, New Dealers, and communists as being of the same ilk. All of these sundry statists sought to impose artificial control on those who had a natural right to be free. In comparison to their shared hostility to "liberalism," the ideological differences that kept statists apart seemed relatively slight. Thus, Flynn asserted with deep conviction in 1945 that those countries that were fighting the Nazis were becoming like them. They had organized themselves anti-individualistically against German and Italian collectivists, in alliance with fellow collectivists in the Kremlin, but the effect of this antifascist belligerence in the United States would be to destroy liberty at home.

The idea that self-described libertarians belonged to the "Right" became widespread in the 1950s, around the time that William F. Buckley, Jr., Russell Kirk, and other political thinkers were trying to construct a "conservative" pedigree for their own movement. Their efforts led to the founding of the *National Review*, which appeared bimonthly, in 1955 and to a doctrinal synthesis combining sympathy for a free market economy with militant anticommunism and Anglo-Catholic religious impulses. Eventually the libertarian purists and the Buckleyites fell out over both philosophical issues and military policies, and, especially once they were ousted from Buckley's made-to-order conservative movement, some libertarians began to refer to themselves as the "Old Right."[22]

Although other libertarians continued to emphasize primarily the distinction between collectivists and anticollectivists, the followers of the economist and polymath Murray N. Rothbard now claimed to hold the true right-wing credentials. This meant, in effect, an anti–New Deal, isolationist Right going back to the interwar period. Those who shared its set of beliefs inclined toward an individualistic, procapitalist world view grounded in free market economics. They eschewed, among other collectivist evils, military projects, deemed to be "the health of the state," and quoted the decidedly leftist author Randolph Bourne in his criticism of the American ruling class during the Great War.

The view that fascism is a distinctly leftist movement did not become an established tenet on the American Right until fairly recently. A noticeable exception to this generalization was Kuehnelt-Leddihn, who tried to bring European conservative ideas to an American public. But his was an exceptional position for a publicist of the American Right, as was the view that fascism was entirely of the Left. More typical was the subsuming of fascism under the catchall heading of "collectivism."

The *National Review* cofounder, Frank S. Meyer, in his tract *In Defense of Freedom* (1962), identified fascists with a "liberal collectivist theory of the state." Supposedly, fascists and Nazis, like communists and socialists, were each advancing some form of Rousseau's theory of the general will. All these ideologues believed in the "underlying real will of the totality, which becomes embodied in the Volk and its leader or else in the Communist Party as the true will of the proletariat."[23] For Meyer, all collectivist ideologies include an attempt to marry a concrete power structure to an abstract, deified will. Political persuasions that glorified this collective will were thought to justify an almost unlimited use of state power, and they had to be understood by reference to the French Revolution and those who prepared the way for this catastrophe.

In the postwar years American conservative publicists treated fascism in conjunction with communism as something wicked; this was clearly the opinion of Meyer and his colleagues. Exactly what kind of bad thing fascism was changed somewhat when the predominantly Jewish neoconservatives came to reconfigure the conservative movement in the 1980s. Thereafter fascism became synonymous with Hitler and the Holocaust, as did other movements and positions that the neoconservatives disapproved of.

Meanwhile, enterprising Republican publicists have attacked their left-wing opposition as fascists by other names. This is exemplified by *Liberal Fascism*, a hefty tome prepared by FOX News contributor Jonah Goldberg that draws extended comparisons between fascist totalitarianism and the Democratic Party. Goldberg's four-hundred-page investigation, whatever its multiple flaws, reveals undeniable diligence. The author consulted a wide variety of secondary literature, including general studies on what the Fascists and Nazis preached and occasionally put into practice. Goldberg also scoured the speeches and policies of leading Democratic politicians and their predecessors going back to the Progressive Era in the early twentieth century in order to prove a correspondence between Democratic policies and Fascist prescriptions.[24] And there was much, according to Goldberg, that the Republicans' opposition, the Fascists, and finally (and perhaps most frighteningly) Hitler agreed on concerning how the state should treat its subjects.

Family planning, the socialization of their subjects, and even preference for particular ethnic groups at the expense of others were positions that Progressive Democrats, New Dealers, followers of Bill and Hillary Clinton,[25] and interwar fascists all embraced at different times and in various ways. The fact that Goldberg refers to the Democratic opposition as "liberals" and "leftists" does not mean that he can't also decry them as fascists. His multiple references to the Clintons tell more about Goldberg's purpose than the appendix that appears at the end of his volume with the 1920 Nazi Party Platform. Because his book was published in 2007, Goldberg only furnishes three isolated references to Barack Obama, who was then an Illinois senator. One might expect that he would have more to say about the "fascism" of the current US president in future editions.

The failings of Goldberg's onetime best seller, aimed at an audience sympathetic to GOP talking points, are all too obvious. His work tries desperately to make disparate things fit together, like Hillary Clinton's "new village" under state auspices and Hitler's *Volksgemeinschaft,* or the affirmative action programs aimed at minorities and pushed by Democrats and Hitler's decision in 1934 to exclude Jews from German professional and political life.[26] Although controversial and often counterproductive, the egalitarian politics of American "liberals" have nothing to do with Nazi race policies, which were pursued to degrade and, if possible, eliminate undesirable groups.

Moreover, Goldberg's charges are profoundly hypocritical since he goes after Democrats, under the label of "liberals" and "leftists," for supporting government policies that have commanded bipartisan support for decades. Periodic expansions of the American welfare state have generally received endorsement from both national parties. Indeed, Goldberg, as a "conservative" journalist, expressed genuine irritation when Kentucky Senator Rand Paul, then a candidate for office, criticized the public accommodations section of the Civil Rights Act of 1964. This was interpreted by Goldberg as a sign of "right-wing extremism," as was Paul's proposal to abolish the sprawling federal Department of Education that came into existence under the Carter Administration. For better or worse, the size and reach of government that Goldberg explicitly or implicitly supports go well beyond anything Democratic presidents enacted in the first half of the last century.[27]

Goldberg also offers a questionable argument in the final chapter about what "has put conservatives and right-wingers of all stripes at a disadvantage." It appears that, unlike the other side, Goldberg's allies "have made the 'mistake' of writing down their dogma."[28] Unfortunately, it is not at all clear that his side, or whatever he imagines that to be, has a unitary dogma outside of belonging to the GOP and reciting sound bites that come from the appropriate media sources or that in this respect they are very different from the other side, which is thought to resemble the fascists, except for the fact that they are allegedly hiding their dogma. Goldberg does provide a pragmatic rule: "that the role of the state should be limited and its meddling should be seen as an exception."[29] The problem here is that he also accepts every major breach of that rule that occurred in the twentieth century from the moment it became part of our bipartisan political legacy. A question that Goldberg never engages (and the addressing of which might cost him some of his readers) is where he would make major cuts. Presumably the military, the Department of Education, and agencies that protect certain groups against discrimination would be off-limits.

Despite these flaws, there is a certain recriminatory vigor in Goldberg's presentation. It builds on a tradition of argument extending back to the 1930s that is integrally related to the American case against the welfare state. We are urged to believe that what passes for American progressive policies are adaptations of fascist corporatism. The present advocates of an expanded American welfare state are pushing in the same direction as were Mussolini and Hitler when they established (or implied that they were establishing) a command economy.[30]

In January 2013, Whole Foods CEO John Mackey made headlines when he accused President Obama of being a "fascist" in light of his harmful meddling with the economy.[31] Another defender of American capitalism, former academic Herb London, published a commentary a few days later linking the "F-word" to Obama. A practitioner of "crony capitalism" in the White House who happily made deals with his prominent business backers, Obama was following Hitler when he extended favors to industrialists.[32] London was absolutely correct in his charges against the Democratic president and in observing that Hitler had played the same games. The biggest question is whether this parallel proves that Obama is a "fascist" as opposed to an opportunistic politician like others in his trade.

Goldberg ends his narrative by recalling that William F. Buckley, Jr., during a televised debate at the Democratic National Convention in 1968, called his debating partner, novelist Gore Vidal, a "crypto-Nazi" and then threatened to "sock you in the goddamn face." Goldberg's book "has served much the same purpose as Buckley's intemperate outburst while striving for more typical civility."[33] The outburst in question was occasioned by a remark of Vidal's accusing Buckley of fascist sympathies. Although the counterattack featured the word *Nazi*, Buckley could just as easily have pulled out the word *fascist*. By then, his magazine and the movement he led were accustomed to identifying fascism with unsavory opponents, a practice picked up once the neoconservatives completed their migration into the Republican Party and began denouncing the New Left as anti-Semitic and antidemocratic. The term "liberal antifascism" first surfaced in the early 1970s and suggested a similarity between the American liberal Left and the violent, nihilistic European government that the United States had fought in World War II.

Since then we have had to deal with an "Islamofascist" enemy, which political activist David Horowitz identified for us when he proclaimed an "Islamofascist Awareness Week" in October 2007.[34] This was designed to combat not only Islamic extremists but also those elements of the Left that still minimize the gathering fascist storm. Republican journalist Don Feder also jumped into the war against "Islamofascism," in the wake of the publication of Goldberg's book, to denounce "left fascism." Feder discerned evidence of this problem in the eruption of political correctness.[35] The "brownshirts of the Left" had begun to trample on free speech by punishing opponents of the gay rights agenda. Although Horowitz and Feder are addressing genuine, worrisome problems in the case of Islamic terrorists and the crusade against unauthorized political and religious opinions, neither unpleasantness would seem to have much to do with European fascist movements of the interwar years. The speaker's resorting to the terms *fascist* or *Nazi* arouses chilling but not necessarily relevant historic memories.

On September 2, 2014,[36] and then again on September 6 in *National Review*,[37] syndicated columnist George F. Will announced that the existential threat to democracy posed by Vladimir Putin's "fascist revival" is even "more dangerous than the Islamic state." Indeed, Putin's "fascist revival will test the West's capacity to decide" whether our civilization even wishes to survive. Nowhere in Will's tirade do we learn how the foreign policy danger posed by the Russian leader entails the establishment of a fascist regime on Russian soil. But Will has even more to hurl at his Russian target. For example, Putin's designs in eastern Ukraine may be driven not so much by nationalism as they are "saturated with Soviet nostalgia." It may be appropriate to ask whether "Soviet nostalgia" and fascism are the same thing. Even more pertinent is the question of whether every expansionist leader becomes Hitler or a fascist by virtue of having expansionist designs.

Those who engage in such heated editorializing, however, are not necessarily treating fascism as a leftist movement. Foreign policy hawks, who once described themselves as being somewhere on the Left, are seeking to justify their realignment. The problem, they would argue, is that those who are now on the Left have betrayed their highest ideals.[38] Apparently the Left has not been sufficiently vigilant in resisting fascist incursions into international trouble spots and American universities; therefore, true antifascists have had to break ranks and join something identified as the American conservative establishment.

Another view that occasionally comes to the fore among media-acknowledged conservatives is that fascism does, indeed, belong to the Left. Unfortunately, this interpretation has been not been refined to a point where it warrants critical attention, as indicated by the following illustration from *The New Criterion* (October 2011). Here, William Gairdner carelessly applies the "f word" to describe all cultural trends that he finds disagreeable: "In what follows, I argue that all the modern, unnatural and therefore anti-human attempts to bend nature and human nature to the will, have been expressed in two basic forms, one macro, the other micro."[39] Characteristic of macrofascism "whether French, Italian, German, or Russian, has always been collective, secular and militant striving through the fearsome top-down power of the State to draw all things into the ambit of a single pattern of national—or in the case of Communism, international—will." This forcing of people and things into a mold has involved the "subjugation and assimilation by force of things spontaneous, private, and natural to artificial and unnatural public designs." Fascism is not a "reactionary response to a perceived loss of natural community" but a particularly destructive form of "a modern Statist dystopia, which relies on well-worn tools of regimentation."[40]

According to Gairdner, the defeat of macrofascism in World War II opened the door to a more subtle form of the same "disease," which has now reached epidemic proportions: "In a pragmatic response to the collapse of the macro form, a softer micro-fascism, also rooted in much earlier intellectual tradition, evolved slowly through the second half of the twentieth century and is now in full bloom as our most pervasive and most invisible political religion." In the newly formatted fascism, rebellion takes place against what Gairdner perceives as the natural order, and this rebellion takes place by allowing individuals to act on their whims without any moral restraint. Microfascists have turned the "Christian insistence on the moral freedom of each individual" into a justification for indulging one's appetites *ad libitum*.[41]

Microfascists have also encouraged "social atomization" by lamenting the unnaturalness of organic ties and reducing persons to administered units relegated to computer files. Gairdner sees fascism's "slave-making technique as being in operation today where egalitarian radicals have negated the natural and eternal biological differences between the genders." Microfascists have simultaneously bestowed on women "the right to triumph over the natural consequences of their own sexual behavior by removing the natural burden of their unwanted children."[42]

Gairdner's jeremiad against "microfascism" reaches a crescendo in its closing paragraphs in which we encounter the following statements: "In short, multiculturalism has mutated into multi-fascism, a trend that is creating mini-nations within nations, many of which as in France are now violent 'no go' zones for police. Nature has come galloping back." Moreover, a statement that was appended to an abortion decision by the Supreme Court giving people the "right to define one's own concept of existence of meaning, of the universe and of the mystery of human life" encapsulates the fascist essence. It involves a "cosmic inversion" authorizing a "pro-godlet ruling that subjected the meaning of all of nature and the universe to individual will, while at the same time pulverizing that meaning into demos-bits."[43]

One can easily locate in these assertions older traditionalist complaints against the unfettered human will. Gairdner's treatment of this subject includes unacknowledged borrowings from conservative heroes of the recent past such as Irving Babbitt, Russell Kirk, and Eric Voegelin, all of whom made related criticisms about the heretical Christian foundations of the present age. Although stated as oracular pronouncements, Gairdner's comments about an atomized but also rigorously controlled society and his reservations about the ideal of total individual autonomy encompass more than a word of truth. Indeed, one could agree with his social views without believing that Gairdner is telling us anything meaningful about historic fascism, except for the facts that he has chosen to make it synonymous with everything he dislikes.

The view that fascism exalts the will and is therefore incompatible with Christian and Aristotelian morality is certainly not a *novum*, nor is the idea that fascists attracted followers by evoking a sense of community for those who felt uprooted. This is a major theme in *Escape from Freedom*, the *pièce de résistance* of the Frankfurt School exile Erich Fromm, and an insight that suffuses Hannah Arendt's post–World War II masterpiece *Origins of Totalitarianism*. Gairdner is certainly not being original when he delineates as "macrofascism" what others treated more systematically in the mid-twentieth century. Looking at his firm denial that fascism was a "reactionary response," moreover, one feels obliged to ask for evidence for his easily challenged assertion. A further question may be in order: even if we assume that fascists and the revolutionary Left both prioritized the will, is Gairdner right when he asserts that the movements he rejects are mostly identical—or that communism was a subgenus of fascism? Perhaps we are speaking in this case about two very different movements that stress equally direct action in order to overcome certain obstacles on the path to taking power.

Even less convincing is Gairdner's attempt to interpret recent developments that distress him as infallible symptoms of "microfascism," given the definitions of fascism he has already furnished. What he deplores in the present age seems to have nothing to do with fascist ideals understood as the organic, hierarchical nationalism preached by Mussolini and José Antonio Primo de Rivera. Feminism, gay rights, and extreme individual expressiveness are unrelated to the unnatural "regimentation" that Gairdner denounces at the beginning of his essay. Categorizing too much expressive freedom as "fascist" does not change its differentness from what it is supposed to be exemplifying or approximating.

This verbal looseness makes one suspect that "conservative" journalists are retaliating against those who pummel them with the "f word." But this retaliatory practice should not be confused with seriously searching for the meaning of a political term. Such quarreling illustrates what intellectual historian Panajotis Kondylis has styled a *"Machtfrage"* (question of power), a struggle over the right to define meaning as a way of advancing a partisan cause.[44] This is yet one more example of how the study of fascism has been turned into a political football, a habit that unfortunately is no longer confined to the European antifascist Left. By now it may be pandemic.

CHAPTER FIVE

The Failure of Fascist Internationalism

Latin Fascist Internationalism as a Literary Vision

Although a huge bibliography on fascist movements exists, one aspect of this subject that has received relatively little attention is the quest for a fascist universalism. This search became particularly noticeable in the early 1930s and coincided with developments then taking place in European politics. Among these were the call for pan-European unity, the search for a new politics (or what Oswald Mosley in England characterized as a "New Party" bridging the socialist Left and the nationalist Right), and the hope on the Right for a fusion of fascist corporatism with Catholic doctrines in the wake of the Lateran Pacts in 1929. Although not all these interests were equally important for all advocates of fascist internationalism, they did reinforce each other in establishing the idea that fascist government did not have to be limited to one nation. Nor did fascist countries have to fight each other in a struggle for survival or hegemony. They could all cooperate in building a new European order and, in the near term, opposing the threat represented by international bolshevism.

These hopes are present in what may have been the most compelling fascist novel ever written, *Gilles*, which was authored by Pierre Drieu La Rochelle (1898–1945) in 1939 and reissued under the German occupation of France in 1942.[1] A sprawling work of seven hundred pages recounting the war experiences, steamy affairs, forays into the politics of the Third Republic, and, finally, the conversion of its protagonist, Gilles Gambier, to fascism, Drieu La Rochelle is depicting his life here in an idealized form. A major difference is that while Gilles in the epilogue is about to perish defending Burgos with the Nationalists during the Spanish Civil War, the author committed suicide in 1945, before he could be arrested (or killed by communist vigilantes) as a German collaborator. A bookish man who, like Gilles, lusted after women, and who, like Gilles, was gravely wounded as a soldier in World War I, Drieu sets out to fashion a heroic version of his own persona. Like Gilles, who was married to a wealthy Jewish woman, Drieu had been married, not once but twice, to Jewish ladies with inherited wealth, although, no less than Gilles, he looked down on Jews as a group, the rise of which he thought coincided with the disintegration of the true France.

In one of the last scenes in this gargantuan novel, foreign volunteers with the Spanish Falange escort Walter, a Belgian Rexist who sympathizes with the Nationalists and is "fighting for Catholic civilization," from the island of Ibiza to Marseilles.[2] Walter is on an unidentified mission and ends up in Ibiza after having escaped Republican-held Barcelona. He displays his mettle by manning a machine gun and helping the Falange take the island. On the boat with other fascist sympathizers, one a Pole and the other an Irishman, Walter discusses why he and his companions were attracted to the fascist movement. Although each professes a belief in the Catholic Church and agrees that it is "indestructible," their first, immediate loyalty is to the "fascist revolution." The Irishman, O'Connor, announces: "I believe fascism will result in a redemptive revolution and that the Church should profit from this occasion to renew itself totally. Walter, from the first moment we met, you expressed exactly my thought, namely, that we're for the virile Catholicism of the Middle Ages."[3] Whereupon Walter, fidgeting with excitement, blurts out: "Fascism will bring about a veritable revolution, a complete turning of Europe on itself [*tour complet de l'Europe sur soi-même*], combining the most ancient and the most modern, but this will happen only if [it] includes the Church."[4]

The question is then posed by the Polish fascist: What would be the consequences if "the Church refuses its support"? The Pole answers his own question by explaining that "if the Church errs politically as it has done so often in the past, we'll have to allow it, at least for the moment, to fall. One can take things or leave them with the Church, which is eternal. If the Church asks us to fight with the communists against the fascists, we could never oblige. We shall have to be excommunicated, as was the fate of many good Christians."[5] Walter asks rhetorically in response: "Just as you would not confuse the Church as an institution with its temporary political and spiritual directions, would you not concede to fascism the same consideration in terms of its universal principle and powers, even if it sometimes abuses them? I'm afraid that if you don't help fascism triumph in your own countries, you may be doing something very different, which is defending your countries against fascist powers even at the risk of allowing antifascist forces to prevail."[6]

The fascist boat travelers then come back to the possible conflict between their own nations and "fascist powers." What exactly would the Pole do if his country (stating a hypothesis that didn't seem entirely outside the realm of possibility when the novel was written) sought an alliance with Soviet Russia against Germany? The Pole indicates that he would not support a war in which the cost of opposing Germany would be to "allow the Red army to invade Poland." Such a hypothetical situation would endanger both his nation and the Church. Walter then introduces the crucial point that "the triumph of fascism should never be confounded with the victory of one nation over other nations."[7]

The Pole goes on to explain that the "hegemony of an idea has always been confused with the rule of a particular nation. Democratic hegemony has resulted in the hegemony of England. It may therefore be necessary to choose between fascism and nationalism." O'Connor then breaks in with a comment: "Nationalism is already obsolete. What the democratic powers have not succeeded in accomplishing in Geneva [with the League of Nations], the fascist powers will [be] able to do. They will establish the unity of Europe."[8] O'Connor mentions what to his mind would be the grim alternative to a European-wide fascist breakthrough: "If the fascist powers are vanquished, would the result be anything less than the hegemony of Russia? Or the rule of such ignoble democracies as France, England, or America?" The Irishman exclaims at this point: "For me the triumph of the United States after a World War would be as frightful as the victory of Soviet Russia."[9]

"This would be the same thing," rejoins Walter, who then announces almost trancelike to the others, "As for me, I have withdrawn from nations. I belong to a new military and religious order which has been set up somewhere in the world and which pursues against all odds the reconciliation of the Church and fascism and their dual triumph throughout Europe." Walter, moreover, has not abandoned all hope that the German government, which is viewed as embodying a defective form of fascism, will ultimately see the light: "Against the invasion of Europe by the Red Army, we may need to promote a birth of European patriotism. This could happen if Germany provided a full moral guarantee that it would honor the integrity of all other

European countries. Only then would it be possible for Germany to fulfill the exalted role that has devolved on her through her power and the tradition of the Germanic Holy Roman Empire, which is to direct the path of a future Europe."[10] Although not entirely demonstrable, it is possible that Drieu inserted these lines into the epilogue after the fall of France, when his future and that of his country depended on the indulgence of the Third Reich. While in Paris during the war years, he petitioned the German occupation to pursue a policy of international cooperation similar to the one that Walter proposes. Needless to say, the proposal was ignored, while the petitioner was treated as a laughingstock.[11]

This conversation is describing an epiphany for Gilles and his authorial creator. Both move from residual French nationalism toward the recognition of fascist internationalism. In Drieu's novel, Gilles expresses the sentiments of his aged guardian, Carentan, a Norman peasant who is mourning the depopulation of rural France. The only parent whom the orphaned Gilles ever knew, Carentan remarks to him as they walk through the countryside, "Yes, France is dying. Let's go to the next village. I'll show you house by house, family by family, the death of France." This death, the reader learns, was taking place for multiple reasons, some of which Gilles finds in the corruption and decrepitude of the French Third Republic.[12]

This parlous situation is seen as embodied in the fictional but representative president Maurice Morel, a Radical Socialist, that is, a member of a mainstream party, and "a bourgeois who pretends to be a socialist or a socialist who turns out to be a bourgeois, the fool who with his own weak and timid hands tries to rebuild the house he has demolished." Bribery, embezzlement, and opportunism are for Gilles the defining characteristics of France's unpalatable government. The tendency of the president and his ministers to vent "fearful, peevish tirades" on the Germans and "their incapacity to make generous initiatives toward or work effectively against a defeated but still powerful enemy" underscore how utterly incompetent the Third Republic had become.[13]

Not surprisingly, Gilles expresses admiration for the French nationalist, monarchist, and man of letters Charles Maurras (1868–1952). Drieu informs us that Gilles (like Drieu) reads Maurras's publication *Action Française* generally with approval.[14] An outspoken Provençal, Maurras despised the Third Republic, glorified the French Catholic past, and called for a governmental change that would unite the true France, the *pays réel*, against the "democratic rented flat [*meublier démocratique*]," as Gilles refers to the French administrative state that had been put up for sale by hirelings. Gilles gives vent to all the same sentiments that he finds in his Provençal hero. Also, like

Maurras, he views Anglo-Saxons, and, even more, their American cousins, as cultural enemies of the French nation and scorns Jews as, at best, never completely French and, at worst, agents of the Soviets. It might have been Maurras speaking when Gilles announces to his Marxist friend Lorin, "The creative vein being exhausted among Europeans, the way has been opened to Jewish shoddiness [*camelote juive*]."[15] Despite his obvious affinity for Maurras, Gilles is also critical of him for being "mired in the past" and refusing to understand the need for a new politics in the interwar age. Although equally contemptuous of the Republic, he rejects Maurras's preoccupation with monarchical restoration.

About halfway through the novel, Gilles becomes the editor of a publication, *L'Apocalypse*, which treats the French Republic with intense hostility. Through this vehicle, Gilles "launches a frontal attack against democracy and capitalism but also against mechanistic thinking and scientism."[16] Gilles informs his Marxist companions that "although I do not believe in Marxism and detest it with all my being, I wish with no less passion that the Marxists bring down the present society. . . . This is a task, destroying bourgeois society, which one could not demand of the fascists at the present time, since except for Hitler's accession to power in Germany, nothing much is known about this movement in France."[17] Yet when Gilles, for want of another profession, opts to be a political pamphleteer, having already abandoned a post in the government bureaucracy, he "belongs to no group or human category."[18] He still views himself as vehemently against plutocracy and corrupt politicians more than in favor of any particular cause. He was a nationalist with certain traditional prejudices but allied to neither Right nor Left.

This becomes particularly clear in how Gilles reacts to the riots in Paris following the Stavisky Affair in February 1934. These were violent demonstrations that brought together Marxist revolutionaries and right-wing militants in the veterans' organization Croix de Feu and among Maurras's followers. The spark leading to these outbursts, which some feared might bring the republic to its knees, was the revelation of a massive fraud committed by a Russian Jewish scam artist, Serge Alexandre Stavisky.[19] Someone long associated with underworld activity, Stavisky sold false bonds in the amount of hundreds of millions in francs, mostly to French insurance companies. These bonds were unloaded in 1933 in the city of Bayonne, whose mayor and other local officials had urged companies to buy the worthless papers. The discovery of the fraud and suspicion that government officials were implicated incited tumultuous reactions from both the Right and the revolutionary Left. When Stavisky died in mysterious circumstances in January 1934, rumors immediately circulated that government leaders were somehow responsible. It was thought that the police shot Stavisky at the orders of politicians who were involved in the costly scam.

When the new premier, and a Radical Socialist Édouard Daladier, dismissed the Paris prefect of police Jean Chiappe, who was known to be on the political Right and was investigating Stavisky's possible highly placed collaborators, the crisis came to a head. Two days of rioting broke out mostly around the Place de Concorde; in Drieu's novel, the protagonist is swept up into this orgy of outrage. Gilles hails the demonstrations as proof that "the people have been aroused from the torpor," that they "can no longer resist the urging of the Furies," and "that those pouring into the streets have discovered they still have blood in their veins."[20] Because "the troops are now mixed together," Gilles points out hopefully, "communists are rubbing shoulders with nationalists. . . . It would take little for these forces to blend together in the face of the common enemy of all youth, an old, corrupt radicalism."[21]

As the rioting rages, Gilles urges a longtime friend who had thrown in his lot with the Radical Socialists to embrace the change that was unfolding outside his office. They were being impelled "to leave the routine of old parties, manifestoes, meetings, articles and discourses. And a power of formidable size was taking shape." At the same time, "the barriers will forever be broken between right and left and the torrents of life will course forward in every sense." Gilles then asks his friend excitedly, "Don't you feel the swelling surge? We are becoming the torrent. One can push it in any direction one wants but one must push it immediately at any price."[22]

Although Gilles is enraptured by the upsurge of anger against the insipid, blatantly dishonest Radical Socialists, there is no indication that even as an insurgent he has moved toward a firm ideological commitment. He simply hopes to see the nationalists and revolutionary Left work together toward bringing down a despised regime. Gilles admires the polemics of the nationalist Right and shares its distaste for Jews, Americans, and Marxist materialism. But he also views the French nationalism of an earlier generation as "obsolete" [périmé] and in need of being retired.[23] In the novel he stresses the task of addressing the challenges of the present time by seeking the cooperation of other European countries. In the last few pages Gilles experiences a fascist internationalist conversion while standing with the Spanish nationalists in Burgos. He admits to having given up on France, "which will retire from the front lines burnt by communist revolvers and at the instigation of Jews."[24] His own nation, Gilles laments, "doesn't even care about saving itself, and a new victory would mean no more to it than defeat."[25]

But what concerns Gilles at this point is no longer France. It is Latin civilization, some of which continued to thrive in the rural regions of his country. Moreover, the political unit that Gilles cares about most is the entire continent: "For him there was Europe. Since 1918 he really believed in Europe." But this entity or civilization Gilles refused to equate with the League of Nations: "Geneva was a sordid petty abstraction which humiliated all powerful life forms. It was necessary that nations recognize each other under a complex sign guaranteeing the autonomy of all sources, particular and universal."[26] It is the hope of a fascist European order that sustains Drieu's protagonist at the end of the novel. What is left unsaid is how exactly this new order would come about. Equally relevant but only cursorily mentioned in *Gilles* is whether a fascist Europe was possible without the project being taken over and barbarized by Hitler's Third Reich.

Drieu's paradigmatic fascist novel conveys fascist internationalism even in its favored religious views. Although there are numerous scenes of Gilles walking by churches and mourning the dwindling number of worshippers or the decay of the largely abandoned buildings, this is mostly a convention of the *romanciers nationalistes* going back to Maurice Barrès in the late nineteenth century.[27] Certainly Drieu did not initiate the practice on the French Right of pointing to old village churches and adjoining cemeteries as evidence that something had been lost in the modern age. That he occasionally attends a Mass and insists that his second marriage be consecrated in a church (since he was divorced from his first wife, it is not clear how this would be allowed) does not betoken that Gilles is a believing Catholic. He adheres to the ideas of his guardian, who believes in the recurrence and universality of certain religious legends without professing any specifically Catholic dogma.

This religious outlook features a savior who suffers for humanity and is then resurrected but is not anchored in any firm, well-defined belief system. And from Carentan's remarks, it would seem that although a devotee of comparative religious studies, Gilles's guardian does not welcome Jewish elements into his preferred legends. Although not immediately obvious from Carentan's statements about the Old Testament, this exclusionary position may be inferred from his visceral distaste for Jews as the creators of modernity. The eclectic religious thinking in Gilles and Carentan was a widespread trait among those on the Latin Right who did not accept Catholicism in any strict dogmatic sense. Such thinking was typified by Maurras and, even more graphically, by the Italian mystic Giulio Evola (1898–1974). Both of these figures were of the Right and in some sense Catholic but not explicitly Christian. Evola tried to fuse Indian theosophy and yoga with pagan asceticism,[28] and Maurras was condemned by the Church in 1927 as a nationalist and religious skeptic who tried to rally support for his monarchist cause by invoking France's historical ties to Catholicism. It might be best to understand Gilles's praise of "Latin civilization" in this eclectic, nonorthodox sense. This is how he sees spiritual questions even when he takes his stand with the fervently Catholic Spanish nationalists. It is not Catholic doctrine that he wishes to defend but the Latinity of Europe as understood in a cultural sense but not in the sense of Catholic belief.[29]

The tension between clerical fascists and neo-pagan fascists, who occasionally sported Catholic colors, became dramatically apparent when conservative Austrian Catholics who later lined up with the Austrofaschisten attacked the fascist internationalist journal *Antieuropa*, launched by Mussolini's longtime friend Asvero Gravelli in 1929. Whereas Gravelli and his associates were against "the old Europeanisms" while working to generate support for fascist teachings, the Austrian Catholic journal *Schönere Zukunft* accused the editors of "preaching the neo-pagan doctrines of Giulio Evola." Austrian critics charged these fascist publicists "with standing close to Evola in their beliefs and proceeding from post-Hegelian idealism in their own peculiar manner."[30] The polemic "*Neuheidnische Strömungen im italienischen Faschismus*" excoriated the neo-paganism of Gravelli and Gentile's adaptations of Hegelian philosophy for Italian fascist purposes. It is not clear that those who complained about neo-pagan fascists necessarily distinguished between the heresies of Evola's and Gentile's philosophies. Both were seen as equally poisonous from the standpoint of the Catholic Right.

Not surprisingly, the first issue of *Antieuropa* tried to forestall such reproaches by noting *Il Duce*'s revulsion for Protestantism. In "*Mussolini contra Luterò*," contributor Giuseppe Attlio Fanelli notes the dislike for the Protestant Reformation displayed by the Italian fascist leader, who stood for Roman order and Latinity. Everything that fascism opposed was ascribed by Fanelli, no less than by Maurras and Drieu, to the Protestant Germanic spirit. Democracy, individualism, and an unfettered economy were all the tares of a European culture that was incompatible with Latin civilization and its outgrowth, fascism. Some effort is made in this critique to join fascism and the Catholic Church, especially since the Italian state was about to conclude the Lateran Pacts. But what emerges from the polarities herein highlighted is the subordination of Catholic beliefs to the concepts of Latinity and *Romanitas*. Gravelli affirms in his introductory declaration that his publication stands for "the salvation of the Latin Catholic West." But this sentiment is expressed a few lines later as "the struggle for Europe but a struggle fortified by the purposes and characteristic conceptions of the spirit that inspires Europe, the spirit of Rome and the spirit of fascism and its head."[31]

Drieu has Gilles meet his death while professing his syncretistic creed. In his final statement of faith, Gilles cries out, "Yes mother of God made man, God who suffers in his creation, who dies and is reborn. I am always a heresiarch. The gods who die and are reborn: Dionysus and Christ. Nothing happens except in blood. It is necessary to die in order to be reborn. The Christ of cathedrals, the great deity white and virile. A king and the son of a king."[32] This "heretical" profession of faith is nothing more or less than the pagan religiosity that had begun to surface in fascist circles. It was strikingly eclectic and blended Catholic sensibility with neo-pagan content.

Those who held such views appealed to the ideals of the Middle Ages, but how that epoch and its ideals were depicted depended on usable images. Virility, hierarchy, and a spiritualized view of nature, far more than religious orthodoxy, characterized that medieval epoch. Within fascism, and especially in its Latin forms, a Christian replacement religion was taking shape. This replacement religion borrowed from Catholicism but not from Protestantism, a religion that Latin fascists typically disdained. What resulted was a reconfigured but still culturally identifiable Catholicism. And without announcing its presence, it offered a path to European unity on the premise that a historical tidal wave would soon move all Europeans in the direction of fascism.

The Italian Quest for an International Fascism

In a rewritten dissertation of close to five hundred pages that has been made available online, *Italienischer Faschismus als "Export"-Artikel (1927–1935)*, German scholar Beate Scholz offers an exhaustive study of the export of Italian fascism as a pan-European movement. The sheer scope of Scholz's thematic treatment, which covers a multiplicity of publications and institutes promoted by the Italian fascist state, indicates that fascist internationalism had widespread support among Italian fascist politicians and European fascist intellectuals. Government-sponsored groups like the Comitati d'Azione per l'Universalità di Roma, the Centre international d'études sur le fascisme in Lausanne, and the Istituto Nazionale di Cultura Fascista in Rome, publications like *L'Universale, Antieuropa*, and, at least occasionally, *Critica Fascista* and theorists and scholars, like Asvero Gravelli, the professor of Italian literature at University College of London and a leading exponent of fascist theory, Camillo Pellizzi, Berto Ricci, and Giuseppe Bottai all personified in different but sometimes intersecting ways the view that fascism as a style of thinking and organization had international significance. Scholz views these lavish defenses of fascist internationalism as a creative enterprise but one that was intended by those at the top to be window dressing for the consolidation of Mussolini's personal rule.[33]

According to this reading, *Il Duce* was first and foremost interested in expanding his personal power both at home and on the international stage. The strenuous efforts to define and apply fascism as an international force coincided with what Emilio Gentile designates as the *accelerazione totalitaria*, namely, the quickening movement toward total power that was inherent in Mussolini's rule.[34] In the 1930s Mussolini placed the Italian administration increasingly under his personal control and tried to reduce the Gran Consiglio and other bodies with which he was supposed to cooperate into mere extensions of his authority. One is left with the impression that Mussolini had no compunctions about abandoning his internationalist outreach once it ceased to be personally useful. After Mussolini invaded Ethiopia and entered an alliance with Nazi Germany, the need for an internationalist cover for his activities vanished. Thereafter, he appealed to strictly national interest while absorbing some of the naturalist, racist ideology of his stronger German ally.

It may be possible, however, to chart a middle course in interpreting the Italian government's sponsorship of fascist internationalism. Mussolini may have been attracted to this internationalist project for a period of time but eventually turned away from it when it diverged from other, more urgent plans. From the late 1920s into the mid-1930s, publications and institutes that were intended to promote fascism internationally received generous subsidies from the Italian government. Moreover, Mussolini showed considerable interest in launching the Montreux conferences and nurturing the Comitati d'Azione, which were instrumental in organizing these and other periodic international gatherings of fascist sympathizers. After the conclusion of the Lateran Pacts, *Il Duce* himself accentuated the ties between the Roman Catholic Church and fascism as an international force. Whether or not he was also interested in centralizing power does not detract from the fact that Mussolini, for a time, exhibited considerable enthusiasm for the ambitious enterprise discussed by Scholz.

The inspiration for this undertaking came from several different directions. One of them, which became particularly important for defining the turn toward fascist internationalism, was Italian fascism's rapprochement with the Catholic Church. A linkage would be established and reaffirmed in Italian political publications, especially after the Lateran Pacts, which embraced fascism, *Romanitas*, and the Roman Catholic hierarchy. Fascism supposedly stood for the same principles on the political level that the

Catholic Church embodied on the spiritual level, and this Roman internationalism, according to its advocates, was not reducible, no matter what the freethinker Gentile believed, to idealist philosophy and other abstract German imports. At least in its Catholic manifestations, fascist universalism stood in explicit opposition to Gentile's actualism, which stressed changing historical moments rather than eternal truths.[35] But, according to A. James Gregor, the anti-Gentilian periodical *Critica Fascista* borrowed from what it condemned. It upheld the explicitly Gentilian theory of "cultural imperialism" when it predicted that fascist ideas would prevail throughout Europe, even if the Italian state never expanded by a single square mile.[36]

Gravelli, who viewed himself as "the architect of fascist internationalism," trusted that his movement would restore order to endangered Catholic societies, the "historical laws of which had been stood on their head." Catholic fascists viewed the Italian movement and its counterparts as, among other things, a political and moral arm of the Counter-Reformation, a second opportunity for the Church to return Europe to "Roman traditions." Gravelli and his fellow contributors to *Antieuropa* invoked a "mystical revolution" that was sweeping across Europe under the impetus of fascism. Indeed, the continent would soon become "a gigantic battlefield between East and West" in which only the fascists would be able to prevail in the name of Christ, Rome, and the cross against foreign cultural and political forces.[37] Whereas *Antieuropa* noted the operation of "fascist ferment" throughout Europe and South America and urged Mussolini to place himself in the vanguard of this tendency, it was assumed that Latinity and Catholicism, as expressing a Catholic world view and Roman-Latin history, would occupy a special place in the transmission of fascist teachings.

It is possible to fit fascist denunciations of democracy, liberalism, and socialism, which are all targeted in Gravelli's tract *"Verso l'internazionale fascista,"* into this alternative vision of a new Roman internationalism. The vision that fascism invoked was based on social order and the subordination of the individual to the community. A vigorous exponent of the beneficent Catholic character of Italian fascism and its possible applications to other European countries was the English thinker James Strachey Barnes. In essays for the *Edinburgh Review* between 1928 and 1930, Barnes treats that era's evolving Italian fascism as a "world view" that others in Europe would do well to adopt: "Fascism may be defined generally as a political and social movement having as its object the reestablishment of a political and social order, based on the main currents of tradition that have formed our European civilization, traditions created by Rome, first by the Empire and subsequently by the Catholic Church."[38] In his articles and in a widely noted book on fascism that Barnes wrote in 1931, which was glowingly reviewed in *Critica Fascista*, Barnes praises the Catholic and Roman elements of fascism and the attendant corporatist organization of economic and commercial life as an attempt to move away from the atomistic, democratic thinking that still prevailed in his country. The fascists were in the forefront of those who were rejecting "the democratism of Rousseau" and "the rule of the mob" that Aristotle so vigorously warned against in *The Politics*.[39]

There were two forms of European internationalism that the Italian fascists regarded as rivals, one of which was judged to be innocuous and the other that was decried as an existential threat. The less threatening competitor was the Paneuropean Movement, which was founded in the 1920s by the multiethnic, multilingual Austro-Hungarian Count Richard Nikolaus von Coudenhove-Kalergi (1894–1972). A celebrity of mixed Japanese, Bohemian-German, Greek, and Flemish extraction, Coudenhove-Kalergi deplored the bloodbath that had been caused by European nationalisms in the First World War. In response to European nationalist excesses, he organized groups of notables who would be receptive to a plan for European unity that he laid out in his book *Pan-Europa* (1923).[40]

In 1926 the author of this tract held a widely publicized conference in the heart of Europe (and of the multinational empire to which his family had belonged), Vienna. Part of the appeal of his European internationalism stemmed from Coudenhove-Kalergi's efforts to reach out across ideological camps. By the late 1920s he had brought over to his cause Albert Einstein, Thomas Mann, Sigmund Freud, Archduke Otto von Habsburg, and the French foreign minister, Aristide Briand, who was appointed honorary president of the pan-European organization. After the Second World War Coudenhove-Kalergi remained in the spotlight by gaining approval for his cause from Winston Churchill and Charles de Gaulle; in the 1950s the advocates of a Habsburg restoration in Austria adopted large chunks of the pan-European program.

Despite Gravelli's disparaging remarks in *"Verso l'internazionale fascista"* about the vagueness of the pan-European plan and despite his stated fear that Briand would use his influence as an internationalist to establish French hegemony on the continent,[41] the editor of *Antieuropa* generally sympathized with Coudenhove-Kalergi. In his postwar memoirs, the father of the Paneuropean Movement ventures the opinion that "the protégé of Mussolini showed himself to be a convinced Pan-European. He read my writings and was secretly my disciple."[42] There is more than a word of truth here. Gravelli's collaborator at *Antieuropa*, Roberto Suster, coined the term "fascist Pan-Europeanism," and in a plan sent to Mussolini for propagating fascist thought, the "architect of fascist internationalism" adopted the same usage. Scholz argues that as Gravelli lost favor with his former comrade-in-arms in the early fascist movement who later became *Il Duce*, he may well have considered "selling his fascist project in another ideological market."[43] This may not be as strange a notion as it first appears. Fascist internationalists not only tried to build bridges to the Catholic Right, but they also eagerly joined international agencies in the League of Nations that they thought would serve their purposes. This, of course, would end when Mussolini attacked Ethiopia and veered into the Nazi orbit. But Gravelli never gave up on his pan-European inclinations, for example, when he proposed locating his center for fascist internationalism in Switzerland rather than in Rome. One need not wonder that Mussolini for several years removed his patronage from this ideological adventurer and returned him to favor only in the late 1930s.[44]

Yet for fascist internationalists there were rhetorical enemies and then real enemies. European internationalist organizations led by well-bred gentlemen, not leftist troublemakers, did not arouse in most fascists the same hostility as the *internazionale rossa* guided by the Soviet Comintern. Like Mussolini, Gravelli occasionally characterized Italy as a have-not nation fighting the plutocratic democracies. But, as Robert Soucy contends in a biography of Drieu and in a later study of French fascism in the 1930s, Latin fascist diatribes against the bourgeoisie should be read with a feeling for hyperbole. Fascists railed against the decadent bourgeois, but it was the decadence of the class under attack, not its social position, according to Soucy, that disturbed the revolutionary Right. Fascists were able to rally to their banner both the propertied class and shopkeepers in Spain and Italy, and throughout the 1930s, fascist leaders in France were moderating their attacks on the class that gave them most of their backing.[45] It is therefore not surprising that Gravelli and other fascist internationalists held their fire when discussing the non-Marxist pan-European project of Coudenhove-Kalergi.

The fascists' preferred enemies were on the revolutionary Left, and this was an adversary they imitated as well as battled. In no way does Nolte exaggerate in his studies the centrality for generic fascists of the revolutionary Left as both a threat and a model to be imitated. Typical of this attitude was a statement by Gravelli in an editorial in 1932 that "we must respond and renew ourselves or else perish" in the face of the gathering Marxist-Leninist storm. Scholz explains how Gravelli and his collaborators at *Antieuropa* recycled what had been drawn from the Left in trying to build an effective counterforce against it. Like Lenin, these fascist activists wished to produce a party of action that would spearhead a European-wide transformation of an already moribund bourgeois society. Italians would have the honor of becoming "the vanguard of European fascism." Like Trotsky, Gravelli called for "permanent revolution" and warned against viewing what fascists had already done as a finished product.[46]

In a proposal for a missionary international fascist organization sent to Mussolini, Gravelli contended that fascism was helping overcome the "ideological misconceptions of liberalism and liberal democracy that had arisen from the French Revolution." It was substituting for both democratic disorder and the Marxist class conflict the promise of "authority, order and justice" and doing so within a properly structured nation. Given their trans-European scope, "we fascists do not consider ourselves a splendid exception; nor do we intend to isolate ourselves in the independence of our victory and movement. Rather we affirm that Italian fascism will be the auxiliary agent in the rise and self-assertion of analogous movements in other countries."[47]

Significantly, Gravelli and other fascist internationalists proclaim "permanent revolution" to be a fascist as well as leftist principle. In the contest between Rome and Moscow, which was apparently looming large, fascists are urged to view their work as something that has to be completed at home and abroad. In this race to the top, liberalism is dismissed as a spent force that was giving way to the revolutionary Left. Only the fascists would be able to stop this process and become the beneficiaries of the collapse of what was already decaying.[48] Needless to say, the call for "completing [*attuarsi*] the national revolution at home, which came from Bottai, Gravelli, Spirito, and other militants, did not please Mussolini as he was working to appease his already insecure subjects in the wake of the Depression. His decision to remove some of the exponents of permanent revolution from high places in the 1930s may have issued from his fear of rocking the boat as Italy was plunged into high unemployment and serious economic setbacks along with the rest of Europe and the United States.

Oswald Mosely as an Apostle of Fascist Internationalism

Although hardly an Italian or Latin fascist, despite willingness to take funding from the Italian fascist government, the English aristocrat Sir Oswald Ernald Mosley (1896–1980) may have carried the idea of fascist internationalism farther than any other fascist leader. His biographer, Robert Skidelsky, underscores repeatedly in his massive work the absolute dedication of his subject to European unity between the wars and, even more, in the post–World War II period. Someone who has been described as an "authoritarian modernizer," particularly in the 1920s and 1930s, Mosley offered his proposals for extensive economic planning for a new Europe as a Labourite member of parliament (MP), then as head of the New Party in 1931, and after 1932 as leader of the British Union of Fascists (BUF).[49] His efforts at maintaining European peace in the 1930s were motivated by the desire to avoid a second European bloodbath. This motive was genuine, as Skidelsky points out, however intermixed it may have been with Mosley's naïve view of Nazi Germany and the attraction exercised on his second wife, Diana Mitford, by Hitler's personality.

A combat veteran of World War I, Mosley repeatedly expressed his determination to keep Europe from ever again plunging into the carnage that he was personally involved in between 1914 and 1918. Contrary to others of his class, Mosley openly supported the independence of Ireland and argued that this move would contribute toward peace between the English and their Irish cousins, whom he thought the English could only hold onto at the cost of increased violence and enmity.[50] Not surprisingly, the Irish were disproportionately represented in the BUF. This fact was attributable to Mosley's past sympathy for Irish independence as well as the threatened social position of the working-class Irish in London's East Side.

Before his venture in uniting all fascist groups in England under his organizational umbrella in 1932 and before donning with his followers a black shirt in imitation of the Italian fascists, Mosley was a rising political star first in the Conservative Party and then, after he broke from the Tories, in the Labour Party of Ramsay MacDonald.[51] He held parliamentary seats in both parties, and even after he had formed his own party in favor of an activist government in 1931, he was cultivated by English political leaders, including Winston Churchill, who was then out of favor with the Tories. FDR was a close American friend of the Mosleys, and in the 1920s Oswald and his first wife, Cynthia (who died of acute appendicitis in 1933), traveled with the future American president on yacht cruises.[52] The vivacious Cynthia was the daughter of George Nathaniel (Marquess of Kedleston) Curzon, former viceroy of India and the figure who, at Versailles, for better or worse, set the boundary between the new state of Poland and Soviet Russia.[53]

Prior to his involvement with the BUF, which appealed to a different social element from the one in which he had been accustomed to move, Mosley had lived in largely aristocratic circles. After his embrace of fascism, he lost longtime political associates, like the diplomat and author Harold Nicolson, who nonetheless remained a personal friend. Another close associate and a Soviet sympathizer, John Strachey, left Mosley's orbit in 1931, when it became obvious that the movement Mosley was leading was not only about national boards for overseeing English economic development and guaranteeing fair wages. As head of the New Party, Mosley already underlined his distance from the Soviet experiment and Marxism, which he considered to be inimical to the British nation.[54]

His choice of fascism was based on the assumption that the road to modernization and, in the short term, the way out of the Depression for England lay in embracing the fascist rather than the Soviet model. This choice was clearly stated in *The Greater Britain*, a tract that Mosley prepared in 1932 as he was establishing the BUF. Here Mosley stressed the need for decisive leadership, which the old ruling class could no longer provide, and the willingness to put aside the kind of parliamentary horse-trading that Mosley associated with modern democracy.[55] Despite his leap into the fascist abyss and his decision to take £60,000 per year for two years from Mussolini's government, Mosley was funded by English men of substance well into the 1930s. A newspaper magnate and fellow aristocrat, Lord Rothermere, conferred on Mosley's cause subsidies and generally favorable publicity in his paper the *Daily Mail*. Mosley even enjoyed initial backing from a prominent Jewish businessman, Israel Sieff, but lost that after he made abrasive references to Jewish interests in one of his speeches.[56]

Characteristic of the BUF in the 1930s was a palpable division between the high and low roads that the movement followed. The organization was open to all loyal British, whatever their ethnic or religious backgrounds, and Mosley was emphatic in his rejection of racialist doctrines, however diligently he pursued rapprochement with Nazi Germany. Moreover, the party organ in which his influence was apparent, *Fascist Week*, dealt with economic planning and building a new fascist Europe. Although his party guard clashed with armed Jewish protesters in London's East Side and, being usually outnumbered, got the worst of it, Mosley protested that he was not personally anti-Jewish.[57] As his son Nicholas notes in his biography of his father, one could scour the pages of *Greater Britain* without encountering even "one reference to Jews. In Hitler's *Mein Kampf*, written ten years previously, it is explicit that Jews are the enemy. In *Greater Britain*, the enemy is decadence. This decadence is in society; in oneself."[58] The same lack of interest in a specifically Jewish problem can be discerned in Mosley's lecture "The Philosophy of Fascism," delivered at the English Speaking Union in 1932.

But there was the shadow side of the BUF, largely identified with Mosley's Director of Propaganda William Joyce and reflected in a fascist publication overseen by Joyce, *Blackshirt*. An Irish American who settled in London and became a fierce English nationalist, Joyce bore on his face the scars of wounds inflicted by leftist militants. His anger at being disfigured was channeled into a fixation with Jews as the enemy of the British people, a fixation that may have been confirmed in Joyce's mind by what seemed to be the coordinated assaults on BUF rallies by Jewish and communist toughs. Nicholas Mosley notes the "obsessive anti-Semitism" that slipped into speeches and articles published in *Blackshirt*, and although these references to "aliens imported from Palestine" and "hairy troglodytes" who have crept out of Germany indicated a "style" of speaking rather than a "deliberate policy," these remarks understandably gave offense.

Readers are further told that although "responsible and moderate members of the BUF" recognized "the predicament should not be ignored," Mosley never really addressed the verbal and behavioral intemperance of some of his assistants.[59] The reason, Nichols Mosley suggests, is that his father felt that in the face of street attacks, he needed "party stalwarts such as Joyce of whom there could be no doubt of their almost reckless courage."[60] An equally obvious reason for Mosley's indulgence may have been his lack of familiarity with the social class attracted by the BUF. Although he could harangue crowds with the best of them, the aristocratic Mosley had never had to deal with angry working-class types until he recruited for the BUF. It is entirely plausible that he thought that someone like Joyce connected with the masses better than he could.

For all that, observes Nicholas Mosley, there was nothing intrinsically anti-Jewish in the fascist planning that Mosley proposed,[61] nor is there any proof that he ever received funds from Nazi Germany, a charge raised against Mosley while he and his wife were incarcerated in squalid conditions as Nazi agents between 1940 and 1943.[62] Over the objections of Labour members of the English cabinet and the National Trade Union Club, Mosley and Diana were released from prison in November 1943. They were then allowed to spend the duration of the war under house arrest in their own residence. By the time of his release, however, Mosley was so ill with phlebitis, a condition he had developed during the First World War, that there was some concern that he might die in his place of confinement. Significantly, it was never made clear what crime he or Diana committed that would have justified their humiliating incarceration during the war.[63]

Curiously, Skidelsky, who published his biography seven years before Nicholas Mosley came out with his work, provides a different picture of Mosley's post–World War II career. Skidelsky emphasizes Mosley's vigor as an advocate of European unity, starting with his tract published in October 1947, *The Alternative*.[64] In February 1948 Mosley made headlines as head of the Union Movement, a group that was working to rebuild Europe as "one nation." Mosley was still working then to come up with his version of a dirigiste economy coupled with imperialism. Not surprisingly, in his post–World War II writings the reader sees unveiled a vision of a unified Europe that would feature centralized economic planning and the continued availability of African resources for the benefit of European growth. Mosley modified this plan to take into account the need to have Africa benefit from this process of European renewal. At the same time, he remained strongly opposed to the immigration that was then underway from the Third World into England. He expressed the wish that Africa and Europe both prosper in their own regions but not together in the same countries with Europeans; in the 1970s he emphatically advocated the repatriation of West Indians to their place of origin.[65]

Most of these positions looked antiquated by the time they were presented in the twenty years that followed the Second World War. Skidelsky notes that Mosley's proposals seem to be throwbacks to the late nineteenth century and that democratic imperialism that had been advocated by Joseph Chamberlain and other empire builders in the waning years of Victoria's reign. The appeal to a European identity that came into play in Mosley's post–World War II activism was no match for the emerging European Community, an international organization of European states that was thriving by the 1950s and was strongly promoted by a very powerful United States.[66]

Mosley offered in its place a variation on de Gaulle's vision of a "Europe of nations" but one that came paired with the unlikely hope of being able to hold onto overseas colonies. This became increasingly unlikely at a time when European countries, including England, were disengaging from their empires in the face of rebellions from indigenous populations. Mosley's resistance to having his country "resettled" by Africans and West Indians was a popular stand for a time—and one that enjoyed the endorsement of, among other illustrious figures, Winston Churchill. But here, too, Mosley came away empty-handed as the political culture in England and elsewhere in western Europe began moving in the direction of "diversity." And even before that happened, the immigration of a Third World workforce into England, prompted partly by economic need, would have been hard to reverse. Finally, plans for centralized economic planning could no longer be presented as an "alternative" in postwar Europe. The socialists who came into power on their own or belonged to ruling coalitions were already offering large chunks of Mosley's programs. The fact that they did so from the Left rather than from the revolutionary Right probably made their measures more popular.[67]

The greatest impact that Mosley exerted on postwar culture may have come from a journal, *European,* that he and his wife edited between 1953 and 1959. A gathering point for what the Mosleys viewed as the independent

Right, *European* provided a congenial venue for all strands of generic fascism. Here one found discussions of interwar syndicalism, considerations on the continued relevance of nationalism, and attempts to fuse nationalist and internationalist themes in what remained of an identifiably revolutionary Right world view. Ezra Pound (an English Catholic poet who fought for the Spanish nationalists), Roy Campbell, Otto Strasser (Hitler's opponent in the Black Front), and the future historian of fascism A. James Gregor were among those who wrote for the Mosleys' magazine.[68] Some of the contributors were also featured in *National Review*, and Mosley's autobiography, *My Life*, was produced in an American edition, courtesy of the conservative press Arlington House in 1972.[69] In the course of promoting his autobiography, Mosley, who was then in his seventies, gave lectures on his politics in both England and the United States and made a memorable appearance on William F. Buckley's *Firing Line*.

Despite some of Sir Oswald Mosley's publishing successes during his later years, Nicholas Mosley begins his work by quoting a statement from the *New Statesman* (May 11, 1979) that Oswald Mosley "must be the only Englishman today who is beyond the pale."[70] This furnishes the title of his son's work, *Beyond the Pale: Sir Oswald Mosley 1933–1980*, and affects the treatment of Oswald's later years, which are shown to have been less gratifying than Skidelsky's biography or Mosley's autobiography suggests. It is hard not to believe that Mosley was widely viewed as "beyond the pale" by the time of his death at age eighty-four. In an avowedly antifascist Europe, this aging activist of the revolutionary Right was not likely to appear on the dinner guest lists of prominent politicians and journalists or have been invited to their homes and public discussions. And so it is entirely credible that by the end of his life, he had become, as the *New Statesman* observes perhaps more matter-of-factly than approvingly, a social outcast.

The Obsolescence of Fascism

The fate of Mosley brings the reader back to the framework in which fascism prospered in the interwar years. Its reemergence in Europe, and especially in England, in the postwar years may have been an anachronism. Fascist ideology did not wear well outside of its time and culture, a limitation that should have been obvious from the beginning of Mosley's political adventure. He visited fascist Italy and was received by *Il Duce* in the 1930s as an exotic follower. The Italian government thereafter provided Mosley with modest subsidies for about two years, perhaps as a test case to see whether fascism as an international movement could strike roots in a Protestant northern European clime. The BUF returned the favor by adopting the Italian fascist Camicia Nera and a party song that sounded like the fascist anthem *"Giovinezza."*[71] Then, on a subsequent trip to Nazi Germany, under the influence of Diana, Mosley expressed interest in Nazi Germany as a society of the future. Although Mosley doggedly opposed England's entry into the Second World War, Nazism influenced his thinking less decisively than did Italian fascism.

But neither national revolution provided the English leader with much more than symbols and rhetoric for his work. Economic planning and centralized leadership were the priorities that led Mosley from the New Party into founding the BUF. Although he understandably tried to downplay his association with continental fascism after the war, there is no reason to doubt the following statement in his autobiography about his attempt to frame specifically English programs for his fascist movement: "I could find nothing in Italian fascism comparable with the policies I devised in my period in government. These policies, which we recommended throughout Britain in the seven years of our fascist movement from 1932 to 1939, were of an entirely different order of thought and action."[72] Further: "The similarity between us and the continental movements began and ended with the need to fight for ideas to be heard at all, and this common experience of the Red assault gave us a certain mutual sympathy."[73]

One longtime link between Italian fascist internationalism and Mosley's embrace of a fascist model may have been the Italian professor who ran the London section of *Fasci all'estero*, Camillo Pellizzi. Pellizzi defended his conversionary activity as Italian cultural outreach. He also saw it as exemplifying his hope that fascism could be made into an exportable corporatist model.[74] But the English case offered no justification for this blithe assumption. Mosley's attempted adaptation of Italian fascism, as a body of symbols and organizational techniques, looked like a caricature of what belonged to a Latin Catholic world. This was true, although the BUF's creator might have understood the situation differently. Mosley believed that he had begun with an economic program, and once he had turned his back on certain features of the Left, fascism was the label he conferred on his brand of authoritarian economic management. But a Latin and Italian character was there from the time Mosley decided to call his program and organization "fascist." As Scholz documents, support for Pellizzi's work came from the Italian government for one reason only: to expand its political influence in England.[75]

It is often argued that England could not become fascist because it had a well-established parliamentary government and a strong tradition of civil liberties. While there is no need to exclude this explanation entirely, other factors were at least equally telling. The dominant culture was so unlike the milieu in which generic fascism flourished that a fascist regime in England, if one had somehow taken root there, would have looked like a foreign import. It would have been the twentieth-century equivalent of a Spanish Catholic monarch taking power in late sixteenth-century England.[76] This foreignness was less of a problem in, say, Romania, where representatives of the Revolutionary Right like Corneliu Codreanu, Alexander Cuza, and Ion Motza successfully incorporated Latin fascist ideas into a Romanian nationalist movement. These would-be Latin fascists studied in France where they absorbed key themes of the French nationalist Right around the time of the First World War. Cusa and Codreanu were particularly impressed by the anti-Semitic literature that was then available in another Latin land.

Because of the seething tensions in their country between a Jewish shopkeeper class and the Romanian peasantry, Romanian fascists built their League for Christian Defense in 1923 and the Legion of the Archangel Michael in 1927. In both cases they merged their Latin authoritarian doctrines and impulses with a reaction to local social problems. Eugen Weber has maintained, in his insightful studies of Romanian fascism, that the Revolutionary Right in Romania had powerful populist appeal.[77] It was viewed as the protector of impoverished peasants against a bourgeoisie that often came from Tsarist Russia or Austria-Hungary and was seen as exploiting the rural population. The socioeconomic world depicted by Weber bore little resemblance to interwar Protestant, predominantly bourgeois, England. Indeed, in the Romanian context, the "men of the Archangel" appeared to be modern versions of the French Jacobins of the late eighteenth century.

Unlike England, Romania was rural and poor and, not insignificantly, had stressed (or exaggerated) its Latin roots ever since gaining independence in the 1860s. Romanian intellectuals were always intent on differentiating their country from its Slavic and Magyar neighbors by playing up its onetime association with the Roman Empire and the Latinity of its language. Although there was no perfect match between, on the one side, Italian fascism and the Falange, and, on the other, the work of their Romanian admirers, there was at least overlap between the original Latin version and its Balkan adaptation. Rural poverty and a proud Latin heritage characterized all these fascist-prone societies.

An adaptation of Latin authoritarianism therefore could take root in Dacia and Moldavia and develop into a national political force. This occurred when the Iron Guard sprang up from nationalist groups in the 1920s and became a critical factor in the formation of interwar Romanian governments. By the time Antonescu moved against the Iron Guard in 1940, the Guardists were on the verge of seizing power in Bucharest. The contrast between this surging Romanian force and the politically impotent BUF is striking. The most promising electoral results that the BUF posted for its candidates were in its stomping ground in East London in March 1937. Union candidates picked up about 8,000 votes while Labour candidates gained majorities in all the districts where the BUF was also represented.

There was, however, a larger explanation as to why fascism failed in England. After the Second World War, all fascist movements, fairly or unfairly, carried the stigma of being associated with Nazi tyranny. But even if that were not the case, the economic programs of fascist groups did not differ significantly from what were then standard welfare state measures. Where self-identified neofascists may have differed from other welfare-state parties was in their persistent warnings against being flooded by Third World immigration. But given that they were already being tarred with the Nazi brush, what remained of postwar fascism never gained enough respectability to be taken seriously on immigration or most anything else.

Equally noteworthy is the fact that fascists could never present themselves as convincing internationalists. In the postwar rush toward European internationalist organizations and ideologies, fascism looked hopelessly behind the times. Because it appealed to organic nationhood and engaged in national economic planning, fascist internationalism necessarily remained a secondary theme. That doesn't exclude the possibility that a revolutionary Right might arise in the future that would feature a less nationalistic focus. Rather, it means that the fascists, because of their history as national revolutionaries, predictably failed at redefining themselves as internationalists of the Right.

This point has been famously disputed by two distinguished historians, Michael Ledeen and A. James Gregor. Both have stressed, to varying degrees, fascism's internationalist potential as well as revolutionary substance.[78] Each concentrates on Italian fascism as a movement rather than an opportunistic regime and looks to Gravelli and Pellizi as bearers of a fascist idea that would embrace all Europeans. Unfortunately for this argument, it cannot show that fascism made headway as an internationalist rival to the revolutionary Left beyond those regions that were already culturally disposed toward the movement. Nor do the proponents of this view prove that fascism in practice was truly revolutionary as opposed to a variant of the authoritarian Right with revolutionary fizz. Gregor tries to bestow on fascism global importance by presenting Third World developmental dictatorships as latter-day manifestations of interwar Italian fascism. This thesis, as argued in the second chapter, is far from a settled matter and assumes continuities that may not have been present. Equally relevant is the fact that Gregor's paradigmatic fascist theorist, Gentile, was emphatically nationalistic and skeptical of the Catholic and internationalist tendencies that became attached to his movement.

To his credit, Gregor does recognize that appeals to *"l'Internazionale fascista"* often served as a smoke screen for pursuing national goals. He asserts that both socialists and "paradigmatic fascism" were "equally diaphanous. Nationalism alone was vital."[79] Although this might have been true in practice and although Gregor's comparisons of Leninism and Italian fascism are sometimes instructive, there is a huge difference between the two movements with regard to their visions of the future. Leninism featured a truly universal vision; fascism did not, except intermittently and in an improvised fashion.

Although Italian fascism revealed an internationalist aspect, Beate Scholz also underlines that fascist internationalism had minimal effect on the Italian fascist government. Scholz further demonstrates that the Italian regime stopped supporting rhetorical and theoretical internationalism when it was no longer expedient to do so. Her massive research leaves the impression that fascists at the top treated the internationalist initiatives pushed by a few intellectuals with profound cynicism. That may have been equally true for the less than consistent manner in which Leninists approached foreign policy. But there was a difference between the two movements in terms of their ideological commitments: unlike fascist internationalism, the Bolsheviks' internationalism was not accessory baggage but resided at the very core of their revolutionary doctrine. Soviet Russia, especially under Lenin, actively pushed world revolution through the Comintern and never abandoned the internationalist reference point of revolutionary socialism.

Fascism would have become obsolescent even if we assume counterhistorically that Nazi Germany had not dragged European fascism down with the Third Reich. Fascist movements could not move far enough away from their organic nationalist origins to become fundamentally different from how they began. By the time the remnants of European fascist organizations signed the Venice Declaration in March 1961, pledging mutual assistance in building a fascist Europe, their persuasion had become a ghost of its former self.[80] A supernationalist fascism pledged to a united Europe may have seemed an oxymoron by the time Mosley got around to fitting fascism and internationalism into one package. In any case few takers were on hand for what the signatories of the Venice Declaration offered postwar Europe. Postwar fascist or neofascist movements, even when they appealed to pan-European sentiments, had scant electoral appeal next to the European Left and the US-supported Christian Democrats.

The one exception may have been the Italian neofascist Movimento Sociale Italiano, which did survive as an electoral force into the 1960s and 1970s. But here a qualification may be in order. By the time something even faintly derivative of Italian fascism created a ruling coalition as the Alleanza Nazionale under Gianfranco Fini, it had lost any substantive connection to neofascism. What became known as "postfascism" no longer even resembled the postwar Movimento Sociale Italiano. The former member of that group who became Deputy Prime Minister in 2001 and Foreign Minister in 2004 was no longer recognizable as the heir to interwar fascism.

One can readily perceive the historical limits of fascism in an exchange between Gravelli and another fascist publicist, Bruno Spampanato, writing in *Critica Fascista* in 1932. The *Antieuropa* director proclaimed grandiloquently that fascism is the true internationalism because it represents the "international of nationalisms."[81] This term applies "insofar as fascist internationalism signifies the network of existing friendships among nations and their people, which are informed by the defense of fascist ideas that have been freely accepted." To this Spampanato retorted, "There is no fascist international. This international was dreamt up by bourgeois with faulty digestive systems around 1922, and it is still today seriously discussed in some journals on the extreme right or extreme left afflicted with literary pretensions."[82] Although Gravelli was echoing an address given by Mussolini in 1930 describing "fascism as Italian in its particular but universal in its spirit" and although no one can know for sure what Spampanato meant by the "extreme right and extreme left," his observation about the ineluctably nationalist character of fascism was spot-on.

CHAPTER SIX

The Search for a Fascist Utopia

Conservatives and Fascists

In *Ideology and Utopia* Karl Mannheim distinguishes between two key terms in investigating the sociology of knowledge and various forms of utopian thinking. Mannheim opposes "ideologies," which are designed to justify a "level of being" for those groups that embody them, as opposed to "utopian" visions that point to alternatives to the existing order of things. Utopias are always "*seinstranszendent*"—that is, they carry their bearers beyond a situation in which they find themselves uncomfortably confined toward a future that is eagerly awaited.[1]

These conceptions (which address more than individual vagaries) are common to social and/or religious groups and may be temporally or spatially grounded. Although Western literature affords many illustrations of paradisiac societies in which particular authors and their sympathetic readers situate their dreams, Mannheim concentrates on utopian visions that are temporally based and were or are socially important. All these visions highlight a golden or godly future or else an idealized past that is imagined to be about to return in a purer form than it had existed before. The examples of utopias that Mannheim explores are the apocalyptic expectations of sixteenth- and seventeenth-century Protestant radicals, the hope for an Age of Reason embraced by the eighteenth-century liberal bourgeois, the harmonious hierarchical society evoked by German and French conservatives in the early nineteenth century and thought to be "realizable" in a postrevolutionary future, and the Marxist view of a socialist world order. For Marxists, the advent of socialism would end the "prehistory" of the human race that had been spent laboring under economically dominant classes.[2]

Although Mannheim lays out in detail all his utopian visions, the one that interested him most was the "romantic-conservative counterutopia." This was constructed as a "defense" by conservatives who saw their order under assault. It was conceived as a mechanism by which a threatened class and its defenders could counter their opponents intellectually and theoretically. In contrast to liberals and revolutionaries who placed their utopian hopes in the future, conservatives identified their ideal world with what was already present and had been transmitted from the past. They mocked liberals as manufacturers of false realities and urged their followers to focus on "that which is in a state of becoming."[3] Such renowned conservative theorists as Karl von Savigny, Adam Müller, and Friedrich Stahl appealed to history as the supreme teacher and mocked artificial constitutions and ready-to-wear governments that relied on individual reason.[4]

Mannheim cites (selectively) the philosopher Georg Wilhelm Friedrich Hegel as the conservative theorist par excellence. This German philosopher systematically presented reality as a process of becoming in which reason operates from within and animates one's life experience. In their emphasis on a "living past" or on a past that had to be restored, conservatives were counterutopian, as opposed to anti-utopian. What their opponents rejected as irrational or archaic was, for them, something worthy of preservation. The conservative notion of utopian "transcendence" was inextricably bound up with the here and now. In *Ideology and Utopia* Mannheim underlines that the conservative "pattern of what is becoming" is a "historic pattern that is not constructed but which grows like a plant out of an inner center."[5]

Further:

> This conservative pattern of utopia, in which thought is an idea submerged in reality, is only understandable in terms of its struggle with other coexisting patterns of utopia. Its direct antithesis appears to be the liberal, rationalistic idea. If a moral imperative is something to be experienced by each individual, the emphasis among conservatives was shifted to being. Only because it exists, is something of higher value, whether because as in Hegel there is rationality already present in it or because as in Stahl one is drawn to the fascinating effects of irrationality. "There is a wonderful sense we have," says Stahl, "that something truly exists. This is your father, your friend, through whom you have arrived at this position in life. Why am I this? Why am I exactly what I am? And the apparently incomprehensible

nature of this situation can only be grasped by recognizing that our being cannot be reduced to thought, that it is not logically necessary but has its source in a higher, free power."[6]

Mannheim furnishes graphic illustrations of the conservative world view that arose in the early nineteenth century, and he interprets it as something that started out as a reluctant exercise in counterutopian thinking. In the way Stahl invokes the hidden mysteries of being one can easily recognize the outlines of twentieth-century existential thought. Indeed, in the insights of this Jewish convert to Protestantism and gray eminence of the Prussian aristocracy of the 1850s, one can even glimpse the outlines of Martin Heidegger's *Being and Time*. Being should be conceptualized as an object of experience that the reader can explore by recognizing its operation in both oneself and the world around one.

There are other bridges between conservative apologetics and later utopian thought. Mannheim observes that Marx's concept of socialism, which he tried to ground in historic reality, drew heavily from conservative thinking. Marx and his followers recycled arguments against both abstract thinking and the supposedly immutable laws of the free market that were being developed in conservative polemics. A conservative critique of the Enlightenment's vision of human advancement made an appearance of sorts in Marx's examination of liberal capitalism. In its Marxist reformulation, this conservative legacy would be joined to a revolutionary socialist picture of social progress and a recognizably leftist view of the social good.

There are certain methodological questions that arise from Mannheim's account of a conservative utopia. The critical insights that are ascribed to conservatism look less like a real utopia than like a creative defense of what Mannheim calls "ideology." The conservative defense of an "idea submerged in being" or an existing reality that lies beneath the surface of what is conventionally taken for reality is not really "utopian." This interpretation of human existence is intended as a counterpoint to the world order envisaged by leftist and liberal visionaries. The outlines of a conservative utopia were, however, present in the writings of some conservative critics of the French Revolution, but Mannheim does not cite these writers in *Ideology and Utopia*. Arguably, the concept of a "conservative utopia" would entail the vision of history culminating in a final godly age—as seen, for example, in the evocation of the "opposite of revolution" introduced by Joseph de Maistre in *Considerations on France* (1797) or in the final age speculation that emanated from South German Catholic conservatives during the Restoration Era. These writers refer to a perfected social order held together by a theocratic center that is brought into existence through a providential act.[7] Mannheim does not offer these more plausible examples of what he styles conservative "utopianism," which may have seemed less interesting to him than conservative ideas that he does treat.

Further, the conservative historical vision that Mannheim does expound relates to his attempt to develop a workable sociology of knowledge *(Wissenssoziologie)*. Mannheim tells the reader that one can grasp the social aspect of ideas by studying their accompanying utopian elements, and he quotes his mentor Alfred Weber, who proposed an integrated approach to visionary concepts.[8] What was relevant for study purposes in each vision should be judiciously applied in order to broaden the reader's understanding of social reality. Despite this catholic approach, Mannheim gives favor to two utopian schemes more than he does to any other. He is drawn to the conservative and Marxist views, believing that each is grounded in historical analysis. Note that for Mannheim the conservative vision was a methodological tool—not simply a historical curiosity.

Moreover, his investigation of a conservative counterutopia can lead the reader toward understanding fascism in its time. Nolte's "escape from transcendence" in the context of his exposition of the fascist world view bears at least some resemblance to Mannheim's treatment of conservative rootedness. Both represent counterstrategies to the revolutionary Left and the abstract rationalism and constitutional constructivism of a liberal culture. In Nolte's picture of fascism, the rejection of a future-based transcendence takes a starkly naturalistic form and is linked to a world of endless struggle. But like Mannheim's concept of a conservative defense of being and becoming, Nolte's escape from transcendence is vitalistic and stresses historical particularity.

Two Marxist critics, Georg Lukacs in *The Destruction of Reason* and Herbert Marcuse in *Reason and Revolution*, locate the beginnings of fascism in the "conservative" turn taken by German thinkers in reaction to the Left Hegelians of the 1840s. Progressive disciples of Hegel found in his identification of reason with historical practice an incentive for introducing democratic and socialist reform. Unfortunately, these forward-looking thinkers were opposed by reactionary polemicists who celebrated inequality and other remnants of the aristocratic past. This energetically applied counterstrategy resulted in a glorification of irrationality and a mystical sense of authority. German philosophy and social thought, according to its critics, took a fateful turn toward justifying "what is," providing this situation could be made to fit an idealized past. According to Lukacs, the derailment of sound critical thinking, abetted by some of Mannheim's favorites, led eventually into the fascistic affirmation of what is naturalistic and based on brute power.[9]

Mannheim's classification of utopias betrays a defect that warrants further comment. The supposed utopianism that came from classical conservatives was not what Mannheim suggests it was. Producing a defense of an aristocratic society under attack is not the same as evoking a future that is critically different from the past. Classical conservatives and Marxists viewed the future in strikingly different ways, and it is not at all clear that conservatives looked toward the future so much as back toward the past. There is also a comparable degree of difference in how conservatives and fascists approached different dimensions of time. Conservatives were defending a society that had existed up until their time but was undergoing revolutionary change. Conservatives, but not Marxists, valued time and duration and, above all, the existential and moral support of inherited institutions. In contrast to the Left, they conceived of historic time as "something reaching back from the present into the past" while for the Left the crucial relation was "the segment of the present that extends into the future."[10] Mannheim's conservative utopias were quintessentially conservative rather than utopian, and Panajotis Kondylis appropriately cites them in his magisterial study *Conservatism*, where he treats classical conservatism as a prolonged theoretical reaction to the French Revolution.[11]

Fascists, by contrast, were not defending a traditional conservatism under assault but were reacting to a situation that developed after a bourgeois society had already established itself. Fascists came along after a radical Left had already arisen and was challenging the existing society. Although fascists occasionally collaborated with landowners and vestiges of the aristocracy, they pinned their hopes chiefly on other social groups. They were a *revolutionary* Right as opposed to the defenders of an ordered society, and what this Right wished to impose as their vision of order was, for the most part, improvised. Theirs was a constructivist Right that followed from the revolutionary nature of their movement and its search for a social base.[12] Like a communist society, a fascist order had not yet been fully established; none had been tried before Mussolini set up his regime in the 1920s.

Fascists shared the aversion to egalitarian ideals among Mannheim's subjects, but they offered as an alternative an invented hierarchy, not the continuation of an eighteenth-century *Ständestaat* or the restoration of a prerevolutionary French class system. These were not options that fascists had available to them, even if they had wanted to exercise them, although it is doubtful that, given the social origins of most of these actors, they would have been happy with a truly conservative social and political order.

The nationalism that fascists espoused would have been seen as a leftist position when Mannheim's subjects were railing against the French

Revolution. Entirely typical of this counterrevolutionary attitude was Maistre's rejoinder to the claim by Jean-Jacques Rousseau that the "nation is sovereign": "a wonderfully convenient word [sovereignty], since one can make of it what one wants. In short, it is impossible to imagine a system better calculated to annihilate the rights of the people."[13] Whereas conservatives in 1810 or 1830 had nice things to say about "the people," what they meant by that term was the inhabitants of a traditional stratified society living by immemorial custom. For the old Right in contrast to the fascists, the *Volk, popolo, narod, nép,* or *peuple* was not a mystical source of spiritual energy that informed the "nation." This concept referred to subjects who obeyed those who held positions of authority. Although some members of an already descending aristocracy turned to European nationalist movements in the late nineteenth century, such a turn was a desperate tactic that would not lead to a restoration of power and did not bring any long-term success.

Representing this old order as one of its last paradigmatic embodiments was the Pomeranian aristocrat and landowner Ewald von Kleist-Schmenzin (1890–1945), who was executed as an opponent of the Nazi regime two weeks before the end of the Second World War. Kleist-Schmenzin, who sprang from one of the most illustrious noble families of Pomerania, remained throughout his life a staunch monarchist, a right-wing critic of the Weimar Republic, and a firm advocate of a representative government based on social estates. Like others of his class, Kleist-Schmenzin looked back nostalgically to the nineteenth century for his political models, and, like Friedrich Stahl, a thinker he deeply admired, he stressed the "Order of Creation" in which the divine creator established for humankind a hierarchical, organic way of life.[14] Kleist-Schmenzin's view of society exalted the aristocratic, agrarian past, which had already begun to pass, and he deemed such modern ideologies as democracy and liberalism to be "preliminary stages on the way to Bolshevism."[15]

Like Kuehnelt-Leddihn, Kleist-Schmenzin considered Hitler and the Nazi movement to be the bodying forth of the ideas that sprang from the French Revolution—albeit in an updated form. In spring 1932 Kleist-Schmenzin backed a last-ditch effort by the non-Nazi Right, led by Chancellor Franz von Papen and General Kurt von Schleicher, to impose a provisional dictatorship on Germany, starting in Prussia, that would exclude the Nazis as well as parties of the Left. This plan for control from the traditional Right failed, and in January 1933 President Paul von Hindenburg made the disastrous decision to give Hitler, who was head of Germany's largest party, a chance to form a coalition government. When the Nazis seized power in what was made to look like a legal revolution, Kleist-Schmenzin opposed "the born democrat" Hitler.[16]

When Hitler's tyranny began to destroy his adversaries, Kleist-Schmenzin let it be known that he expected such behavior from a plebeian demagogue. Most annoying to him was Hitler's racism, which he linked to a vulgar biological materialism and the triumph of the revolutionary ideal of equality. Aryan racists, according to Kleist-Schmenzin, had simply taken over the democratic fixation on equality and ascribed it to all members of a supposedly superior race. Hitler's biologically based utopianism was nothing more than "an attempt to approximate the liberal concept of the greatest happiness of the greatest number."[17]

Kleist-Schmenzin did not offer his colleagues and followers any comforting vision of a future harmonious age. Even his monarchism was nothing more than a vague hope, which he believed could be fulfilled only if the appropriate candidate for the throne presented himself. But the Hohenzollern Crown Prince Louis Ferdinand seemed interested in nothing more than getting by under the Third Reich, and Kleist-Schmenzin came to refer contemptuously to this "anonymous" pretender to the German throne who never exhibited the "unconditional devotion to a cause" that Kleist-Schmenzin noticed among Nazi activists. During the last years of his life, Kleist-Schmenzin tried unavailingly to negotiate between the perpetually endangered German Resistance and English leaders, who rejected the overtures of Hitler's increasingly desperate opponents.

But Kleist-Schmenzin's pessimism arose from other causes beside his futile mission to undo Hitler's rule. He viewed the future bleakly because his class and his country seemed doomed to destruction once the Nazis took over. When a Nazi court sentenced him to death as a conspirator, Kleist-Schmenzin accepted the verdict stoically. Rather appropriately, he was executed with the guillotine, an instrument of death identified with the French Revolution, which this victim of the Third Reich blamed genealogically for having engendered the Nazi state.

Given his truly reactionary understanding of state and society, it would be misleading to describe Kleist-Schmenzin and others of his background as "nationalists" without first clarifying this term. Although Kleist-Schmenzin for a time supported an openly nationalist party, the German National People's Party, he never felt comfortable as a member of a chauvinistic mass organization. He joined that particular party because, in theory, it favored a monarchical restoration, which, for Kleist-Schmenzin, was a way back to the nineteenth century. He made clear, however, that his own position was not the nationalism then in vogue but "conservatism as a world view, which views all things from an unchanging standpoint that is infused by the spirit of religion."[18] For Kleist-Schmenzin, an ordered world was based on a creator, a preindustrial society, and an inherited structure of authority.

Nationalism was a tactic embraced by conservatives after the conservative critique of revolutionary innovation reproduced by Mannheim's and/or Kleist-Schmenzin's nostalgic vision no longer had purchase in a changing society. In England the aristocracy held onto some of their power for a few generations longer than elsewhere because of their good fortune in living in a country that won both world wars, albeit at a heavy price, and by becoming "Tory Democrats." Even on the continent, impoverished aristocrats tried to buy time for themselves by marrying into the wealthy bourgeoisie or making matches between their children and the progeny of Jewish bankers. But there is a difference between slowing the descent toward the bottom and reversing course.

Fascists were on the Right by virtue of having opposed the Left in theory and practice, but that was not the same as standing for a past that was already in decline. Fascists were not linked to any one social class and moved back and forth, as in Italy, when they tried to satisfy followers from varied social backgrounds. Finally, fascism was a situational rather than a theoretical movement. Unlike the Marxists, fascists did not claim to be teaching a scientific form of socialism held together by historical and economic laws. Although Mussolini's minister of education and court philosopher, Gentile, was a respected idealist philosopher, it is entirely possible that Gentile would have held that reputation, and perhaps even a higher one, if he had never espoused Italian fascism. And it is easily imaginable that a fascist movement would have existed and flourished even without the theoretical works of Gentile or the nationalist, corporatist pronouncements of the Spanish Falange.

A Generic Fascist Template

The reader may ask here whether fascism had its own vision of the future and, if it did, whether that vision was contingent on a notion of progress shared with the Left. Could the fascist vision be discovered in such theorists as Giovanni Gentile and José Primo de Rivera, who set out to explain the order they were laboring to build? Of all fascist thinkers, Gentile, who worked with Mussolini for two decades and ghostwrote *Il Duce*'s tracts and speeches, may have been the most noteworthy fascist thinker not only because of his reputation as a neo-Hegelian philosopher but also because of his learned formulations of fascist doctrines. Gregor, a biographer of Gentile, presents him as someone who focused on the fascist future. Gentile professed belief in democracy, stressed the modernity of the fascist state, and viewed the Italian fascist regime as having emerged from the rebirth of Italy as a free nation in the second half of the nineteenth century.

Gentile contrasted the Italian *Risorgimento*, which he claimed had inspired his philosophical work, with the French revolutionary experience. According to Gentile, Italian patriots tried to construct a nation built on the consciousness of duty, as opposed to the abstract "rights of men and citizens" proclaimed by French revolutionaries in 1789. But Gentile insisted with no less vigor that the transformation of Italy into a nation-state represented a radical break from a reactionary past. The Catholic scholar Augusto Del Noce treats Gentile as a quintessentially modernist thinker, someone who came to define for his fellow citizens a modern alternative to older, Catholic traditions of thought.

Del Noce demonstrates convincingly that from the early twentieth century well into the period of his engagement as a fascist philosopher, Gentile shaped Italian modernist thinking. Among those whom he influenced were his longtime collaborator in publishing projects and, later, Italy's leading antifascist, liberal philosopher Benedetto Croce. It is not surprising that some of Gentile's disciples ended up as Marxists—or, like Ugo Spirito, postwar communist sympathizers.

Del Noce quotes skeptically the judgment of socialist thinker Norberto Bobbio, who relegates Gentile to "the other Italy" in which rhetoric was allowed to take the place of philosophy. This substitution supposedly resulted in the Italian counterpart of what Marx derided as the "German ideology," a provincial form of thinking that insulates its followers against more cosmopolitan ideas and, in the Italian case, led to a fascist takeover. Del Noce reminds his readers that someone whom Bobbio considers to have been a "bad philosopher" with "an educationally corrupting philosophy" was long regarded inside and outside of Italy as a towering thinker.[19] Gentile's philosophical systems, be it *attualismo* or its later variation, immanentism, were hailed by Italy's lay society as modernist successors to Catholicism. Del Noce views the Italian Left's postwar attacks on Gentile as an attempt by progressives to dissociate themselves from their predecessors, who had been compromised by fascist contacts.

According to Del Noce, Gentile's early work, *La Filosofia di Marx* (1899), should not be regarded as an unqualified dismissal of Marx's thought. In this composition Gentile distinguishes between the valid Hegelian core of Marx's early writings and the "disastrous deviations from Hegelian thinking," which pushed Marx as early as the 1840s toward historical materialism. Gentile does not reject Marx entirely but seeks to save him from the "superficiality" [*superfetazione*] he exhibited once he reduced historical causation to material social relations. This, explains Gentile, resulted in Marx's "metaphysic" of materialism that took the place of exploring the role of spirit in history. Gentile later disguised his return to Hegel, in the form of a spiritually driven dialectic, by claiming that he was returning to the anti-positivist side of nineteenth-century Italian thought.

In all phases of Gentile's intellectual evolution, Del Noce discerns the selective and sometimes arbitrary incorporation of modern thought traditions ranging from Spinoza's pantheism to Descartes's subject/object dichotomy to labored variations on Hegelian philosophy. In Gentile's neo-Hegelianism, no end state of being is ever reached, and spirit goes on actualizing itself ad infinitum. Although repelled by Marx's materialism, Gentile still recognized in Marx someone who prefigured his own evolution, from belief in a reflective or self-reflective absolute mover in history to the understanding of history as action and struggle. Gentile's ambivalent relation to Marx supposedly indicates the attraction exerted by a post-Christian philosophy on its major Italian practitioner even at the beginning of his career.

Moreover, Gentile viewed the state, particularly once fortified with his philosophical work, as fully able to provide for the educational needs of the young. He chafed at what he thought were the unjustified pretensions of the Church following the Lateran Pacts in 1929, particularly the Church's insistence that it should be responsible for the moral formation of Italian children. His article *"Due Anni Dopo"* and his letters and conversations with Mussolini stress the point that the concordat with the papacy had engendered "an irreconcilable contradiction." The Church and the "ethical fascist state" each claimed for itself the right to be the primary source of public moral education. Either one or the other would have to yield, and there was no doubt whom Mussolini's minister of education and chief ideologue thought should give ground.

A more sympathetic and more stylistically accessible study of Gentile can be found in A. James Gregor's *Giovanni Gentile: Philosopher of Fascism*. Despite Gregor's now well-established view of Italian fascism as the entry point for non-Marxist socialist tyranny in the Third World, the author praises Gentile as a scholar, a humane individual, and a "moderating influence" on Italian fascism. Gregor properly notes the differing levels of tyranny associated with fascist regimes, and unlike the Nazis or other "anti-democratic reactive developmental nationalisms," which include Stalinism and Maoism, Italian fascists were not genocidal, nor were they conspicuously brutal, preferring to exile their opponents rather than kill them. Gregor ascribes the "mildness of Italian fascism" to the "intrinsically humane qualities" of the Italian people and the fact that "the barbarity of the civil war in Italy that preceded the March on Rome—and that which terminated the Second World War—might well have convinced everyone of that."[20]

Still, Gregor tries to link what he describes as a mild Italian dictatorship (his characterization of this rule as "mild totalitarianism," although placed in quotations, is clearly oxymoronic) to other more oppressive forms of "systematic, anti-individualistic collectivism." Supposedly all such movements are descended in varying degrees from the Italian experience and have at least some reference to Gentile's *La Dottrina politica del fascismo* and his other works on the fascist idea. But Gentile, as we learn from Gregor, tried to humanize collectivism by adding an "ethical concern" that was absent from Marxism; indeed, he attempted (vainly) to make fascism into a movement that was held together by duty and moral solidarity.[21]

From Gregor's ambivalent attitude toward Gentile and his statements about how his professor, the famous German-Jewish refugee historian Paul Oskar Kristeller, wept upon learning that his onetime *maître à penser*, Gentile, had been assassinated by antifascist partisans, it is apparent that Gregor admired his subject.[22] Equally obvious is the fact that the fascist movement that is best known to Gregor is fundamentally different from what Nolte characterizes as "radical fascism." The moral and theoretical gulf between them was at one time truly immense, even if Gregor, like Nolte, places both the German and Italian movements and regimes, with some reservations, into the same "fascist" basket.

Gentile was an Italian nationalist, and, as Gregor notes, his first book published in 1898, expanded from his doctoral thesis and submitted and accepted by the University of Pisa, *Rosmini e Gioberti*, was a valiant (but not particularly convincing) attempt to demonstrate the achievements of Italian philosophical thought in the first half of the nineteenth century.[23] Arguably this had nothing to do with exalting "proletariat nations" but was a common exercise at the time among the advocates of emerging and reemerging nations. Irish, Jewish, Slavic, Hungarian, and other nationalistically minded publicists were claiming to have made similar discoveries at the end of the nineteenth century about how their forebears were artistic and intellectual luminaries whom larger and more influential nations had unfairly ignored. Gentile did not initiate this custom, nor did he push it beyond what others were doing to instill their nations with self-esteem in the same time period.

Fascist Alternative Visions of the Future

The more relevant question for this study is whether Gentile incorporated a modernist perspective that guaranteed a happy future for the human race. This future for leftist visionaries would entail the creation of a world society consisting of politically and socially homogeneous populations. The inhabitants of this society would enjoy the same individual or human rights and have access to similar amenities. This is recognizable as the kind of future that galvanized the Marxists and democratic Left. Mannheim points out that leftist visionaries borrowed their utopia from a liberal, bourgeois belief in progress that was inherent in the Enlightenment. They altered this vision by conferring on it a more egalitarian and more confrontational form. We can locate the same vision in Nolte's description of "practical transcendence" and the way biblical prophecy was reconstructed in modern political ideologies as the advent of a socially just world order.

It is hard, however, to find such an optimistic view in fascism, even after taking into account its progressive side and even after differentiating fascism from the traditional Right. Whether or not fascists differed from that older Right may be less pertinent for this study's purposes than whether or not they belonged to the Left. Fascists vigorously defended particularity and hierarchy, which rendered them theoretically and in practice the Left's opponents. It is therefore extraneous to this book's argument whether or not they also took the same positions as traditional conservatives. Fascists who came along later confronted a more radical Left than the relatively tame liberalism that conservative polemicists had targeted.

The counterargument of European conservatives, including an American who was sympathetic to their persuasion, George F. Kennan, that fascists were on the Left as beneficiaries of the French and, possibly, Bolshevik Revolutions, does not invalidate this study's interpretation. What German-Jewish political theorist Leo Strauss once defined as an essentialist conservative world view would apply to generic fascists no less than classical conservatives: they "regard the universal and homogeneous state as either undesirable, though possible, or as both undesirable and impossible." Moreover, "conservatives look with greater sympathy than liberals on the particular or particularist and the heterogeneous." Fascists indeed stressed particularity with a vengeance and did so in the face of already weakened traditional social institutions.

They worked toward this goal partly by reviving archaic-looking arrangements that were meant to counteract the further pulling apart of what was particularistic and hierarchical. From whence came their interest in corporatist structures, which during the interwar period attracted followings in Latin America and most of Catholic Europe?[24] In their studies of the Falange, Arnaud Imatz and Stanley Payne note the keen enthusiasm shown by José Antonio and Ledesma Ramos for Catholic social teachings pointing toward corporatist organization and communal participation in economic decision-making.²⁵ José Antonio delved tirelessly into the works of nineteenth-century defenders of organic, participatory schemes aimed at protecting the working class against predatory capitalism. Such conservative Catholic critics of capitalism as Albert de Mun, François René de la Tour du Pin, Frédéric le Play, and Bishop Wilhelm Emmanuel von Ketteler of Mainz all figured among the heroes of the Falange's architects.

"National syndicalism" seems to have been the Falangist response to the "social problem," which, not incidentally, fit the ideological grid of Charles Maurras, the French conservative nationalist who presented nationalism and syndicalism as "the two forces destined to guide the future."²⁶ Exactly how one could implement this form of corporatism, fusing a nineteenth-century anarchist plan for local control of economic developments with vocational structures for political participation, is never fully worked out. But the Falangists developed a strong belief in syndicalist organization. By this means, it was hoped, one could advance Catholic social teachings while reviving the national spirit through a non-liberal, non-Marxist economic model. Since much of the Falange's leadership was killed off at the beginning of the Spanish Civil War, its leaders never had the opportunity to refine their economic planning. Unlike the corporatist blueprints periodically issued by the Italian fascist government, the more rudimentary economic schemes of the Falange originated with a movement that never ruled.

Catholic or thinly disguised Catholic corporatist thinking was a recurrent presence in the Latin fascist repertoire that was usually accompanied by an emphasis on spirituality. These affirmations were intended to contrast fascism with Marxist materialism (or, in Gentile's case, an equally hated positivism). The concept of a spiritualized universe also contributed to the semi-official philosophy of fascist Italy that took the forms of actualism or immanentism. Nolte's attempt to generalize from a crude Nazi biologism to illustrate a pervasive fascist "escape from transcendence" is not applicable to all forms of fascism. Especially in Latin countries, where generic fascism flourished, what was anathema to its adherents was a specifically leftist form of transcendence.

Croce's description of fascism as *"arretratezza"*—that is, backwardness, may be correct if readers accept his verdict in a nonjudgmental sense, which may not have been Croce's intention.²⁷ Common to all forms of fascism is a rejection of progress, or, more particularly, the kind of progress associated with the spread of equality and cultural and social homogenization. This does not mean that fascists shunned all change and wished to apply Luddite principles to industrial or medical developments. But they resisted the vision of human improvability preached by liberal democrats and revolutionary socialists and tried to put in its place an existential and social alternative.

The alternative they embraced may have been one of the following three. (Although fascist visions sometimes merged, in other cases they remained mutually exclusive.) Nolte privileges the first vision in his studies, which was particularly strong in German Nazism but far less so in Latin fascism—namely, the vision of a biologically driven, continuing struggle among races and ethnicities. Although this vision took a disastrous turn under the Nazi regime, when used to justify genocidal policies, it assumed a more reflective, nonviolent form in such nineteenth-century writers as Count Arthur de Gobineau (1816–1882) and Heinrich Gumplowicz (1838–1909). History, according to these thinkers, would lead not to a final happy age but to continuing ethnic struggle. The only interruption in this strife would come when one group won a decisive victory over another and could prolong its period of dominance. No victory was permanent, and each would give way in the end to a resumption of conflict.

What has been described as class war, noted Gumplowicz, typically reflected the hostility felt by warring sides who viewed themselves as ethnically opposed.[28] Gobineau had reached a similar conclusion when he interpreted the strife between the French aristocracy and the French Third Estate as masking an ethnic conflict between the noble descendants of Germanic warriors and the Celto-Roman population they had subdued.[29] Much of Gumplowicz's later work on ethnic struggle (*Rassengegensätzlichkeit*) attempts to flesh out the arguments in Gobineau's writings of the 1850s. Without denying that the social conflicts stressed by the socialists were real, Gumplowicz subordinated them methodologically to the struggle between groups who viewed themselves as culturally and/or ethnically distinct. Although there is a journalistic and even academic tendency to draw straight lines between Gobineau and Gumplowicz and Nazi ideology, the distance between them is far greater. Focusing on ethnic conflict as the key to human history is not the same as advocating the mass murder of undesirable ethnic groups. Still, the view of history as determined by ethnic strife does mark a tradition of thought that influenced what Nolte defines as "radical fascism."

Another fascist vision, which the author of this book suggests is the most systematically constructed, issues from Gentile's work, particularly from two of his works that were published in 1916, *I fondamenti della filosofia del diritto* and *Teoria generale dello spirito come atto puro*.[30] In both these tractates the reader is given a view of history as unending process—or as the continuing self-reflection of the absolute spirit *in actu*. The ethical will of each individual should be considered not as a single member of a multitude but as something actuated by the state as the "means" through which individuals could rise above their particularities and become part of a spiritual whole.

But neither spirit nor the state should be taken as a permanent "given." All givenness (*datità*) in Gentile's metaphysic is subject to change. A key term for understanding Gentile's dialectic, which takes over and modifies the Hegelian one, is a development (*svolgimento*) without end. In the *Fondamenti*, which was written during the First World War and six years before the installation of a fascist government in Italy, Gentile insists that "the Good or will, whose actualization includes a negative moment, which is Evil, cannot develop without an opposite. If that opposite disappeared, the becoming of the Good would cease and its power would diminish."[31] In *The Doctrine of Fascism*, Gentile expresses his concept of necessary polarities in this manner: "The nation as the state is only an ethical reality to whatever extent it can develop. A state that ceases to develop is doomed to death."[32]

Gentile proposes a generic fascist world view that differs markedly from the crude naturalism that Nolte ascribes to German National Socialism. In a comprehensive study of Gentile's idealism titled *The Social Philosophy of Giovanni Gentile*, H. S. Harris observes that his subject made conscious choices for an idealist and spiritualist as opposed to a materialist perspective and for a collectivist as opposed to an individualist understanding of obligation.[33] Ultimately an act of will causes the philosopher to opt for one perspective over another, for it was apparent to Gentile that he could pursue social and epistemological inquiries with equal plausibility from opposing positions. This in itself indicates the voluntarism that lies at the heart of Gentile's thinking and imprints his politics. It also reflects his choice of spiritualism against materialism or positivism, which was a decision that marked Latin fascism and surfaced in movements like the Iron Guard.[34] In Gentile's thought, spiritualism often looks like pantheism, and it is not surprising that his system has been compared to the divinely infused cosmology of Spinoza. Like Spinoza, Gentile constructs a spiritualized world but one that unfolds dialectically and becomes operative in historical practice.

Note that unlike Hegel's spirit in history, Gentile's dialectic does not end at the present moment with the emergence of the modern state. It remains in a state of development, just like the state itself, which defines itself through practice (*in fieri*). Unlike the Hegelian view of right, in which individual rights are incorporated into the structure of the state, Gentile seeks to transcend "individual velleities" or a "multitude of empirical individuals." All such particularities must be spiritually purified and given true identity through the individuality of the will of the state. Gentile's state is not a towering external presence but operates in the interior of each person as a reflection of the spirit. It represents a higher reality into which the individual parts have to become integrated in order to participate in spirit's work.[35]

Although Gentile's appeals to duty and solidarity are a call to such participation, they do not lead to any end point in the human saga. As Del Noce reminds us, Gentile was full of contempt for the Enlightenment and "never refers to humanitarianism, a religion of humanity or the utopia of a unified and reconciled humanity. With the term 'humanity' he wished to designate the immanence of individuals in the universality of the Spirit." Significantly, Gentile was a savage critic of the League of Nations, which he thought "was founded on the individualistic, anti-historic concepts which prevailed with the abstract rationalism of the eighteenth century and in the resulting idea of a final, perfected society. But since everything in human affairs is in a state of development, one cannot speak of definitive political solutions; nor is it possible to anticipate the character of the next crisis."[36]

In this judgment Gentile was following the teaching of Hegel, who insisted that there should be no higher instance for settling disputes between states than the actions they take in relation to each other. Hegel considered war between European states, as long as it involved self-limited conflict, to be a "tie between the belligerents," presuming their conflict "would pass" and lead to the resumption of peaceful relations.[37] For Hegel and Gentile, the nation-state expresses "a particular spirit" that "operates in the dialectic of finitude." Through their interaction, nation-states bring forth the "spirit of the world that asserts its own right to be the very highest one."[38] Because of the fates and deeds of particular states, as Hegel famously put it, world history becomes a world court.

A third, less well-defined fascist vision is concerned with staving off socially harmful forces by reclaiming the past selectively. All fascist movements did this, but some took this course with more determination than others. The neo-medieval aspects of fascism, which were so prominent in its Latin manifestations, or the simultaneous cult of the Roman Empire, which shared center stage in fascist Italy with Gentile's philosophy and corporatism, were all attempts at updating the past and making it serve counterrevolutionary or anti-leftist ends. Permeating all fascist movements, including the partial outlier that was Hitler's Germany, is the theme of decadence and renewal.

Although in the fascist vision, history is not tending toward the end point of a universal society of equals, there is the possibility of reversing deterioration, be it social, biological, or moral. Renewal was possible if one re-energized one's nation, a task that could but did not have to be promoted through war. Here again the discussion is not about linear developments but about repeated cycles of growth and waning as applied to human societies. These concepts and images were drawn from pre-Christian antiquity, and the philosopher Friedrich Nietzsche tried to substitute them for the Christian or Enlightenment concept of progress.

Another element that went into Latin fascist movements and intensified and reflected their rejection of progress was the once-influential thought of the French syndicalist and social philosopher Georges Sorel (1847–1922).

Although Sorel was affiliated for a number of years with the anarchist wing of the French labor movement, his view of history was as far removed as humanly possible from the Marxist one. Sorel saw human events in a mostly cyclical fashion, and, in his best-known work, *Reflections on Violence* (1908), he praised "violence" as the release of revolutionary energy intended to free society from a self-indulgent, parasitic ruling class.[39] Such revolutionary action could be triggered by the acceptance of the "redemptive myth," a narrative about an improved humanity that Sorel thought would drive the masses into heroic action. Early Christianity had achieved this effect, without inflicting direct violence on others, by inspiring future martyrs with its eschatological vision. Sorel hoped that the call for a "general strike" intended to bring down capitalism would release a similar élan among French anarchists and an enthusiasm that would spread to other enemies of the regime.

Sorel hated the bourgeoisie for its moral flabbiness, which was a condition that he thought was aggravated by wealth. He hoped to see this satiated class dispossessed and stripped of political control. But Sorel took this personal moral stand without a belief in progress or the future triumph of equality in a transformed world. He opposed the status quo because he associated it with decadence and an excess of comfort. But he also believed that any upheaval he incited would eventually produce a new stagnant ruling class. The once-righteous victors would have to be dislodged by a later generation as they became like those they had replaced. This was the closest Sorel came to explicating the laws of history, and in *The Illusions of Progress* (1908) he derided the unfounded optimism of those who attached a happy ending to the never-ending struggle he described.[40]

His ideas about "redemptive myths" that would push the masses toward purifying violence but would not end the cycle of decadence and revolution had profound effects on the revolutionary Right.[41] Sorel's thinking attracted French and Italian intellectuals who accepted fascism as a redemptive myth that justified "national revolutions." Such revolutionaries categorically rejected the Enlightenment's vision of a perfectible humanity that would introduce an epoch of universal social justice. Instead, they focused on the irrational sources of social behavior and fashioning an alternative "myth of the revolution" that could compete with the Marxist-Enlightenment view of a golden future.

Further Thoughts on a Discredited Ideology

Fascism should interest readers not because it characterizes the present or is likely to dominate the future but because of what it once exemplified. It was a movement of the revolutionary Right, a force that now exists in the

West as an isolated or only remotely approximated curiosity. The revolutionary Right does not belong in any way to conventional political discourse in Western countries. Today's mainstream parties do not look like anything that could be described as "fascist" in any historic sense. Although this distancing from the fascist or quasi-fascist past may be ascribed to multiple causes, among these causes is undoubtedly a widespread horror of something that once bestrode the continental European stage. As a past to be avoided, fascism still casts a long shadow, even if that term has been recklessly applied and even if it is increasingly hard to figure out how the current usages are related to the real past. But behind this bugaboo lies a semblance of reality in the sense that what is condemned once belonged to the Right in a way that the GOP or the German Christian Democrats definitely do not.

Fascism was not the only Right that existed in its time, and it is quite possible to recognize in someone like Charles de Gaulle, who fought the Nazi German invaders of his homeland, a truer conservative nationalist than those who rushed to collaborate with the Vichy government. Moreover, interwar political leaders like Horthy, Dollfuss, and Franco all came out of the non-fascist Right, and, as Payne observes, the authoritarian Right that claimed these personalities should not be confused with fascism. Although when push came to shove, authoritarian figures took on fascist trappings, they abandoned these with relief as soon as the occasion presented itself.

Further, as the second chapter points out, not all fascists or *fascisants* everywhere in Europe found themselves fighting on Hitler's side. Some Poles, Belgians, French, and other Europeans who had been sympathetic to Italian or Spanish fascism fought Hitler's armies when they invaded their countries. Those German rightists who wished to emulate Mussolini but distrusted Hitler were killed or scared into submission in 1934. But this did not help their reputations as nationalist enemies of the Third Reich. Anti-Nazi and non-Nazi fascists ended up in the same rogues' gallery with Hitler and Himmler, just as the communists who had once served the Nazis during the period of the Soviet-Nazi Non-Aggression Pact were rehabilitated as the world's most reliable antifascists. This attitude is understandable, everything considered. And everything here refers to the egalitarian democratic spirit of the present age and the function of fascism as a stand-in for whatever is diametrically opposed to the present American or western European political culture.

Nolte has asked, somewhat waggishly, whether Western readers would think differently about Nazism if readers ceased to believe in present values. It is doubtful that most Western peoples would. First of all, the Nazis were too unappetizing to come back as a popular rage (although this defect has not kept Western intellectuals from apologizing for murderous communist regimes), and, secondly, the ethnic mixing in Western countries would make the acceptance of Nazi ideology as a public philosophy unthinkable as well as unworkable. There may be no alternative to the ideology of diversity given the way Western societies have evolved or been pushed in the last seventy years.[42]

Finally, there is no reason to believe that people would abandon deeply ingrained patterns of thought or myth, even if they came into conflict with empirical reality. One obvious reason that Nazism lost its appeal so rapidly after the defeat of the Nazi government was its fundamental incompatibility with what were then widely held beliefs in the Western world. Communists and socialists have not fared as badly in the court of world opinion, regardless of how badly communist regimes have acted. Still, one might hope for a modest change even within the framework created by inherited moral attitudes. Such a change would involve not turning the world on its head but allowing for an ideologically neutralized space in which historical questions could be engaged without recriminations. It would be pleasant to read about fascism in the popular press or in some academic publications without having to encounter the boilerplate clichés of the Popular Front era.[43]

It would be equally nice to be able to discuss the Right in historical perspective without having to endure such ritualistic gestures as branding opponents of gay marriage or putting women into combat as "the Right" or "the ultra-Right." By these ultramodern standards, most people were on the "Right" or even the "far Right," including most of the Left, until recently. It is equally silly to hear libertarians putting fascists on the Left because they sometimes sounded vaguely like social democrats. In interwar Europe, it was altogether possible to be on the far Right while favoring a paternalistic state. There were once socialists of the Right and those of the Left. Interwar men of the Right, such as Oswald Spengler and Ernst Jünger, readily addressed their fellow Germans as a "nation of workers." Spengler praised socialism as a distinctly "Prussian" form of organization, which he contrasted with the capitalist way of life associated with the English and Americans.[44]

This brings the reader back to the question of how fascists could be on the Right, and even on the far Right, if the Right is now identified, at least in the United States, with individual self-fulfillment. There are three answers to this question, all of which may be complementary. First, one should define the Right contextually. Although the Right is always opposed to the Left, the enemy it is resisting may differ depending on time and circumstance. In Italy after the First World War or in Spain in the 1930s, fascists fought revolutionary socialists or anarchists (of the Left); in American society the

Right (to whatever extent such an entity operates) defends the rights of citizens to arm themselves against a leftist state or else it insists on dismantling a welfare state, which advances leftist social policies.

The current Right no longer defends the "State" for a very simple reason. Unlike its associations in certain interwar European countries with traditional authorities and inherited hierarchies, the present form of public administration is no longer associated with the Right. Politicians and journalists now talk about expanding equality and even creating a universal nation while celebrating Third World immigration and "cultural diversity." The administrative state that is intended to further these purposes is a modern democratic creation. It has little or nothing to do with what Gentile apostrophized as a spiritualized "ethical will." Neither Gentile nor Friedrich Stahl was acting as a forerunner of George W. Bush or Barack Obama when he spoke about "the State."

Secondly, there is nothing inherently right-wing about glorifying individual rights and certainly not human appetites. European conservatives have traditionally identified individualism with the Left, which is at war with inherited community. Since the early twentieth century, however, critics of the welfare state have turned to the language of individual rights as a remedy against the overreach of the centralized state. This is a weapon that is found in the American Bill of Rights and one that social traditionalists in the United States have tried to use to stave off undesirable change. Driven to desperation, they appeal defensively to what they don't entirely believe in principle.

Although used as a final recourse, the appeal to constitutionally guaranteed individual rights does not belong to the historic Right. It may indicate the limited options of the critics of the modern administrative state that a self-described American conservative and defender of community, Robert Nisbet, alternated attacks on the "national state" with invectives against unbridled individualism in his 1953 classic *The Quest for Community*. An enemy of all centralization as an atomizing force, Nisbet viewed the cult of the individual as a necessary accompaniment of public administration: "The conception of society as an aggregate of morally autonomous, psychologically free individuals, rather than as a collection of groups, is, in sum, closely related to a conception of society in which all legitimate authority has been abstracted from the primary communities and vested in the single sphere of the State. What is significant here is that when the philosophical individualists were dealing with the assumed nature of man, they were dealing in large part with a hypothetical being created by their political imagination."[45] Nisbet was speaking for himself when, in *The Sociology of Emile Durkheim*, he explained: "Durkheim rejected individualism on every possible ground.

He found it insupportable as a principle of social solidarity, as an ethic or moral value, as a cornerstone of the social order, and not least as the vantage point of social analysis."[46]

While Nisbet viewed fascists as state centralizers in a hurry, he always lavished praise on traditional European conservatives of the nineteenth century.[47] He was not alone in this predilection. In the 1960s the American conservative intellectual movement was split between libertarians and those who were denounced as "statists" or the "authoritarian Right," a group that embraced Nisbet and the Burkean man of letters Russell Kirk.[48] Not surprisingly, the traditionalist camp armed themselves with critiques of universal rights that came from European conservatives and mocked the idea that society is nothing more than a multiplicity of individuals. Even in the United States the association of the Right with individualism has not gone undisputed.

Finally, there is no intrinsic reason to imagine that when Gentile exalted the state as the bearer of an ethical will, he was praising the totalitarian tyranny that existed then in Germany and Russia. His spiritualization of the state has to be seen in the context of his battle against clericalism and his attempt to establish a "philosophical alternative" to Catholicism in the Italian nation-state. One of his longtime passions was educational reform, and Gentile hoped to turn Italian schools into centers for his own philosophically based Christianity, which he chose to believe arose organically out of the *Risorgimento*.[49]

What distinguished this plan from the one introduced far more ruthlessly by secularists in France was Gentile's relatively conservative thinking. As minister of education, he wished to leave a place in national education for the Church as well as for humanistic studies. But Gentile defended no less insistently the totalizing character of the fascist regime, by which he meant its primacy over clerical authority in shaping Italian moral education. Gentile's attempt to invest the state with a spiritual aura must be understood against the background of his struggle in a deeply Catholic country against ecclesiastical influence. Among the beneficiaries of the defeat of the fascists, beside the communists, were the American-sponsored Christian Democrats, a group that Gentile would have abhorred. Even more curious was the fact that Italian fascists, no matter what Gentile might have thought about this arrangement, eventually became the allies of the clericalists in Austria and Spain. Other fascisms, particularly the Falange, took a much more benevolent view of Church influence than the premier Italian fascist philosopher.[50]

The history of fascism illustrates, among other things, the difficulties faced by a rightist movement in opposing the ascendancy of the modern Left. This remains the case even when taking into account the ineptitude and occasional brutality shown by fascist leaders. The sharp ideological disparity between fascism and a more successful modernity is also part of the reason that fascism faded so ignominiously. Its ideas stand in stark contrast to today's dominant values, and it was entirely predictable that in an already rapidly changing European society, fascists failed to build significant mass movements outside of certain unevenly modernized countries. (Here again one must exclude the Nazi totalitarian outliers who were not, for the most part, generic fascists.) Fascism's chances for becoming an overpowering historical force were, in fact, never very promising. Even if the Nazis had not contributed to their destruction, fascists would not have attained the international power they tried desperately to project in the interwar years. In the best of circumstances, they might have survived a bit longer among second- or third-rate powers, as an exotic authoritarian movement, before becoming a footnote in modern history. Fascism's greatest recognition value since its high-water mark has been as a slur—or as an indiscriminately used synonym for Nazi genocide.

The great contest in the West during the second half of the twentieth century was waged without reference to a failed fascist experiment. The overshadowing confrontation featured two internationalist contenders: communism, which was identified with the Soviet Empire, and liberal democracy, which was championed by the United States. This is the way politics played out in the last century in what became the dominant power centers of the age. Even if some fascist enthusiasts had gone on ruling somewhere in Europe, this would not have put them in the same league with the United States or the Soviets. The existence of a fascist homeland would not have changed the major power alignments in the West extending from the end of the Second World War down to the fall of the Berlin Wall. It is also unlikely that the survival of a fascist presence would have prevented a world culture that is distinctly American from becoming a cosmic force.

CHAPTER SEVEN

A Vanished Revolutionary Right

In this study of fascism the author has made obvious arguments and others that are more implicit. The obvious arguments, which are repeated throughout most of the chapters, can be summed up as follows: there is a generic fascism, which resembles the Italian fascist movement and, to a lesser extent, the Italian fascist government. This form of fascism shaped the interwar revolutionary Right, which came into vogue in Europe after the First World War. Moreover, fascism has a distant family relation to traditional conservatism but less ideological connection to German Nazism. It became perhaps inevitably linked in the popular mind to Nazism because of the (hardly predestined) alliance between Hitler and Mussolini. Whether or not Hitler had come along, fascism would have had an extremely limited temporal existence. As a movement and/or regime, it once prospered in countries that were not world powers. Fascism also had a distinctly Latin character, and it is unimaginable that it would have done well in a markedly different culture, say that of the United States or Great Britain.

This book also questions whether Third World dictatorships should be considered as extensions or identifiable relatives of Italian fascism. With due respect to the outstanding scholarship of A. James Gregor, Ernst Nolte was probably right that fascism belonged to a specific temporal-spatial context and therefore should not be applied to developmental dictatorships all over the globe. It was a movement that drew on a European heritage of ideas and built on European social classes and social crises. Generic fascism, if the author may be permitted to use this term, was essentially Franco-Italian. Without such figures as Gentile and Sorel, it is hard to think that a fascist world view would have come into existence. Although Nietzsche, Spengler, and (far less) Hegel all contributed to this *Weltanschauung*, such transalpine thinkers entered Latin fascist movements through a Latin Catholic filter. The resulting fascist product was then carried to northern and eastern Europe, where it became identified with other nationalist movements.

Another argument that cannot be missed in this text is the inadmissibility of applying "fascist" to whatever the speaker finds viscerally repulsive. In Europe this practice has gone so far that antifascism has been turned into a state religion by the governments and media in some western European countries. Antifascism typically entails equating every form of politically incorrect protestation, whether directed against gay marriage or the introduction of Sharia law into European countries, with "fascist" intolerance and then inventing some kind of linkage between the putative outrage and those atrocities committed in Nazi Germany. In such a forced connection the *argumentum ad Hitlerum* trumps any sober attempt at persuasion or dissuasion.

There is, however, a less obvious argument that the author of this book has tried to develop, and it may be stated thus: "Right" and "Left" have essentialist meanings and are not simply relational terms. If readers don't care to accept this, then impassioned journalists and Hollywood celebrities should be free to apply political labels however they like. As the author writes this, a "red states" website is sending him an Internet message that he should oppose by every lawful means necessary the confirmation of Senator Chuck Hagel as American Secretary of Defense. Indeed, every "conservative" should be up in arms against the nomination of this supposedly leftist former senator from Nebraska.

Although the frame of reference that this message assumes may make sense to some partisans, there seems nothing particularly right-wing or left-wing about Hagel's cause. Account must be taken of the fact that the Republican Party went from being an isolationist party to a militant advocate of liberal internationalism while the Democratic Party has moved somewhat in the opposite direction. Hagel is a decorated war hero and, until recently, was a social conservative by current American standards. Despite his patriotic background he became identified with the Left when he called for sizable cuts in the military budget and warned against American military entanglement in the Middle East. Even if Hagel has criticized the support that the United States has given to Israel against Arab states, it is hard to see how this stand would make the former senator into a leftist and his opponents into the opposite.[1]

It is exceedingly difficult to draw proof for one's contention from a current event that in all likelihood is already fading from memory. And then there's the additional problem of being accused of trying to apply one's example in a less than objective fashion. In this case the author of this book readily concedes that the candidacy of Hagel was vulnerable because of questionable judgments the senator expressed about Iran and other foreign policy subjects. Objections about these judgments emerged during the Senate hearing that preceded Hagel's confirmation. But the designated American Right hurled charges against the candidate that just as easily could have emanated from the Left, e.g., about Hagel's alleged homophobia, anti-Semitism, and softness on American Southern racists. Hagel's partisans, by contrast, depicted the senator as a foreign policy realist.[2]

While there is no reason that either side in this affair should be assigned to the Right or the Left by virtue of having been for or against Hagel, arbitrary litmus tests are likely to be applied when substantive definitions are lacking. At that point distinctions become mostly relational between party blocs that claim different ideological locations in a two-party system. This arrangement works, providing voters forget the considerable overlap between the two sides. The Republicans are supposed to be on the Right, but, like the Democrats, they privilege in their discourse equality and human rights and are hardly about to abolish an already extensive welfare state. Such a move is all the less likely since Republican voters insist on having government programs preserved and even expanded for themselves. When Republicans say they're for "getting government off our backs," voters may assume that they are joshing or dissembling. Besides, even if they succeeded in doing the impossible by dismantling the welfare state, what would be "right-wing" about pursuing that course? Such an action might please an authentic Right that was seeking to weaken a government it didn't like. But it would not be taking its negative position for the individualistic reasons that the Republicans would likely adduce if they did what they are not likely to do.

Making sense of this historical context is a task that the author addresses in his book *After Liberalism* (1999). Americans live in an age in which equality or fairness is the prime desideratum, and the welfare state is the proximate means for making people feel good about themselves.[3] Americans believe that the rights they preach are universally valid and should apply everywhere. Both our national parties give the impression that American democracy should be open to as much of the human race as we can fit into our national borders, and if there is any significant partisan difference in the pursuit of this goal, it lies in how the two parties would treat those who are in the United States illegally, mainly those from countries to our south.

Admittedly, we could find other differences between Republicans and Democrats or between the English Conservative and Labour Parties, but these distinctions have become increasingly blurred and are now limited mostly to "policy" approaches. The late Christopher Lasch tried to explain such a consensus as based on the acceptance of the "myth of Progress," which was fed by the desire for material gratification. Western politics are now shaped by the desire for and availability of consumer products and the demand for individual self-actualization.[4] There is also growing consensus about privileging certain values, particularly equality. Because of these presuppositions, partisan camps have come to look more and more alike, and the resulting consensus rests on what were, into the last century, considered leftist values.

The widely shared convictions, which are also honored in Canada and western Europe, may be said to correspond to the essentialist Left, certainly as that term was understood in the period being treated here. Ever since the defeat of Nazi Germany, and even during the struggle against Soviet communism, what were once deemed leftist ideas have been in the ascendant, and Americans and western Europeans have constructed parliamentary polarities on the basis of this given. Only the German government has been totally honest about this process. Chancellor Merkel's chief advisor, Volker Kauder has indicated that after the horrors of the Nazi experience, Germany refuses to have a Right.[5] Its parties must all come out of the Left or else out of a center that presumably tends in a leftist direction. To whatever extent the present Christian Democrats are "Christian," Kauder explains, they are committed to social change of a non-rightist type.

German sociologist Niklas Luhmann, who, like other future German academics, was sent to the United States after the Second World War for training in democratic living, came up with an interesting plan for distinguishing "Right" and "Left" in a parliamentary system. The Right should be "about defending the prevailing order" while the Left should support "emancipation, even for those who do not necessarily want to be emancipated."[6] This would operate, or so it would seem, on a kind of automatic pilot featuring alternating parties that are adorned with distinctive slogans. The sharing of governance that Luhmann had in mind would differ fundamentally from what Giovanni Sartori characterized as "hot politics" and Carl Schmitt viewed as the "Political," defined as the "most intense" friend/enemy relation."[7]

Luhmann favored for his country the adoption of formal arrangements that would allow democratic government to function smoothly. His makeshift operational definitions for the "alternation of the governing and the opposition" reflect the real basis of Luhmann's concerns. After seeing his country wrecked by the Nazis, he wanted no part of essentialist political differences. He therefore proposed something like an American political system for the Germans, one that replicated the mentality as well as the alteration between two party blocs that he encountered in the United States or that he believed corresponded to the American model.[8]

Strangely enough, some of the best treatments of the essentialist Right have come from self-described leftists who are terrified of a resurgent antiliberal enemy. A relevant book is *Les anti-Lumières du XVIIIe siècle à la guerre froide*, which the historian of fascism Zeev Sternhell produced to underline the continuity of rightist thinking, from the earliest reactions against the Enlightenment down to the putative resurgence of the Right in the second half of the twentieth century.[9] Most of Sternhell's laments are *vieux jeu*, and earlier collections of such grievances compiled by Isaiah Berlin, Georg Lukacs, Stephen Holmes, J. Salwyn Shapiro, and a multitude of other authors dealing with the "distant roots" of Nazism or Italian fascism would reveal most of what is recycled in Sternhell's work. Beside Sternhell's non-originality in this department, there is the recurrent problem of his procrustean approach to the history of ideas.[10] It would be easy to cite multiple cases of this problem in his book—for example, the fudged genealogies, by which critics of the Enlightenment are indiscriminately shoved into the same house of horrors under the superimposed face of Hitler. Sternhell lumps together Nazism with far less destructive forms of right-wing authoritarianism such as Mussolini's Italy and Salazar's Portugal, thereby giving the impression that everything associated with the "anti-Enlightenment" has gone in the same catastrophic direction.

One may smile while noting certain inconsistencies in Sternhell's arguments. He rages against the counterrevolutionary Joseph de Maistre, who observed in *Considerations on France*, "There is no man as such; I have only encountered Frenchmen, Italians and Russians and from reading Montesquieu's *Persian Letters*, I now know that Persians exist. As for mankind, I have yet to find such a thing."[11] But in an interview, Sternhell characterizes himself as a "super-Zionist": "Zionism was and remains the right of Jews to control their fate and their future." This is "a right that Jews were deprived of historically and which Zionism restored to them." Are we to imagine that Sternhell's own Jewish nationalism is more in sync with his standard of Enlightenment universalism than it is with Maistre's right to particularity? Moreover, in his oft-cited comment, Maistre is making an anthropological and sociological point, not paving the way for Nazi atrocities.

In the end, however, Sternhell may be confirming Maistre's perception, which borders on the commonplace. People have usually viewed themselves and been seen by others through their ethnic or national identities. Sternhell's insistence that Jews have a collective right to create their own nation-state does not mean that he wishes to place them in a universal state that is equally open to everyone.[12] Sternhell's right to an ethnically specific homeland assumes a right to particularity, although he may be loath to grant Europeans the privilege he would gladly bestow on his own national group. Here Sternhell is expressing selective identitarianism, which is claimed for one's own group in relation to other, allegedly more powerful, groups.

But behind this inconsistent application is the recognition of the truth that the concrete, particularistic, and communal, namely, those attributes that Sternhell attaches to critics of the Enlightenment, shape our human identities. And the perspective that Sternhell ostentatiously disdains can still help investigate actual societies—save for those parts of the world that have undergone advanced modernization. Before the emergence of a globalist, post-Christian, post-national West, Maistre's bon mot would have made sense in explaining how people everywhere lived and thought. It continues to make sense for those groups that have still not been fully exposed to market-, media-, and bureaucratically driven homogenization.

There is also the question of why those who challenge what Sternhell affirms should not be viewed as the heirs of the tradition of rational inquiry. Why is someone who disputes the existence of human rights or points out the limits of egalitarian politics with reasoned arguments no less a child of the Enlightenment than someone who embraces Sternhell's political values? Why, for example, is David Hume, who questions whether "abstract" natural right can be empirically confirmed, less of a "lumière" than those who have rallied to this myth?[13] Apparently being "Enlightened" requires one to nod at noble lies.[14] One might even argue that the attempt to claim intellectual modernity for current political attitudes, starting in the early modern period, is a totalitarian enterprise. It forces patterns of thought and ultimately Western history into the preconceived moral choices of a new priesthood of intellectuals.[15]

Despite such interpretive problems, Sternhell's work has one compensatory merit that may overshadow all its forced connections and accusations of guilt by distant or nonexistent association. It indicates what the Right is, and it makes unmistakably clear that the Right is not the Left but something palpably and sometimes irreconcilably different. The Right for Sternhell is not simply the required other party in a parliamentary setup—for example, the party that favors spousal benefits but not yet marital rights for gay partners, or else Medicare but not quite the Affordable Care Act (Obamacare). The opponents of the Enlightenment represent something that offends

Sternhell deeply, something that may be linked in his mind to the death of family members in Nazi-occupied Poland.

Notwithstanding these personal hostilities, in his studies on the antecedents of French fascism, Sternhell manages to describe in detail both the old Right and its revolutionary offspring. Also, in Sternhell's earlier works, one rarely detects the loathing for the Right or that deep commitment to the Left that permeate his recent professions of globalist faith. The Right was a reaction against what rightists regarded as a materialist world view, and it was driven by opposition to "universal rights" and the desire to preserve historic identities. The Right always viewed with suspicion or contempt the operation of parliamentary systems that allowed vested economic interests and professional politicians free play. One need not endorse these essentialist characteristics any more than Sternhell did to grasp how pervasive they were among enemies of the Left. "Right" is not being used in this context as an invented distinction that allows the "system" to operate without having to worry about "extremists." It is an independent existential and cosmological point of reference.

There is one other observation that should be discussed one last time before this book can be ended. It is about the difference between fascism and the more authentic Right that Mannheim and Panajotis Kondylis discussed in exhaustive detail. In a very obvious sense, fascism was a false Right to the extent that, like postwar American conservatism, it was an invented movement held together by a synthetic, changing ideology. Unlike postwar American conservatism, however, fascists were honest about the fact that they were always in the process of defining their movement through historical practice. Unlike America's dubious conservatives, fascists did not hide behind "permanent values" with changing contents and applications or become the handservants of an established party in a system of party rotation.

But the most serious defect of fascism was exactly the opposite of the job-seeking conformism of the establishment Right in the United States. Fascists viewed violence positively, as a cathartic agent; as Stanley Payne shows in his characterization of José Antonio, Onésimo Redondo Ortega, Ramiro Ledesma Ramos, and other Falange leaders, Spanish fascists shared an almost mystical view of the effects of revolutionary violence. This was clearly an attitude they carried with them from the Left, particularly from the Anarchist-Syndicalist movement, which was quite strong in Latin countries. If fascism became a "counterrevolutionary imitation of the Left," it also carried along leftist baggage, which was more obvious in some fascist movements than in others. Payne cites passages and entire editorials from the Falange newspaper, *El Fascio,* that could have been written by orthodox

Marxists.[16] This leftist shadow and the predilection for revolutionary violence were characteristic of fascist movements, if not necessarily of fascist regimes, that distinguished them from any traditional Right.

Finally, the reader should focus one last time on the rightist gestalt that generic fascism exhibited and Sternhell, however uncomfortably, allows the reader to understand. In their emphasis on particularity, identitarian politics, and hierarchy, fascists expressed recognizably right-wing attitudes. These may not be the attitudes of American libertarians or Republicans trying to reach out to minorities, but they are the historic attitudes of the Right extending back entire centuries.

Saying this neither glorifies nor discredits the views in question. This study does not seek to convert anyone to any political persuasion, let alone turn readers into fascists. Presented here are attitudes and concerns that are integral to the essentialist Right. Fascists embodied, however defectively, some traditional conservative sentiments and did so in a way that those who now call themselves "conservative" usually do not. The exercise here demanded is not likely to please most political journalists and party activists, but the alternative is to allow ideological designations to drift along without fixed meanings. Through some kind of terminological manipulation, one defines "conservatism," "liberalism," "Marxism," or "fascism" however the speaker (or journalist) wants and then coaxes or browbeats others into accepting one's imposed definition. This may be the current practice of majority parties and the pet passion of those who celebrate their virtues. But this cannot be the guiding principle in any treatment of essentialist positions or of their accompanying world views. Anyone seeking to deal honestly with the ideologies that have unfolded since the French Revolution should be willing to think about them historically rather than through the prism of presentist prejudice and partisan enthusiasms. This means recognizing the distinctiveness of distinctive epochs and understanding that the ideological reference points and characteristic visions of one age may not be the same as those of another.

Appendix

Fascism and Modernization

In looking at fascism as a modernizing force, there are two relevant interpretations that this study has thus far left out. One is a cultural perspective, notably adopted by Roger Griffin, that explores the relation between fascism and the reaction to modernity. Like this study, Griffin's work deals with fascism in the context of a particular epoch in the European past. In several of his books, most notably *Modernism and Fascism,* Griffin dwells on the connection between interwar fascism and a revolt against "modernity" that is particularly apparent in the cultural and artistic realm. He defines modernity historically, starting "with the localized emergence in late eighteenth-century Europe of the reflexive mode of historical consciousness which legitimated the French revolutionaries' fundamentalist war against tradition and their deliberate attempt to replace it lock, stock, and barrel with an entirely new epoch."[1]

This process, which "incurred the wrath of Conservative thinkers such as Edmund Burke and Joseph de Maistre," assumed the notion of progress and affirmed the need to slough off the residues of the pre-rational past.[2] Griffin quotes Adorno's astute observation that "modernity is a qualitative, not a chronological category."[3] This glorification of modernity as a transition from barbarism to a morally based, scientific civilization angered its critics and led to heated reactions. Griffin ties the revolt against this "temporalization" of progress to the growing sense that modernity was "decadent." Modernism, which became dominant in the first few decades of the twentieth century, transmitted and gave expression to this antimodern critique; Griffin distinguishes between "modernism" as an artistic and philosophical movement and the pedestrian modernity that modernists came increasingly and loudly to oppose.

He underlines the "paradox" that the modernists were wedded to certain aspects of the modernity they railed against. They were looking for an "alternate modernity" to what they decried as decadent while being neither able nor eager to retreat into the already lost dimension of the past: "the modernist search to combat the threat of nihilism first took shape once Western myths of progress lost their credibility and modernity entered a protracted period of liminoidality. This process was intensified by the growing temporalization of history since the Enlightenment and further accelerated by the social disruptions and rise of materialism promoted by the industrialization of society under new capitalist classes."[4] Griffin presents the reader with another paradox—namely, that most of the most prominent modernists, such as Pablo Picasso, Walter Gropius, and the Cubists, were politically on the far Left. This orientation was natural: "Even though some forms of modernism seem more concerned with reviving tradition or conveying a sense of cultural decay, its overall momentum is futural and optimistic. In whatever medium it operates it works toward—or at least points [to] the need for—the erection of a new canopy of mythic meaning and transcendence over the modern world, a new beginning."[5]

Significantly, the same modernist category is made to apply to artistic and literary figures of the Right, including the ones who were attracted to fascist movements. Is it a matter of secondary interest, as Griffin suggests, that "some forms of aesthetic modernism find a source of transcendence in the artistic exploration and expression of decadence rather than in focusing on utopian remedies to it"?[6] In light of this generic "primordialist definition," the reader may be justified in asking what common features can be found in the Jewish communist Cubist Georges Braque and the pro-fascist warrior against Jewish bankers and literary modernist par excellence Ezra Pound, except that both were artistic pioneers living in the West during the early twentieth century? Certainly not all modernist adventures entailed a rush toward the revolutionary Right or, as in the case of T. S. Eliot, enthusiastic support for monarchy and Anglo-Catholicism. Modernists moved in different political directions depending on other variables beyond their shared modernist propensities. And certainly not all modernists were "futural and optimistic." Some of them, like the German man of letters Gottfried Benn, were perpetually full of bitter bile, and if there is a "canopy of mythic meaning" in the works of Louis-Ferdinand Céline, it has yet to be discovered.[7]

Where Griffin is correct is in assuming that there was a strain of modernism that led inexorably toward the Right. This was particularly true of literary modernists, starting with such illustrious names as Filippo Marinetti, Luigi Pirandello, Gottfried Benn, Ernst Jünger, Louis Ferdinand Céline, Mircea Eliade, T. S. Eliot, Ezra Pound, Wyndham Lewis, and William Butler Yeats. Although Griffin is wrong to identify Jünger, whose hatred for Hitler was undeniable, as a Nazi and Eliot as a fan of fascism,[8] he is nonetheless spot-on that among literary modernists there was a pervasive predilection for the Right. Among these figures certain themes and concerns dominated, especially the quest for spirituality, a desire to return to some aspects of the pre-liberal or pre-democratic past, and disenchantment with a mechanized, rationalized society.

Griffin is particularly helpful in providing details about "reactionary modernism," which is the form of that genus that dovetailed with a predisposition toward the revolutionary Right. Such a movement was "the twin of 'decadence,' not in the sense of the late nineteenth century art movement bearing that name, but because it articulates the urgent need of contemporary society to be regenerated and for history itself to be renewed." Moreover, modernism "is seen as the fruit of modern reflexivity in crisis, the product of a temporalized self-awareness that, responding to the perceived decay of history itself, is thus driven in extreme cases to envisage its 'total' regeneration through an unprecedented process of creative destruction."[9] Griffin argues that the mindset he describes had already entered political thought by the early twentieth century (as witnessed by Nietzsche and Sorel), and, even before the interwar period, one could already observe "modernism overflow the boundaries of the 'aesthetic' category."

There are recurrent tics in Griffin's presentation that should be noted for the sake of a balanced assessment. Among these disfiguring features are tortured syntax, unnecessary name-dropping that often does little to illuminate the argument made, and needless excurses. The author also makes it appear that the rightist sensibility that was lodged in reactionary modernism may jump out of the trash bin to which it has been confined since 1945 and once again wreak havoc on a hapless Europe. The evidence cited for this anxiety is less than compelling, especially since Griffin is just as determined to show that fascism was tied to the nationalist excesses of a past era. It is also quite conceivable that fascists would have come to power even without the aid of modernist artists and literati. Reactionary modernists may have contributed in some way to fascist successes, but they were hardly a determinative factor anywhere. In fact, not all modernists sympathized with the fascists, and not all reactionary modernists ran to join the fascists or Nazis. Although well-disposed toward Action Française and its *maître à penser* Charles Maurras, Eliot loathed Hitler and turned his back on the nationalist Right during the Spanish Civil War once it took aid from Nazi Germany.[10]

Having called attention to these tares, it should be noted that Griffin's study makes several convincing points. Fascist theorists and fascist politicians had an ambivalent relation to modernity, and that relation was reflected in modernist artists. While modernists bewailed modern decadence and denounced what they understood as "liberalism," they were firmly connected to modernity or saw no way out of their temporal-cultural situation. Griffin speaks of the modernist project as an "alternative modernity which holds out the prospect of putting an end to political, cultural, moral and/or physical dissolution, and sometimes looks forward to the emergence of a new type of 'man.'"[11] There is no doubt that one could find elements of this project in the speeches and writings of fascist leaders, most particularly in the document "*What Is Fascism?*" that Gentile prepared for *Il Duce*. Griffin is furthermore correct that fascists and reactionary modernists revealed an "essential rightist" gestalt, although whether this was equally present in the left-wing modernists is open to question.

One may qualify, however, by noting that what Griffin is describing is mostly the modernist influence on the fascist and Nazi movements. By contrast, his account of how the fascists consolidated power by applying modernist ideas is far from convincing.[12] It is based on a selective use of conventional secondary sources that do not demonstrate that modernism led to fascist seizures of power. One could easily imagine Mussolini and Hitler taking and consolidating power without having to invoke modernist images. Where Griffin is far more convincing is in documenting how a fascist aesthetic and style drew heavily on modernist art and modernist sensibilities, from Nazi architecture to Italian fascist graphics and experimental cinema under the Third Reich. A further sign of cultural modernization that Griffin barely touches is the development of the social sciences as a modern discipline in Nazi Germany. It was under Hitler's regime that statistically based sociology and social history got their start at Leipzig and other German universities. It is an irony bordering on the absurd that such a discipline was repackaged as a decisive break from the Nazi-tainted German past when it was promoted in the postwar period. In the late 1940s this relatively new discipline was brought back counterfactually or mistakenly as an effort to "overcome the German past." Helmut Schelsky, who was a pioneering researcher in social statistics in postwar Germany, learned his discipline, like many of his colleagues, under the Third Reich.[13]

It may also be useful to distinguish modernism as an intellectual and artistic movement from the advocacy of modernization, a task that Griffin energetically engages in his book. Because futurists like Marinetti, who celebrated the machine age, lent support to Italian fascism does not mean that the fascist regime adhered to a liberal democratic idea of progress. Nor did it signify that Italian, French, or Spanish fascists hoped to break from the past in order to build a rational, scientifically planned society. Fascists adored antiquities, made a cult out of dead national heroes, and held to an irrational view of the universe. If history revealed to these militants any direction, it was the one they found in Sorel, Nietzsche, and Spengler. That direction was cyclical, and whatever trajectory it followed was determined by human will and "destiny."

A Final Loose End

In contrast to the backward-looking perspective, however ambivalently expressed, of generic fascism, Nazism exhibited a modernizing thrust. While this argument is knowledgeably engaged in the works of Rainer Zitelmann and Michael Prinz, the German academic and journalistic world has generally avoided it. The reason for the neglect and sometimes angry dismissal accorded Zitelmann and other like-minded interpreters of the Third Reich goes back to what Germans have been taught about their present democracy. This is a government that began with a constitution, the formation of which was overseen by the occupying powers after World War II. According to German politicians from across the respectable ideological spectrum and most well-known German intellectuals, the postwar German governments (the same argument was often made for the East German communist dictatorship) represented a necessary and, indeed, redemptive break from the German past. It was the peculiarities of German political and social traditions that had resulted in the crimes of the Nazi regime, and the only way that Germany could avoid returning to its *Sonderweg* (aberrant historical path) was by reconstructing itself totally as a Western democratic society.[1] The abolition of Prussia as a political entity by the Allies after World War II symbolized the efforts of Germany's conquerors to drive home what, for them, was a self-evident point: that the militarism and reactionary social habits identified with the German past, and preeminently embodied in Prussian history and culture, had caused most of the suffering of twentieth-century Europe.

Zitelmann has stood this assumption on its head by presenting Hitler and his government as a radically antitraditional leap into the future.[2] In more than one way, the Nazi state threw up a bridge between, on the one side, the Second Empire and the Weimar Republic and, on the other, the present German state and society. Zitelmann makes a cogent case that Hitler considered himself a revolutionary. The Nazis were not trying to recover the German past but wished to forge ahead into what they believed was a modern, scientifically organized national community. Therefore, when Hitler proclaimed his determination to make "revolutionary" changes, he was stating the truth.[3]

Contrary to the judgments of such German public intellectuals as Ralf Dahrendorf, Dolf Sternberger, and Jürgen Habermas, all of whom reject Hitler's claims to have been a true modernizer, Zitelmann depicts the Nazis as fundamentally and radically antitraditional. It was not the lingering ghost of the German past but the nature of Nazi modernization that generated catastrophic results as well as solid social achievements. Zitelmann takes on Anglophile sociologist Dahrendorf, who in *Gesellschaft und Demokratie in Deutschland* (1965) insists that any modernization under the Third Reich was "unintended."[4] What Nazism aimed at, according to Dahrendorf, was "the restoration of the traditions and the values of the German past." Zitelmann interprets such statements as "a form of moralizing for the masses," which has no "scientific value." He looks at a speech that Hitler delivered on February 1, 1933, which Dahrendorf characterizes as a "profession of tradition," that ends with the following words: "The national government will shield Christianity as the basis of our collective morality, and the family as the nucleus of our national and political structure."[5] Zitelmann notes that, even according to Dahrendorf, Hitler ignored his own call to protect traditional institutions. He made this particular promise soon after he assumed the chancellorship for the purpose of reconciling unfriendly conservative and Catholic voting blocs. Against this "profession of tradition," Zitelmann quotes from the invectives against Christian superstition that Hitler delivered before his colleagues and military commanders between 1941 and 1945.[6]

He likewise cites a leading German social historian of the antinational Left, Hans-Ulrich Wehler, who offers this insight: "In many theories of modernization, the United States following the Second World War was at least implicitly a realized utopia. Just as in the Victorian age when the economic and political leadership of England shaped evolutionary theory and the social Darwinism that came out of it, so modernization theories came to reflect the self-satisfaction and world economic and political dominance of America after 1945. The theoretically and empirically damaging effects of this conception have gone so far that supposedly neutral categories about social and economic change have been turned into evolutionary universals."[7]

The American model, particularly in an idealized form, has only limited usability for understanding modernization in general. And to whatever extent this real or imagined model has been made normative, it has been applied in Zitelmann's country mostly to create an immaculately antifascist political culture. Zitelmann observes that there is no reason to believe that modernization leads to increased political freedom, nor does he think that we can predict the outcome of this process of change while it is still unfolding. As an investigator of modernization in his own country, Zitelmann focuses less on the transformative blessing of twentieth-century Americanization than on the material metamorphosis of Germany during the early years of Nazi rule. Whether we are looking at increased salaries for the German working class, the relative openness of the workforce for women, heightened emphasis on equality of opportunity, the creation of public works projects leading to increased jobs, and a state policy aiming explicitly at full employment and entailing paid vacations, the Third Reich may have been the most modernizing German government of all time. Hitler tried to replace aristocratic army officers and upper middle-class bureaucrats with state servants from more modest circumstances. Of course, the beneficiaries of this reform would be made entirely dependent on both the *Führer* and the Nazi Party; this may help explain why Hitler reached down socially for state servants and military commanders.

Zitelmann points out repeatedly that Hitler despised the old ruling class because of his "self-understanding as a revolutionary" and his longtime position as a social outsider. Indeed, Hitler was even conflicted about the upheaval in November 1918 that overthrew the monarchy, an event he could never bring himself to condemn unreservedly. He praised the socialists who assisted in this process and went on paying and even increasing their pensions after he came to power. Even when he criticized this lurch to the far Left, Hitler distanced himself from those conservatives and monarchists on the Right who rejected the revolution categorically. It was not "the content of the revolution but the defenselessness in which it left his country" that Hitler lamented. In contrast to the French Revolution and the French overthrow of the Empire in 1871, the German revolutionaries did nothing "to save the honor of their nation." Zitelmann quotes Hitler on the failure of the German Socialists to go far enough in sweeping away the imperial government and its governing class while mobilizing their countrymen to withstand a foreign enemy.[8]

This raises doubts about the *"volkspädagogische"* interpretation of modern German history promoted by, among others, Fritz Stern in the United States and most German academic historians specializing in their country's past. In Zitelmann's revisionist view, the Nazi period was not an extension of the cumulative German past but broke quite consciously from what had preceded it. In its modernizing tendencies, the Nazi regime may have resembled the federal republic more closely than it did the German Second Empire or even the Weimar Republic.

A frequent collaborator of Zitelmann, Jürgen M. Falter, has worked to discredit the conventional judgment that Nazi electoral support came preponderantly from the middle class. Falter shows that erosions took place in the Socialist Party bloc in key German elections in the early 1930s and that much of the nonworking-class Socialist Party base (presumably minus the Jewish vote) migrated to the Nazis. The electoral base of the Catholic Center Party and the monarchist National German People's Party held remarkably firm throughout the Depression while the predominantly Protestant middle class, particularly state and private employees, gave evidence of volatility more than adhesion to the Nazis.[9]

Looking at the populous German province of Hesse, which is often cited as paradigmatic for middle-class Nazi support, Falter supplies a more varied picture of political behavior in key elections there than one might infer from reading other social historians. Nazi support throughout Germany suggests that the party was genuinely populist, reaching across class lines. Nazis appealed strongly to revolutionary sentiments by playing on progressive anti-Catholic sentiments in Protestant regions, promising broad economic change, and setting themselves apart from traditionalist forces.

Although the party included anti-Semitic positions, these were not as conspicuous in Nazi electoral propaganda as is often believed. If the German electorate was pursuing a *Sonderweg*, that should have favored Prussian monarchists and Bavarian Catholics rather than Nazi revolutionaries. Note that the conventional views offered about the continuities of German history stress the persistence of German hostility to liberal and democratic ideas, an attitude that is said to have caused German voters to cling to an antidemocratic past. According to Zitelmann, however, the Nazis were as much revolutionary modernists as those who were sent to Germany after the Second World War to reeducate its defeated population. When it comes to defining where Hitler stood on the political spectrum, Zitelmann underlines the difficulty of placing Hitler on the Right or on the Left. Hitler conceived of himself, or so his statements reveal, as a pure revolutionary.[10]

Zitelmann is particularly in his wheelhouse in his massive revised dissertation *Hitler: Selbstverständnis eines Revolutionärs*, providing evidence of Hitler's evolution as a modernizing despiser of tradition. He emphasizes the selectivity of attempts to portray Hitler as someone yearning to return to a mythic or neo-medieval past. Contrary to the image of the Nazi leader as someone who was working to restore an agrarian national community, Hitler emerges in Zitelmann's treatment as a furious industrializer. Although plans for a primitive Aryan *Gemeinschaft* haunted such Nazi functionaries as Heinrich Himmler and Alfred Rosenberg, this orientation affected Hitler minimally. Even in his ferocious anti-Semitism, Hitler tried to justify himself by appealing to "science" that would substantiate his revulsion for Jews and Slavs. Zitelmann also presents Hitler's *Lebensraum* policy in the East, which was aimed at displacing Slavic populations and replacing them with German settlers, as a (for Hitler) reasonable attempt to create self-sufficiency for his people.[11] Again and again Hitler presented himself as a scientifically armed visionary preparing for the German future. Like Stalin, he invoked science and his view of himself as being on the cutting edge of change to defend his inhuman actions.

If Zitelmann faults conventional leftist historians for trying to present Hitler as a predictable extension of the German past, he is equally critical of Nolte for portraying Hitler and the Nazis as Teutonic counterparts of generic fascists. Although Zitelmann seconds Nolte on the need to treat the Nazi period as a comprehensible (*verstehbar*) part of modern history, he disagrees with Nolte's reading of Nazism in fundamental ways. This impassioned disagreement, on Zitelmann's part, has gone largely unnoticed among establishment German historians, who consider all revisionists to be unjustifiably indulgent toward the German past. Such historians take offense when Nolte and Zitelmann insist that German scholars should stop harping on the unique wickedness of their country and its collective past. Despite their shared outcast status, however, Zitelmann and Nolte part ways in the revisionist pictures they offer their readers.

In an essay for the anthology *Die Schatten der Vergangenheit*, Zitelmann targets what he believes are Nolte's oversights. He quotes Paul Joseph Goebbels, Hitler, and other Nazi dignitaries who illustrate their movement's radical revolutionary side. As a German revolutionary, Hitler mocked the "internationalist" aspect of Soviet communism but expressed admiration for Stalin's leadership and, well into the Third Reich, stated his preference for communism over bourgeois liberalism. Characteristic of these quotations is deep repugnance for the German bourgeoisie combined with a lack of sympathy for traditional German elites.

One could find no stronger statements of such sentiments anywhere, including among German communists, than in those tirades against bourgeois ethics that Nazi leaders confided to their diaries or expressed in confidential talks. Although Hitler temporized on his way up with the classes he hated, it is untrue that he was only pretending to be socially radical. Hitler and Goebbels were anti-Christian totalitarian modernizers. Zitelmann seems especially impatient with Nolte's comparisons of the Nazis to the reactionary Right.[12] Hitler and his accomplices were more reckless and far more destructive than any reactionary class because they were in no way inhibited by traditional loyalties. They were able to gain a mass following by considerably improving the material condition of Germans and furnishing them with a hopeful vision of the future.

The American historian Ronald Smelser provides a complementary portrait of Hitler's leader of the German Labor Front (*Deutsche Arbeitsfront*), Robert Ley (1890–1945). In this revisionist telling, Ley was more of a radical and modernizer than historians have conventionally assumed. According to

Richard J. Evans and Ian Kershaw, Ley was a typical tool of the Nazi regime who helped destroy independent labor unions and brought German workers entirely under the grip of the Nazi state. When Hitler suppressed an independent labor force in January 1934 by enacting the Work Order Act, which put labor relations in the hands of government-appointed trustees (*Treuhänder der Arbeit*), Ley went along and continued to promote Hitler's interests among German workers until the end of the war.

Distaste for Ley, which has been expressed by most historians who have written about him, is certainly understandable. He was a raving anti-Semite who rose to prominence as a Nazi bullyboy in his native Ruhr region; his fondness for brawling may have been partly ascribable to brain injuries that he suffered in the First World War. He also employed slave labor in German industry, a charge that the Allies planned to use against him when they decided to try him at Nuremberg. Ley saved his captors the trouble of a trial by taking his own life.

Smelser argues that, although personally unpalatable, Ley remained a committed social reformer throughout his adult years. The National Socialist Industrial Cell Organization (*Nationalsozialistische Betriebszellenorganisation*) that he headed was an attempt to create a Nazi trade union movement that would lure workers away from the socialist-affiliated *Allgemeiner Deutscher Gewerkschaftsbund*.[13] But this did not prevent the Nazi counter-organization under Ley's leadership from pushing workers' demands for higher pay and other benefits as vigorously as its onetime rivals in the Socialist Party. What renders Smelser's conclusions especially compelling is that he almost backs into them. Smelser never misses an opportunity to make his subject look sinister and praises almost ritualistically the American ideal of democratic pluralism. He also happily avails himself of the term "brown revolution," which is meant to suggest that the Nazis were profoundly reactionary but played at being revolutionaries to gull the German workers.

Given these disarming remarks, it is all the more remarkable that Smelser offers conclusions that coincide with Zitelmann's revisionist perspective. Ley as director of the German workers' front "pushed Germany forward into a more modern society," and he did this by frantically working to provide workers with insurance, lessening pay disparities between men and women, offering periodic vacations to the laboring class, and making automobiles affordable for working families. These goals were in no way shelved after the disbanding of socialist unions in May 1933 or even after the introduction of the Work Order Act during the following January.[14]

Reforms continued and were even accelerated afterward not only to "curry favor with the workers, but also to heighten their productivity." Further:

The Labor Front mounted a major, substantial psychological and cultural campaign to raise the self-image of the worker, to underscore the value of work, whether manual or otherwise, and to blur the traditional distinction between blue collar and white collar, between working class and middle class. Again, the purpose was social integration intended to gain support and legitimacy for the regime, and the strategy did result in tightening the connection between the government and the working class. The DAF also tried, in particular through its vocational education programs, to create for German workers a climate of upward mobility, the sense that in the Third Reich a worker could become middle class if he worked his training level, worked harder, and became more efficient.[15]

Another significant long-range aspect of this Nazi program for social modernization, which would extend into the federal republic—along with the *Volkswagen, Autobahnen*, a national holiday on May Day, social insurance, and vacation packages for the *deutsche Arbeiterschaft*—was a social scientific approach to the proper deployment of labor resources. The DAF under Ley would commission and turn out books on labor-related subjects; the organization tried to goad leading academics, like the legal theorist Carl Schmitt, into writing for its series of publications.[16] Although a drunken brawler with a damaged frontal lobe, Ley seems to have been enormously energetic in pursuing his projects. It may be redundant to tell the reader, as Smelser does, that Ley "provided the carrot (or the promise of it) which invariably accompanied the stick" and that the Nazi state became more dangerous as a result of its modernization.[17] No one in his or her proper mind would identify Hitler's empire with sunshine and light. The key question is whether the Nazis effectively worked to modernize Germany. On this point the revisionists make an overwhelmingly strong case.[18]

As a graduate student at Yale in the mid-1960s, the author of this book encountered professors who took a similar position to the one just summarized but did so while offering accounts of the Nazis as the successors of Frederick the Great, Otto von Bismarck, and Kaiser Wilhelm II. Those who taught German history would occasionally anticipate Zitelmann's point but then stifle the impulse to pursue an uncongenial line of thought. They were emotionally and professionally wedded to the continuity thesis about German history and the view already embedded in cement that Hitler was a reactionary in the spirit of earlier German leaders. Zitelmann should be congratulated for having broken the mold in what remains a largely unreceptive academic and journalistic environment in the United States and Germany.

One may also doubt that those heavily documented accounts of the outbreak of World War I that have come from such independent-minded scholars as Christopher Clark and Konrad Canis will lead most academics and journalists toward a more balanced view of shared responsibility for the First World War.[19] German historians in particular seem determined to burden their country with exclusive blame for the Great War no less than for Hitler's acts of aggression. In the face of what Zitelmann criticizes as the "unscientific" manner in which his fellow citizens do history—as exercises in national atonement and Habermasian pedagogy—his attempt to challenge entrenched views, however well-documented, may face a long uphill battle.

Zitelmann should be further congratulated for arguing that totalitarianism is inherent in modernization, an idea that, had it come from the Frankfurt School, would cause no one to clear his or her throat in discomfort. Unfortunately, Zitelmann is not considered fit to notice the link between modernization and total control, which is a connection that Jewish refugees from the Nazis, like Hannah Arendt, were already exploring in the 1950s. Modernization and centralized tyranny are not incompatible tendencies, as Zitelmann reminds the reader no less persistently than Hannah Arendt, Eric Voegelin, and Zygmunt Bauman. The two often travel together.

There are, however, several points that should be introduced to indicate the limits or limited applicability of Zitelmann's arguments. The first point does not contradict Zitelmann's general thesis but simply notes what it does not apply to. Zitelmann may be right about the radical modernizing thrust of Nazism, which Nolte, no more than his antifascist critics, pays sufficient attention to. But this does not disprove that generic fascism, by which is meant primarily Latin fascism, had a different, more reactionary character than its German counterpart. Italian fascism was less modern and not really totalitarian, no matter how hyperbolically Mussolini and Gentile described their cult of the state.

Secondly, Zitelmann does not refute the contention that certain backward-looking, agrarian themes colored Nazi appeals to the German *Volk*. At most he shows that these themes influenced Hitler less decisively than is often believed. But there is evidence that such themes were present in Nazi propaganda. American historians Henry Ashby Turner and David Schoenbaum cite multiple examples of pastoral images being conjured up in Nazi speeches and electoral campaigns;[20] neither historian seems to be looking for anything but the truth in their research. Although Zitelmann may be right in his overall depiction of Hitler as a modernizer, the proof of anti-modernist tendencies in the Nazi movement and propaganda may be too blatant to be dismissed.

Zitelmann further complicates the picture by citing positions taken by Hitler that were also present among figures of the intellectual Right during the Weimar Republic. Hitler's ambivalent opinions about the overthrow of the monarchy can also be found in a profoundly reactionary figure, Oswald Spengler. In *Preussentum und Sozialismus* Spengler treats the establishment of the Republic and the subsequent creation of a *Räterepublik* by Marxist revolutionaries in Munich as a farce. Like Hitler, this glorifier of the Prussian state contrasted the gravity of national revolutions carried out by the French with the amateurish venture of German intellectuals. Spengler never viewed the Germans who ended the monarchy as the *Novemberverbrecher* (the criminals of the November Revolution), which was the judgment of traditional monarchists. Rather, he mocked the German revolutionaries as political bunglers who further weakened an already defeated country.[21]

Pace Zitelmann, Hitler's belief that "dictatorship may be the purest democracy" did not separate him from conservative thinkers of the interwar period. One encounters exactly the same view in the writings of Carl Schmitt, and particularly in Schmitt's post–World War I tract *Die Diktatur*. Such associations do not disprove the characterization of Hitler as a radical revolutionary, but they do raise questions about Zitelmann's attempts to dissociate Hitler entirely from the traditional German Right. There was, in fact, more rhetorical overlap than Zitelmann concedes.

In his underlining of Hitler's view of revolutions, Zitelmann proves, perhaps unwittingly, that there was more ambivalence at work here than any consistent line of thought. Certainly one cannot ascertain a clear direction from Hitler's reaction to an event that Zitelmann examines at length, which was Hitler's decision to back the Reichswehr in 1934 against Ernst Röhm and the SA as a threat to the German military. The ensuing executions took place, according to Zitelmann, while Hitler was still of two minds. The *Führer* was not sure that he was acting correctly, as a self-styled revolutionary, by ordering the destruction of the Nazi Left, including the socially radical SA. He later expressed strong regrets that he had not rallied to the radical revolutionaries during the Night of the Long Knives. Although Hitler demonstrably voiced such second thoughts, he did so years later, after he was already losing the war and beginning to think about where he had gone wrong.[22]

Finally, one might ask whether Nazism's totalitarian character really aided its function as a modernizing force in Germany. Zitelmann leaves unanswered the vexing question of why modernization took a far bloodier course in Germany than, say, in England or the United States. Nor does he escape the force of this question by telling us that "social welfare, a high living standard and an egalitarian development in industrialized countries corresponds well beyond the age of colonialism to under-development and impoverishment in the countries of the Third World as well as a growing inequality on a global scale."[23] Zitelmann cannot demonstrate that what he deplores should be laid at the doorstep of Western industrial countries. He seems to be blaming these countries for the sake of proving his premise—namely, that industrial modernization even outside of Germany exacted and continue to exact a disastrous global price.

Yet, is it possible to compare the price that he asserts has been exacted for this process to the murderous tyranny of Hitler's Germany or Stalin's Russia? Zitelmann seems reluctant to acknowledge that not all forms of modernization have carried the same price tags. What he characterizes as "liberal democracies," whatever their faults, have not modernized under a regime that approached the brutal tyranny that overtook Germany in 1933. Even while recognizing the totalitarian danger inherent in the modern centralized state, certain distinctions between modern regimes should be obvious. Although the totalitarian behavior of politically correct, overbearing Western elites may be deplorable, it is light-years away from the type of totalitarianism practiced by Nazi radical modernizers. Snatching people's minds and infantilizing one's population is not the same as putting them into extermination camps where the inmates are starved and slaughtered. Practicing economic policies that may or may not impact negatively on Third World peoples is not the same as invading neighboring countries and wiping out or enslaving their populations. Zitelmann must surely grasp this difference, even if he can't resist in this instance opposing the masochistic antinationalism of his fellow German intellectuals by offering counterviews that are equally over the top.

There is another point that should be made in this context—namely, that Germany in the nineteenth century was undergoing rapid industrialization, economic growth, and the rise of a large middle class; if its government had not recklessly stumbled into World War I (along with its neighbors), Germany might have continued to develop as a modern nation-state. Its government was in some ways less liberal than those that then existed in the United States and England. Nonetheless, Germany was far closer politically to its Western counterparts than it was to most other countries in the world, including the Russian Empire. Equally noteworthy was the fact that the German working class lived better and was better educated than workers in any other Western country.

There was no predetermined "course of German history" dragging the country toward the totalitarian nightmare that erupted in 1933.[24] During the Second Empire and even before, Germany was modernizing without murdering people; during the Weimar Republic, before the Depression, the country was recovering from a lost war, despite the substantial territorial losses and onerous financial conditions that had been placed on its people by the Versailles Treaty. Germans did not need Hitler or Ley to modernize their country any more than Russia needed Stalin to build factories. Even more relevant is the fact that if the Nazis did contribute to modernization, they did so while perpetrating horrendous things that were not necessary for modernization. That was not a collateral cost but a form of tyranny that took advantage of modern means to seize and hold onto power.

These observations, however, do not overshadow the accomplishment of Zitelmann and his collaborators in calling attention to certain developmental patterns that contradict conventional, and by now stereotypical, pictures of the German past. The lines of continuity between the Third Reich and postwar German societies should be at least as obvious as those running in the opposite direction. Whether looking at the totalitarian apparatus imposed by the Soviets on eastern Germany or the expansive social welfare regime set up in the Federal Republic, the earlier Nazi government left its imprint.

Even those scientific studies of society that were so near and dear to the hearts of postwar German social reformers had a clear foundation in the Third Reich. The gathering and investigation of social statistics was an academic practice that came into its own under the Third Reich; if the Nazi government stressed the practical value of this activity, so too did postwar German universities and political administrations, nor was the selective idealization of America a peculiar characteristic of "Germany's journey toward the West" under postwar democratic custodians. As Zitelmann clearly demonstrates, the Nazis praised the United States as the society of the future, revealing an affinity that went back well into the nineteenth century in Germany.[25]

Significantly, Zitelmann never hesitates to defend the *"Westbindung"* as a geopolitical necessity and stands with those German intellectuals and journalists who wish to preserve the present German relationship with the United States. But he takes this position not as a believer in American virtue or in his country's unfitness to exercise power. Zitelmann is a resigned realist who knows his country will likely never again become a world power. Providing that Germans do not live in slavish obedience to the American hegemons, they may have no better option than remaining allied to Washington.[26] In any case Zitelmann's main concern is not with foreign policy. He is engaging the dogmatic refusal of other historians to consider ideologically unwelcome facts, a tendency that has assumed overshadowing importance in his homeland. The implications of his arguments go well beyond his concept of "historical science" and his calls for a paradigm shift in the study of the Nazi period. Zitelmann is challenging the crusade against the national past that his country's government, educational institutions, and media are all engaged in pursuing.

Notes

Notes to Introduction

1. Ernst Nolte, *Der Faschismus in seiner Epoche*, 10th ed. (Munich: Piper, 2000), 35–42, 61–67, 491–95.

2. Ibid., 419–24, 505–12; Ernst Nolte, *Die Krise des liberalen Systems und die faschistischen Bewegungen* (Munich: Piper, 1968), 35–69.

3. See Nolte, *Der Faschismus in seiner Epoche*, 486–514; Nolte, *Die Krise des liberalen Systems und die faschistischen Bewegungen*, 70–126; and Ernst Nolte, *Der europäische Bürgerkrieg 1917–1945: Nationalsozialismus und Bolschewismus* (Berlin: Propyläen, 1987), 46–106. My indebtedness to Nolte as an interpreter of fascism and the European Civil War does not extend to his book of reflections, written when the historian was already in his late eighties, *Späte Reflexionen: Über den Weltbürgerkrieg des 20. Jahrhunderts* (Wien: Karolinger Verlag, 2011). Here Nolte suggests that Hitler was pursuing a defensive strategy against bolshevism and its Jewish supporters, even when this supposed act of resistance involved mass murder. Throughout his career, Nolte seems to have been more critical of the Second Empire than the Third Reich, a fact that may be attributed to the death of his young brother in military service on the Russian front. But his late-in-life aberrations and enthusiasms need not affect our judgment of Nolte's core writings on fascism and the interwar confrontation between fascists and antifascists. Contrary to Nolte's characterizations, the German Nazis were a borderline case for studying fascism and both more vicious and more single-mindedly committed to modernization than Latin fascists.

4. See Alan Wolfe, "The Revolution That Never Was," *The New Republic*, June 7, 1999, 37–38.

5. See Renzo De Felice, *Mussolini*, 4 vols. (Turin: Giulio Einaudi, 1995); Arnaud Imatz, *José Antonio: La Phalange Espagnole et le national-syndicalisme*, enlarged edition (Paris: Edition Godefrey de Bouillon, 2000); Arnaud Imatz, *José Antonio: entre odio y amor. Su historia como fue*, preface by Juan Velarde Fuertes (Barcelona: Áltera, 2006); Pío Moa, *Las origines de la Guerra civil española* (Madrid: Encuentro, 1999); Pío Moa, *El derrumbe de la Segunda República y la Guerra Civil* (Madrid: Encuentro, 2001); Stanley Payne, *Fascism in Spain, 1923–1977* (Madison: University of Wisconsin Press, 1999); and Zeev Sternhell, *La droite révolutionnaire: Les origines françaises du fascisme* (Paris: Seuil, 1978).

6. See, for example, A. James Gregor, *The Ideology of Fascism: The Rationale of Totalitarianism* (New York and London: Free Press, 1969); A. James Gregor, *The Fascist Persuasion in Radical Politics* (Princeton, NJ: Princeton University Press, 1974); Roger Griffin, *The Nature of Fascism* (New York: St. Martin's Press, 1991); and Roger Griffin, *Fascism, Totalitarianism, and Political Religion* (London: Routledge, 2005).

7. See Imatz's interview with Moa, "L'historien de la Guerre d'Espagne qui fait scandale," in *Nouvelle Revue Historique* 17 (March/April, 2005), 27–29; and Imatz's "La guerre civile démythifiée," in *La guerre d'Espagne revisitée* (Paris: Economica, 1989), 7–54.

8. This comparative view of Nazism and Stalinism is already present in Franz Borkenau's work *Totalitarianism* (London: Faber and Faber Limited, 1940).

9. Juan J. Linz, *Totalitarian and Authoritarian Regimes* (Boulder, CO: Lynne Rienner Publishers, 2000), 159–263.

10. Ibid., 24; and Norberto Bobbio, Renzo De Felice, and Gian Enrico Rusconi, *Italiani, Amici Nemici* (Milano: Donzelli, 1996), 29.

11. Typical of this genre is C. L. R. James, *State Capitalism and World Revolution* (Chicago: H. Kerr, 1950); and for the recasting of this expectation on the post-Marxist Left, see my work *The Strange Death of Marxism: The European Left in the New Millennium* (Columbia, MO: University of Missouri Press, 2005), particularly 54–118.

12. David Rising, "Germans Today See Nazi Defeat as Liberation," *The Times of Isreal*, May 7, 2015, http://www.timesofisrael.com/germans-today-see-nazi-defeat-as-liberation/.

13. See Theodor W. Adorno, et al., *The Authoritarian Personality* (New York: Harper, 1950); and Christopher Lasch's comments in *The True and Only Heaven: Progress and Its Critics* (New York: Norton, 1991), 456–63.

14. See Hannah Arendt, *The Origins of Totalitarianism* (New York: Harcourt Brace Jovanovich, 1973), 256–57.

15. See John P. Diggins, *Mussolini and Fascism: The View from America* (Princeton, NJ: Princeton University Press, 1972); and Wolfgang Schivelbusch, *Entfernte Verwandtschaft: Faschismus, Nationalsozialismus, New Deal 1933–1939* (München: Carl Hanser Verlag, 2005).

16. See Justin Raimondo, *Reclaiming the Right: The Lost Legacy of the Conservative Movement*, expanded edition (Wilmington, Delaware: ISI Books, 1998); John T. Flynn, *Forgotten Lessons: Selected Essays of John T. Flynn*, edited by Gregory P. Pavlik (Irvington-on-Hudson, NY: Foundation for Economic Education, 1995); and John T. Flynn, *The Roosevelt Myth: 50th Anniversary Edition*, edited by Ralph Raico (San Francisco: Fox & Wilkes, 1998), especially 138–41, 188–91.

17. See Jonah Goldberg, *Liberal Fascism: The Secret History of the American Left, from Mussolini to the Politics of Meaning* (New York: Doubleday, 2007). For a critical dissection of Goldberg's work, see *The American Conservative* (July 2010), http://theamericanconservative.com/article/2010/jul/01/00035/.

18. François Furet, Ernst Nolte, and Marc de Launay, *Fascisme et communisme* (Paris: Plon, 1998), 33–41, 129–41.

19. Augusto Del Noce expands on his view of fascism as a progress-oriented, modernist movement in his posthumously published biography, *Giovanni Gentile: Per una interpretazione filosofica della storia contemporanea* (Bologna: Il Mulino, 1990).

20. Nolte, *Der Faschismus in seiner Epoche*, 515–58.

21. See Furet, et al., *Fascisme et communisme*, 61–67.

22. *Courrier International*, December 14–31, 2014, 12.

23. Ibid.

Notes to Chapter One

1. Nolte, *Der Faschismus in seiner Epoche*, 42–60, 515–20; Nolte, *Die Krise des liberalen Systems und die faschistischen Bewegungen*, 33–69, indicates how far on the antinational, pro-Marxist Left Nolte stood in the 1960s.

2. See Nolte, *Die Krise des liberalen Systems und die faschistischen Bewegungen*, 134–199.

3. Nolte, *Der Faschismus in seiner Epoche*, 515–48.

4. Furet, et al., *Fascisme et communisme*, 83–84.

5. Ibid. See also the interview with Furet in *Ideazione* 3, no. 4 (Summer 1996), 19–28.

6. In a study of the Romanian Iron Guard, Mircea underscores his subjects' preoccupation at Montreux with an international Jewish threat. See "The Iron Guard and the 'Modern State,'" *Journal of Comparative Fascist Studies* 1 (2012), 65–90.

7. See Renzo De Felice, *Storia degli Ebrei sotto il fascismo* (Turin: Einaudi, 2005); Alastair Hamilton, *The Appeal of Fascism: A Study of Intellectuals and Fascism, 1919–1944* (New York: MacMillan, 1971); the thematic issue on fascism edited by Frank H. Adler in the journal *Telos*, 133 (Winter 2005); and Ernst Nolte, *Der Faschismus: Von Mussolini zu Hitler* (Schnellroda: Antaios, 2003).

8. See John Lukacs, *The Last European War: September 1939–December 1941* (Garden City, NY: Anchor Books, 1976); and Nolte, *Der europäische Bürgerkrieg*, 46–105.

9. The template for Nolte's linkage of the three "fascist" movements is already present in Walter Frank's *Nationalismus und Demokratie im Frankreich der dritten Republik (1871 bis 1918)*, (Hamburg: Hanseatische Verlag, 1933). Frank's work celebrates the newly installed Nazi regime as having its origins in the French nationalist Right during the Third Republic. Curiously, the French Right that Ernst Jünger and other conservative German revolutionaries of the interwar years profoundly admired was ferociously anti-German and sought to avenge the Franco-Prussian War. The scholarship of Zeev Sternhell, published since 1972, buttresses with further evidence the fascist line of descent coming out of late nineteenth-century France.

10. Gregor, *The Ideology of Fascism*, 14–15.

11. Ibid., 365–74.

12. Stanley G. Payne: *Fascism, Comparison and Definition* (Madison: University of Wisconsin Press, 1980), 3–41.

13. For the relevant works of Zeev Sternhell on French fascism, see *Maurice Barrès et le nationalisme français* (Paris: Fayard, 2000); *La Droite révolutionnaire*; *Ni droite ni gauche: L'idéologie fasciste en France* (Paris: Seuil, 1983); and "Sur le fascisme et sa variante française," *Le Débat* (November 1984).

14. Payne, *Fascism, Comparison and Definition*, 211.

15. See Nolte, *Der Faschismus: Von Mussolini zu Hitler*, 367.

16. Ibid., 368.

17. Ibid., 369. A parallel argument about the powerlessness of the Right in contemporary Germany can be found in my book *The Strange Death of Marxism*, 96–118.

18. Nolte, *Der Faschismus: Von Mussolini zu Hitler*, 369–70.

19. Gregor, *The Ideology of Fascism*, 365.

20. Ibid., 365; and A. James Gregor, *Italian Fascism and Development Dictatorship* (Princeton, NJ: Princeton University Press, 1979).

21. Gregor, *The Ideology of Fascism*, 375.

22. Ibid., 375. For a related argument, although one not as densely documented, see Luciano Pellicani, "Fascism, Capitalism, Modernity," in *European Journal of Political Theory* 11, no. 4 (October 2012), 394–409.

23. See Jeffrey Herf, *Reactionary Modernism: Technology, Culture, and Politics in Weimar and the Third Reich* (Cambridge, UK: Cambridge University Press, 1986); and Roger Eatwell, *Fascism: A History* (New York: Allen Lane, 1996).

24. See Rainer Zitelmann, *Adolf Hitler: Eine politische Biographie* (Göttingen: Muster-Schmidt, 1989) and *Hitler: The Policies of Seduction* (London: Allison & Busby, 2000). Also informative in this regard is the thoughtful essay by Karlheinz Weissmann "Nationalsozialismus und Moderne," in *Alles was rechts ist* (Graz und Stuttgart: Leopold Stocker Verlag, 2000), 225–41.

25. Daniel Guérin, *Fascism and Big Business*, 2nd edition (Atlanta: Pathfinder Press, 1994); Franz L. Neumann, *Behemoth: The Structure and Practice of National Socialism, 1933-1944* (New York: Oxford University Press, 1944); and Rolf Wiggershaus, *Die Frankfurter Schule: Geschichte, theoretische Entwicklung, politische Bedeutung*, 6th ed. (München: Beck'sche Verlagsbuchhandlung, 2001), 311-32.

26. Renzo De Felice, *Mussolini il fascista* (Turin: Einaudi, 1968), 386-89; for a study of Gentile's attempts to minimize the role of the Church as an Italian national "spiritual center" even after 1929, see V. Pirro, "Stato e Chiesa in Giovanni Gentile," in *Nuovi studi politici* 2 (April/June 1996), 27-40. Gentile's reservation about conceding to the Church's ethical and philosophical authority in education can be read even in his apparent defense of the Lateran Pact, "La Conciliazione," in *Origini e dottrina del fascismo*, 11th ed. (Rome: Quaderni dell'Istituto Nazionale Fascista di Cultura, 1934).

27. See Alexander Stille, *Benevolence and Betrayal: Five Italian Families under Fascism* (New York: Picador, 2003), 22.

28. On James Burnham's incorporation of Trotsky's view of Soviet Russia into his theory of managerialism, see *The Managerial Revolution: What is Happening in the World* (reprint, Westport, CT: Greenwood Press, 1972), particularly ii-vii; and Samuel T. Francis's monograph, *Power and History: The Political Thought of James Burnham* (Lanham, MD: University Press of America, 1984). See also Rudolf Hilferding's "Das historische Problem," *Archiv für Politik* (1953), 295-324; and for Nolte's obvious sympathy for Marx and his "humanistic lodestar," see *Der Faschismus in seiner Epoche*, 521-28.

29. See my treatment of Hilferding's evolution from a Marxist theorist into a critic of the managerial state in *Multiculturalism and the Politics of Guilt: Toward a Secular Theocracy* (Columbia, MO: University of Missouri Press, 2002), 86-88.

30. In a special supplement to the *New York Review of Books*, November 18, 1971, "Chile: Year One," communist historian Eric Hobsbawm asks the American Left to back the Salvador Allende-regime in Chile, which, in contrast to other recent socialist experiments, is not judged to be a form of "political exotica." The same phrase surfaced in a conversation that I held with Hobsbawm that is reported in my book *Encounters: My Life with Nixon, Marcuse, and Other Friends and Teachers* (Wilmington, DE: ISI Books, 2009), 184-85.

31. Gregor, *The Ideology of Fascism*, 8-10.

32. Ibid., 26-29; and the text of *Carta del Lavoro* is provided in the appendix to De Felice's *Mussolini il fascista*, 533.

33. Ibid., 533-34.

34. See the portrait of the fascist Left in Danilo Breschi, *Spirito del novecento: Il secolo di Ugo Spirito dal fascismo alla contestazione* (Soveria Manelli: Rubbettino, 2010), 40-83.

35. Ibid., 39-41; Giordano Bruno Guerri, *Giuseppe Bottai, fascista* (Milano: Mondadori, 1996).

36. Indicative of Spirito's desire to replace "private self-affirmation" with awareness of the corporate good embodied by the state are his essays "Economia programmatica," in *Nuovi studi*, nos. 3-5 (June-October 1932), and "L'iniziativa individuale," in *Critica Fascista* 10, no. 24 (December 15, 1932).

37. Robert Sidelsky's *Oswald Mosley* (New York: Holt, Rinehart and Winston, 1975) is the most comprehensive and balanced study of a controversial English political figure.

38. Two informative studies of Father Charles Coughlin and his anticapitalist economic views are Charles J. Tull, *Father Coughlin and the New Deal* (Syracuse: University

of Syracuse Press, 1965); and Marc Dollinger, *Quest for Inclusion: Jews and Liberalism in Modern America* (Princeton, NJ: Princeton University Press, 2000).

39. The fullest biography of Ledesma Ramos is by José Maria Sánchez Diana, *Ramiro Ledesma Ramos* (Madrid: Editora Nacional, 1975).

40. See, among other relevant sources, Raoul Girardet, "Notes sur l'esprit d'un fascisme français 1934–1939," *Revue française de science politique* 5 (1955), 529–46; Robert Soucy, "The Nature of Fascism in France," *Journal of Contemporary History* (April 1966), 27–55; and Robert Soucy, "French Fascist Intellectuals in the 1930s: An Old New Left?," *French Historical Studies* 8, no. 3 (Spring 1974), 445–58.

41. See Erik von Stein Hansen, *Hendrik de Man and the Crisis in European Socialism, 1926–1936* (Ithaca: Cornell University Press, 1968).

42. This is quoted in Breschi's *Spirito del novecento*, 69.

43. See W. Brian Newsome, *French Urban Planning, 1940–1968: The Construction and Deconstruction of an Authoritarian System* (New York: Peter Lang, 2009); Richard Griffiths, "Fascism and the Planned Economy: 'Neosocialism' and 'Planisme' in France and Belgium in the 1930s," *Science and Society* 69, no. 4 (2005), 580–93.

44. See Diggins, *Mussolini and Fascism*; and Schivelbusch, *Entfernte Verwandtschaft*.

45. Quoted in De Felice, *Mussolini il fascista*, 364; on the fate of Italian socialist exiles who tried to arouse antifascist awareness by attacking Mussolini for his invasion of Ethiopia, see Laura Pisano's essay "La cultura degli esuli italiani di fronte alla espansione coloniale del fascismo (1935–1939)," in *Fascismo ed Esilio: Aspetti della diaspora intellettuale di Germania, Spagna e Italia*, editor Maria Sechi (Pisa: Giardini Editori, 1988), 13–38.

46. Schivelbusch, *Entfernte Verwandtschaft*, 34–36.

47. Guido Valabrega, *Ebrei, fascismo, sionismo* (Urbino: Argalía, 1974); for Mussolini's more general view of Italian interests in the East, see Renzo De Felice, *Il fascismo e l'Oriente: arabi, ebrei, indiani nella politica di Mussolini* (Bologna: Mulino, 1988).

48. Ernst Hanisch in *Der lange Schatten des Staates: Österreichische Geschichte, 1890–1990*, series editor Herwig Wolfram (Wien: Ueberreuter, 1994), painstakingly distinguishes *"Austrofaschismus"* from other more violent forms of fascism. Dollfuss's regime was "authoritarian" but, unlike fascist Italy, did not exhibit any expansionist aspirations.

49. On the overthrow of the Horthy regime and the Arrow Cross's advent to power, see Thomas Sakmyster, *Hungary's Admiral on Horseback: Miklós Horthy, 1918–1944* (New York: Columbia University Press, 1994); and Istvan Deak's essay in *The European Right: An Historical Profile*, eds. Hans Rogers and Eugen Weber (Berkeley and Los Angeles: University of California Press, 1965), 364–405; and Eugen Weber, *Varieties of Fascism: Doctrines of Revolution in the Twentieth Century* (Princeton: Van Nostrand, 1964).

50. See Paul M. Hayes, *Quisling: The Career and Political Ideas of Vidkun Quisling*. (London: Newton Abbot, 1971); and O. K. Hoidal, "Vidkun Quisling's Decline as a Political Figure in Prewar Norway, 1933–1937," *The Journal of Modern History* 43, no. 3 (September 1971), 440–67.

51. See Payne, *Fascism, Comparison and Definition*, 136.

52. See Jean Stenger's essay on Belgium and the Rexistes in *The European Right*, 128–67; Jean-Michel Etienne's detailed treatment of the sectarian character of this Walloon phenomenon in *Le mouvement rexiste jusqu'en 1940* (Paris: A. Colin, 1968); and Carl Strikwerda, "Corporatism and the Lower Middle Classes: Interwar Belgium," in *Splintered Class: Politics and the Lower Middle Class in Interwar Europe*, ed. Rudy Koshar (New York and London: Holmes & Meier, 1990), 210–39.

53. Payne, *Fascism, Comparison and Definition*, 137. Particularly informative recent books on Vichy are Bernard Bruneteau, *L'Europe nouvelle d'Hitler* (Paris: Edition du Rocher, 2003) and Robert O. Paxton, *Vichy France: Old Guard and New Order* (New York: Columbia University Press, 2001). See also John F. Sweets's provocative article "Hold that Pendulum! Redefining Fascism, Collaborationism and Resistance in France," *French Historical Studies* 15 (Fall 1988), 731–58; and Sarah E. Shurts, "Redefining the Engagé: Intellectual Identity in Fin de Siècle France," *Historical Reflections* 38, no. 3 (Winter 2012), 24–40.

54. See Stanley G. Payne, *The Spanish Civil War* (New York: Cambridge University Press, 2012), 111–30; and Stanley G. Payne, *The Franco Regime: 1936–1975* (Madison: University of Wisconsin Press, 1987).

55. See Stanley G. Payne, *Falange: A History of Spanish Fascism* (Stanford, CA: Stanford University Press, 1961); Payne's essay on the Falange in *The European Right*, 168–207; and the concluding chapter of Imatz, *José Antonio: La Phalange Espagnole*, 450–598.

56. See Mihai Fatu and Ion Spalatelu, *Garda de Fier, organizatie terrorista de tip fascist* (Bucharest: Editura Politica, 1971); Armin Heinen, *Die Legion Erzengel Michael in Rumänien: Soziale Bewegung und politische Organisation* (Munich: Oldenbourg Verlag, 1986); Leon Volovici, *Nationalist Ideology and Antisemitism: The Case of Romanian Intellectuals in the 1930s* (Oxford UK: Pergamon Press, 1991); and Eugen Weber, *The European Right*, 501–74. In a well-researched essay, Weber presents the established view of the Guard as arising out of a Romanian rural culture and embodying the vision of an idealized past. The young Romanian scholar Mircea Platon is challenging this view, in a forthcoming monograph in which Platon locates the Guard's strength and vision in the rising urban elites of interwar Romania.

57. See Armin Heinen, *Rumänien, der Holocaust, und die Logik der Gewalt* (Munich: Oldenbourg, 2007).

58. "Fascist Ideology In France," *UKEssays.com*, http://www.ukessays.com/essays/history/fascist-ideology-in-france-history-essay.php.

59. See Etienne, *Le movement rexiste jusqu'en 1940*, 175–93; and *The European Right*, 160–67.

60. Payne, *Fascism, Comparison and Definition*, 191.

61. In a work published during the Salò Republic, *I profeti del Risorgimento italiano* (Florence: Sansoni, 1944), Giovanni Gentile traces the fascist movement back to its radical democratic antecedents in the nineteenth century. See also Emilio Gentile's *Il mito dello stato nuovo* (Roma-Bari: Laterza, 1999), 3–7, for a discussion of the invocation of nineteenth-century radical democrats among apologists of the fascist "national revolution"; and Danilo Breschi's entry "Fascismo" in *Dizionario del Liberalismo* (Soveria Manelli: Rubbettino, 2011), 440–48. Breschi is particularly informative when writing about Gentile's adoration of Mazzini, as seen in his lecture given at Florence in 1925, "Che cosa è il fascismo?" See also by the same author, "Fascism, Liberalism and Revolution," *European Journal of Political Theory* 11, no. 4 (October 2012), 410–25. Here Breschi stresses the failure of Italian liberalism in halting the fascist ascent to power. According to Breschi, some liberals were "self-deluded" and naïvely accepted the view that the fascists were authentic children of the *Risorgimento*; others, like longtime premier Giovanni Giolitti, grossly underestimated fascism's revolutionary energies.

62. See, for example, the attacks by Erik von Kuehnelt-Leddihn on both "ochlocracy" and the totalitarian implications of democracy in *Leftism Revisited: From De Sade and Marx*

to *Hitler and Pol Pot* (Washington, DC: Regnery, 1991); and *The Menace of the Herd* (Milwaukee: Bruce Publishing, 1943). On my conversations and correspondence with this thoughtful, imposing nobleman, who published in numerous languages well into his nineties, see my *Encounters*, 97–98, 115–122.

63. See Lee Congdon's insightful biography *George Kennan: A Writing Life* (Wilmington: ISI Books, 2008), 24–27. Unlike other interpreters of Kennan, Congdon stresses the nineteenth-century conservative prism through which his subject viewed the international scene. He cites the favorable references in Kennan's writings to Salazar and Helmuth von Moltke and treats these far from incidental statements as expressing Kennan's world view.

64. Helmut Rumpler, *Österreichische Geschichte 1804–1914: Eine Chance für Mitteleuropa* (Wien: Ueberreuter, 1997), 488–89, 502, 508.

65. Ibid., 490; and Andrew Whiteside's essay on Austria in *The European Right*, 309–12.

66. Among the many works dealing with the beginnings of Catholic corporatism are Heinz Herberg's *Eine wirtschafts-soziologische Ideengeschichte der neueren katholischen Soziallehren in Deutschland* (Duisburg: A. Behrens, 1933); August M. Knoll, *Der soziale Gedanke im modernen Katholizismus: Von der Romantik bis Rerum Novarum* (Wien: Reinhold, 1932); and Hans Reichel, *Die Sozietätsphilosophie Franz von Baaders: Seine Lehren über Geschichte und Gesellschaft, Staat, und Kirche* (Tübingen: Laupp, 1901).

67. Carl Schmitt, *Verfassungslehre*, 8th edition (Berlin: Duncker & Humblot, 2010), 5–6.

68. Ibid., 252–56, 265–71.

69. This train of events is presented in detail, mostly from the standpoint of the artificially revived Italian fascist regime in Renzo De Felice's *Mussolini l'alleato*, vol. 2 (Milan: Einaudi, 2008). On Giovanni Gentile's efforts to inspire the Italian army and Italian civilian population during the Salò Republic, see Benedetto Gentile, *Giovanni Gentile: Dal discorso agli italiani alla morte, 24 giugno 1943–15 aprile 1944* (Firenze: Sansoni, 1954).

70. See Sebastian Haffner, *Defying Hitler: A Memoir*, trans. Oliver Pretzel (New York: Picador, 2003); and the testimonies of two persecuted National Bolshevik leaders, Karl Otto Paetel, *Nationalbolschewismus und nationalrevolutionäre Bewegungen* (Germany: Siegfried Bublies Verlag, 1959); and Ernst Niekisch, *Widerstand* (Sinus Verlag, 1982). It may indicate the extent of the triumph of antifascism over older leftist ideologies that the works of Paetel and Niekisch are now only available from what Wikipedia describes as "far right-wing" publishers. Although the National Bolsheviks were strongly pro-Soviet, and although Niekisch supported the East German communist regime, certain militants, because of their fervent German patriotism, may have fallen into disrepute.

71. Franklin H. Adler, *Italian Industrialists from Liberalism to Fascism: The Political Development of the Industrial Bourgeoisie, 1906–1934* (New York: Cambridge University Press, 2002); De Felice, *Mussolini il fascista*, 223–43, 268–79. De Felice considers the *Carta del Lavoro* that were partly an attempt to settle Italian labor-management disputes to have been a "naïve, schematic" design intended to paper over class resentments; Ibid., 278–79. The regime obviously desired *"una conciliazione delle classi contrapposte."* On this policy and Gregor's view of the economics of fascism, see my review of Gregor's *The Faces of Janus: Marxism and Fascism in the Twentieth Century* (New Haven, CT: Yale University Press, 2000) in *American Outlook* (March/April, 2001), 58–60.

72. Two English-language works on the ultimate survivor, Hjalmar Schacht, are Edward Norman Peterson, *Hjalmar Schacht: For and Against Hitler* (Boston: Christopher Publishing House, 1954); and the partly autobiographical *Hjalmar Schacht: Confessions of the "Old Wizard"* (Boston: Houghton Mifflin, 1956). Although Schacht did aspire to become Hitler's eco-

nomic advisor in 1933, there was no common ground between his beliefs and Nazi ideology or any form of fascist corporatism. A cofounder of the disproportionately Jewish German Democratic Party after World War I, with the middle names "Horace Greeley" bestowed on him by his pro-American parents, Schacht was hardly the kind of person whom Hitler would have picked to oversee the German economy because of ideological compatibility.

73. See Robert O. Paxton, "The Five Stages of Fascism," *The Journal of Modern History* 70, no. 1 (1998), 1–23.

Notes to Chapter Two

1. Renzo De Felice, *Interpretations of Fascism*, trans. Brenda Huff Everett (Cambridge, MA: Harvard University Press, 1977), 3–99.

2. Ibid., 175–92.

3. Arendt, *The Origins of Totalitarianism*; and Hans Buchheim, *Totalitäre Herrschaft: Wesen und Merkmale* (Munich: Kosel Verlag, 1962).

4. Arendt, *The Origins of Totalitarianism*, 372.

5. These characteristics are specifically enumerated as section heads in Carl J. Friedrich and Zbigniew Brzezinski, *Totalitarian Dictatorship and Autocracy*, 2nd ed., revised by C. J. Friedrich (Cambridge: Harvard University Press, 1965).

6. See Herman Finer's *Mussolini's Italy* (New York: H. Holt, 1935); Augusto del Noce, *Il problema ideologico nella politica dei cattolici italiani* (Turin: Bottega d'Erasmo, 1964), and *Il problema dell'ateismo* (Bologna: Il Mulino, 1990).

7. *Encyclopaedia of the Social Sciences*, ed. Edwin R. A. Seligman (New York: MacMillan, 1931) 5:137; and Erwin von Beckerath, *Wesen und Werden des faschistischen Staates* (Berlin: J. Springer, 1927).

8. Ibid., 138; and Giovanni Gentile, *Il fascismo al governa della scuola* (Bologna: Il Mulino, 1990).

9. See Emilio Gentile, *God's Democracy: American Religion after September 11* (Westport, CT: Praeger, 2008). In *The War for Righteousness: Progressive Christianity, the Great War, and the Rise of the Messianic Nation* (Wilmington, DE: ISI Books, 2003), Richard Gamble traces the blending of Protestant millenarian ideas with the concept of American exceptionalism as far back as the urgent calls for American intervention in World War I. Gentile's scorn for recent appeals to this "American religion" may be driven by hostility toward George W. Bush and his Republican administration or else to short historical memories. Both American national parties have resorted to the same messianic rhetoric in formulating America's global mission; each has taken the lead in upholding the American creed at different times. See also Walter A. McDougall, *Promised Land, Crusader State: The American Encounter with the World since 1776* (Boston and New York: Houghton Mifflin, 1997). On the parallel developments in the two American parties, see Jeff Taylor's critical study *Politics on a Human Scale: The American Tradition of Decentralism* (Lanham, MD, Lexington Books, 2013).

10. See Grant N. Havers, *Lincoln and the Politics of Christian Love* (Columbia, MO: University of Missouri Press, 2009), 25.

11. Michael Burleigh, *Earthly Powers: The Clash of Religion and Politics in Europe, from the French Revolution to the Great War* (New York: Harper Perennial, 2005), 9.

12. See, for example, Eric Voegelin, *The New Science of Politics* (Chicago: University of Chicago Press, 1952); and Eric Voegelin, *Science, Politics and Gnosticism*, trans. by William J. Fitzpatrick (Chicago: University of Chicago Press, 1968).

13. See Les K. Adler and Thomas G. Paterson, "Red Fascism: The Merger of Nazi Germany and Soviet Russia in the American Image of Totalitarianism (1930s–1950s)," *American Historical Review* (April 1970), 1046.

14. See Franz Borkenau's comparisons of Nazism and Soviet communism in *The Totalitarian Enemy* (London: Faber & Faber, 1940); and Peter Coleman's *The Liberal Conspiracy: The Congress for Cultural Freedom and the Struggle for the Mind of Postwar Europe* (New York: Free Press, 1990). The attacks made on the C for CF owing to its CIA funding do not disprove that the group had a left-of-center point of origin.

15. George Orwell's *Homage to Catalonia* (New York: Harcourt Brace 1980) is the classical statement of anti-Soviet leftist loyalty, starting with statements about its author's antifascist commitment and concluding with an attack on the Soviet-controlled communists for having caused "the wrong side" to win in Spain.

16. See Gerhart Niemeyer, *Between Nothingness and Paradise* (Baton Rouge: Louisiana State University, 1971), especially 76–103.

17. See Robert Nisbet, *The Making of Modern Society* (New York: NYU Press, 1986), especially 186–97, 202; Jacques Ellul, *Propagandes* (Paris: Colin, 1962); Michael Oakeshott, *Rationalism in Politics and Other Essays* (Indianapolis: Liberty Fund, [1932] 1991), and Helmut Schelsky's now out-of-print, onetime classic on the totalitarian implications of the planned economy, *Das Freiheitswollen der Völker und die Idee des Planstaates* (Karlsruhe/Baden: Volk und Zeit, 1946).

18. This is precisely the argument in Robert Nisbet's *The Present Age: Progress and Anarchy in Modern America* (New York: Harper and Row, 1988), 45–62. See also Michael Oakeshott, *Rationalism in Politics and Other Essays*, particularly 97–132; and Herbert Butterfield, *International Conflict in the Twentieth Century, a Christian View* (New York: Harper and Brothers, 1960).

19. Hans Buchheim, *Totale Herrschaft: Wesen und Merkmale* (Munich: Kösel, 1962), 115; see also Ulrich von Hassell, *Vom Anderen Deutschland. Aus den nachgelassenen Tagebücher 1938–1944* (Freiburg im Breisgau: Atlantis Verlag, 1946).

20. Quoted in *Totale Herrschaft: Wesen und Merkmale*, 115–16.

21. See Arendt, *The Origins of Totalitarianism*, 31–34.

22. This connection is already established in the introduction to *Totalitarian Dictatorship and Autocracy*, most explicitly on 25.

23. See Arendt, *The Origins of Totalitarianism*, particularly 305–391.

24. An essay of mine that treats the decontextualized application of fascist labels, perhaps all too flippantly, is in *The American Conservative*, July 4, 2005, 23–26.

25. See Arendt, *The Origins of Totalitarianism*, 19.

26. Ibid., 19–20.

27. This is clearly the argument of volume two of Christian Tilitzki's *Die deutsche Universitätsphilosophie in der Weimarer Republik und im Dritten Reich* (Berlin: Akademie Verlag 2002). Tilitzki, who deals mostly with the broadly defined "Philosophiefakultäten" in German universities from the Weimar Republic through the Second World War, documents the growing indifference of the Nazi authorities to academic appointments, particularly after they had begun to lose the war. See also Arendt, *The Origins of Totalitarianism*, 305–437.

28. See Ernst Jünger's wartime diaries, published as *Strahlungen* (Tübingen: Heliopolis, 1949); J. P. Stern's biography *Ernst Jünger* (New Haven: Yale University Press, 1953); and the discussion of Jünger's interwar "conservative revolutionary" but outspokenly anti-Nazi and emphatically non–anti-Semitic politics in Armin Mohler and Karlheinz Weissmann's *Die Konservative Revolution in Deutschland 1918–1932* (Graz: Ares Verlag, 2005), 180–230.

29. See Paul Hollander, *Political Pilgrims: Western Intellectuals in Search of the Good Society*, 4th ed. (New Brunswick: Transaction Publishers, 1997).

30. Stéphane Courtois et al., *Le livre noir du communisme* (Paris: Robert Laffont, 1997).

31. See Roland Leroy, "Bouillon de culture," *Le Journal du Dimanche*, November 7, 1997; and *Le Monde*, November 14, 1997, 8.

32. See Vladimir Tismaneanu, *Iliescu, Communism, Postcommunism* (Boulder, CO: University of Colorado Press, 1996), 167–69; and Peter Gross, *The Great Shock at the End of a Short Century: Ion Iliescu in Dialogue with Vladimir Tismaneanu on Communism, Post-Communism and Democracy* (New York: Social Science Monographs, 2004).

33. See Mircea Eliade, *Mythes, rêves et mystères* (Paris: Gallimard, 1972), 21.

34. See Leonard Schapiro, *Totalitarianism* (New York: Praeger Publishers, 1972), 18–38, 99.

35. Ibid., 117.

36. Among works that make this argument are Amos Perlmutter, *Modern Authoritarianism: A Comparative Institutional Analysis* (New Haven: Yale University Press, 1981); Juan Linz, *Totalitarian and Authoritarian Regimes*; Larry Diamond, Jonathan Hartlyn, Juan Linz, and Seymour Martin Lipset eds., *Democracy in Developing Countries: Latin America*, 2nd ed. (Boulder, CO: Lynne Rienner, 1988); and Jeane Kirkpatrick, "Dictatorships and Double Standards," *Commentary* (November 1979). Unlike the other works being cited, Kirkpatrick's famous essay does not argue in favor of pushing authoritarian governments toward democratic transformations. The author views these autocracies as mostly caretaker regimes, which do not pose an international danger that is equivalent to communist revolutionary dictatorships. Although often grouped together with liberal internationalists, Kirkpatrick stood in opposition to the neoconservative call for a "global democratic revolution."

37. For extravagant statements of this democratic revolutionary sentiment, see Joshua Muravchik, *Exporting Democracy: Fulfilling America's Destiny* (Washington, DC: AEI Press, 1991); Ben J. Wattenberg, *The First Universal Nation: Leading Indicators and Ideas about the Surge of America in the 1990s* (New York: Free Press, 1991); Carl Gershman and Michael Allen, "New Threats to Freedom: The Assault on Democracy Assistance," *Journal of Democracy* (April 2006); and William Kristol and Robert Kagan, "Toward a Neo-Reaganite Foreign Policy," *Foreign Affairs* 75, no. 4 (July/August 1996), 18–32.

38. De Felice, *Interpretations of Fascism*, 175–92.

39. This thesis about a perverted form of modernization leading to fascism is found in Danilo Breschi, "Fascismo," *Dizionario al liberalism italiano*, 440–48; A. Cardini, *Il grande centro: I liberali in una nazione senza stato: il problema storico dell'arretratezza politica (1796–1996)* (Bari and Rome: Lacaita, 1996); Herf, *Reactionary Modernism*; Denis Mack Smith, *Modern Italy: A Political History* (Ann Arbor: University of Michigan Press, 1997); and Hans Ulrich Wehler, *Modernisierungstheorie und Geschichte* (Göttingen: Vandenhoeck und Ruprecht, 1975).

40. See Herbert Butterfield, *The Whig Interpretation of History* (New York: Norton, 1965); and Michael Bentley, "Herbert Butterfield and the Ethics of Historiography," *History and Theory*, 44 (2005), 55–71. Perhaps the most grotesque attack on Butterfield for failing to defend American democratic values against changing political foes can be found in Gertrude Himmelfarb's polemic "Whigged Out," in *New Republic*, 231, 15 (2004), 30–41. In *Herbert Butterfield: History, Providence, and Skeptical Politics* (Wilmington: ISI Books, 2011), 223, Kenneth B. McIntyre makes the wry observation that Himmelfarb loathed But-

terfield for "not displaying sufficient hatred of the Germans during the first half of the twentieth century and for repeating this wickedness by insufficiently hating the Russians in the second half of the same century."

41. See Volker Hauff, *Sprachlose Politik* (Frankfurt: Fischer, 1979), 25; and Kurt Sontheimer, *Die Unversicherte Republik* (Munich: Piper Verlag, 1979).

Notes to Chapter Three

1. Wiggershaus, *Die Frankfurter Schule*, especially 49–113; Martin Jay, *Adorno* (Cambridge: Harvard University Press, 1984). Two sympathetic, informative studies of the Frankfurt School and critical theory are Russell A. Berman, *Modern Culture and Critical Theory: Art, Politics, and the Legacy of the Frankfurt School* (Madison: University of Wisconsin Press, 1989); and Martin Jay, *The Dialectical Imagination: A History of the Frankfurt School and the Institute of Social Research, 1923–1950* (University of California Press, 1996).

2. Wiggershaus, *Die Frankfurter Schule*, 134–46, 171–81.

3. Ibid., 214–15, 565–617; Herbert Marcuse, *Reason and Revolution: Hegel and the Rise of Social Theory* (Boston: Beacon Press, 1970); Herbert Marcuse, *Counterrevolution and Revolt* (Boston: Beacon Press, 1989); and Herbert Marcuse's "Hegels Ontologie und die Theorie der Geschichtlichkeit," in *Die Gesellschaft* (1923), 136–74.

4. See Rolf Wiggershaus, *Adorno* (Munich: Beck'sche Verlagsbuchhandlung, 1998); and Lorenz Jäger, *Adorno: A Political Biography*, translated by Stewart Spencer (New Haven: Yale, 2004); and Paul Gottfried's review of Jäger in *The American Conservative*, December 6, 2004, 30–33.

5. Cited in Wiggershaus, *Die Frankfurter Schule*, 429.

6. Ibid., 432.

7. Ibid., 435–36.

8. Ibid., 430.

9. See J. J. Bachofen, *Myth, Religion, and Mother Right*, trans. by Ralph Manheim and introduced by Joseph Campbell (Princeton, NJ: Princeton University Press, 1992).

10. See the following works by Erich Fromm: *Die Entwicklung des Christusdogma: Eine psychoanalytische Studie zur sozialpsychologischen Funktion der Religion* (Munich: Beck'sche Verlagsbuchhandlung, 1965); *Psychoanalysis and Religion* (New Haven: Yale University Press, 1950); *The Sane Society* (NY: Holt, Rinehart & Winston, 1954), 15, 54–57; and "Die sozialpsychologische Bedeutung der Mutterrechtstheorie," in *Zeitschrift für Sozialforschung*, no. 3 (1934).

11. Adorno, et al., *The Authoritarian Personality*, 891–960.

12. See Jürgen Habermas (with Ludwig von Friedeberg, C. Oehler and Friedrich Weltz) *Student und Politik: Eine soziologische Untersuchung zum politischen Bewusstsein Frankfurter Studenten* (Berlin: Neuwied, 1961); "Pädagogischer 'Optimismus' vor Gericht einer pessimistischer Anthropologie. Schelskys Bedenken zur Schulreform," in *Neue Sammlung*, 251–78; and Helmut Schelsky, *Die Skeptische Generation: Eine Soziologie der deutschen Jugend* (Düsseldorf: Eugen Diederichs Verlag, 1963).

13. *The Authoritarian Personality*, 676–67; Gottfried, *Multiculturalism and the Politics of Guilt*, 100–129. Adorno has a tendency to attach the prefix "pseudo" to any political stance that displeases him, which he ritualistically attributes to a "fascist potential" and "repressive and ultimately destructive wishes," ibid., 676. A respondent is presumed to be a

good socialist, and therefore mentally stable, if he or she calls for nationalizing the means of production. But the "semi-fascist parole officer" whom Adorno interviews is judged to be a "pseudo-socialist" because "of his outspoken albeit inarticulate wish that the system of free enterprise and competition should be replaced by a state-capitalist integration where the economically strongest group, that is to say, heavy industry, takes control and organizes the whole life process of society without further interference by democratic dissension or by groups whom he regards as being in control only on account of the process of formal democracy but not on the basis of the 'legitimate' real economic power behind them," ibid., 677. Aside from its clunky Teutonic wording and tortuous syntax, Adorno's observation suffers from the further defect of having nothing to do with the parole officer's comments. The respondent expressed approval for the "collectiveness" of the New Deal but opined that "private business could do it better than the government" when it came to national economic recovery. It is impossible to find evidence of mental pathology or fascist sympathy in this extremely measured, ambivalent response, which in the 1930s represented a centrist political position. It is also unclear why someone who advocates nationalization of productive forces, which was Adorno's preferred economic policy, is being more open to "democratic dissension" than someone who is less economically radical. By this standard, Joseph Stalin may have been the most tolerant figure of the age.

14. See Max Horkheimer's "Allgemeiner Teil," in *Studien über Autorität und Familie* (Paris, 1936); and (together with Adorno) *Dialektik der Aufklärung: Philosophische Fragmente* (Amsterdam: Querido Verlag, 1947).

15. Wiggershaus, *Die Frankfurter Schule*, 733–87.

16. See Lasch, *The True and Only Heaven*, 460–61; and S. M. Lipset, "Working Class Authoritarianism," in *American Sociological Review* 24 (1959), 482–501.

17. For Adorno's picture of his scholarly life in America, see "Wissenschaftliche Erfahrungen in Amerika," in *Stichworte* (Frankfurt, 1969).

18. "The F Scale," *Anesi.com*, http://www.anesi.com/fscale.htm.

19. See, for example, Allison G. Smith and David G. Winter, "Right-wing Authoritarianism, Party Identification, and Attitudes Toward Feminism in Student Evaluations of the Clinton-Lewinsky Story," *Political Psychology* 23, no. 2 (June 2002), 355–383; A. M. Manganelli Rattazzi, A. Bobbio, & L. Canova (2007), "A Short Version of the Right-Wing Authoritarianism (RWA) Scale" *Personality and Individual Differences* 43, no. 5; Herbert Kelman and Janet Barclay, "The F Scale as a Measure of Breadth of Perspective," *The Journal of Abnormal and Social Psychology* 67, no. 6 (Dec. 1963), 608–15; and M. Deutsch, "Trust, Trustworthiness and the F Scale," *The Journal of Abnormal and Social Psychology* 61, no. 110 (July 1960), 138–40. In recent decades the F-scale has been renamed with some variation as the PR Scale, but the employers of this test for prejudice freely admit its derivation from Adorno's measurements. See Edward Dunbar, "The Prejudiced Personality, Racism, and Anti-Semitism: The PR Scale Forty Years Later," *Journal of Personality Assessment* 65, no. 2 (1995), 270–77. Stephen J. Whitfield, in "The Theme of Indivisibility in the Post-War Struggle against Prejudice in the United States," in *Patterns of Prejudice* 43, no. 3 (2004), 201, 223–47, raises the question of why all crusades against "prejudice" in the United States, starting in the 1940s and 1950s, begin with the assumption that dislike for a particular minority regarded as vulnerable by social psychologists and journalists is thought to indicate an abnormal hatred for all other groups. Whitfield refers to Adorno, et al., *The Authoritarian Personality* as a source for this now widespread belief.

20. See Bob Altemeyer, *Right-Wing Authoritarianism* (Winnipeg: University of Manitoba Press, 1981); and, by the same author, *The Authoritarian Specter* (Cambridge, MA: Harvard University Press, 1996).

21. For the antinational sentiments of Trittin and his defenders, see *Junge Freiheit*, November 23, 2012, 6; and the fakten/fiktionen site http://2011/08/jürgen-trittins-tiefrote-vergangenheit-und-seine-antideutsche-umschlage. Although these sources are clearly hostile to Trittin, his statements suggest a profound, indeed astonishing, revulsion for his country and all European national identities.

22. See the Kampf gegen Rechts site http://www.kampf-gegen-rechts.de/ and the declaration of war on nationalism in *Jungle World*, a website publication that is close to the German Greens and the Party of Democratic Socialists, October 29, 2009, http://jungle-world.com/artikel/2009/44/39686.html.

23. For a particularly bitter treatment of this subject by a figure of the interwar German Right who was savagely contemptuous of the Nazis but badly abused during the American Occupation, see Ernst von Salomon, *Der Fragebogen* (Reinbek: Rowohlt, 1953), 578–667. Salomon's attack on his American captors elicited an impassioned rejoinder in *Time* in 1955: "It Just Happened," *Time* (January 10, 1955), http://content.time.com/time/magazine/article/0,9171,861117,00.html.

24. For a provocative, critical study of the Allied Occupation, see Caspar von Schrenck-Notzing, *Charakterwäsche: Die Reeducation der Deutschen und ihre bleibenden Auswirkungen*, enlarged, 2nd ed. (Graz: Ares Verlag, 2005), 23–78, 127–72; for a far more favorable but also balanced view of the German democratic society that emerged after the Occupation, see Walter Laqueur, *Europe since Hitler: The Rebirth of Europe* (NY: Penguin Books, 1982), 89–100, 312–16, and 472–90.

25. Richard M. Brickner, *Is Germany Incurable?*, introduced by Margaret Mead (NY: J. B. Lippincott, 1943).

26. Schrenck-Notzing, *Charakterwäsche*, 106–8.

27. Ibid., 308.

28. Ibid. For criticism of the attacks on the German Federal Republic as neofascist by another famous refugee from the Third Reich, see the study *Affinität wider Willen? Hannah Arendt, Theodor W. Adorno, und die Frankfurter Schule*, edited by Lilian Weissberg, *Jahrbuch* (Fritz Bauer Institut, 2011).

29. For a confirmation of the affluent, culturally privileged environment in which Adorno grew up in Frankfurt, see Wiggershaus, *Adorno*, 11–26; and the sketch of Horkheimer in Wiggershaus, *Die Frankfurter Schule*, 55–66. A scandal broke out in 2006 when the Berlin magazine *Cicero* documented Habermas's involvement with the Third Reich, http://de.wikipedia.org/wiki/J%FCrgen_Habermas. A far more extensive relation with the Nazis, including acts of spying on university colleagues and working to create a Nazi-controlled German Protestant church, has been uncovered concerning the forerunner of the antinational school of German history, Fritz Fischer. See Klaus Grosse Kracht, "Fritz Fischer und der deutsche Protestantismus," *Zeitschrift für Neuere Theologiegeschichte* 10, no. 2 (2003), 196–223. A perceptive essay by David Pan for *Telos* (Spring, 1999) no. 115, 7–35, "Adorno's Failed Aesthetic of Myth," notes the tension between Adorno's skepticism about modernity as expressed in the *Dialectic of the Enlightenment* and Habermas's celebration of modernity as liberation from the past. Adorno's positive engagement with the cultural past and Habermas's contempt for premodernity may reflect, among other things, their differing levels of exposure to a traditional humanistic education.

30. Habermas's opening salvo against Nolte in what became the Historikerstreit was published in the weekly *Die Zeit* (July 11, 1986). A collection of Habermas's broadsides against Nolte and Nolte's defenders are available in *Eine Art Schadensabwicklung: Kleine politische Schriften* (Frankfurt: Suhrkamp, 1987). Also relevant to this dispute is Steffen Kailitz, *Die politische Deutungskultur im Spiegel des 'Historikerstreits'* (Wiesbaden: Westdeutscher Verlag, 2001).

31. http://www.sms.at/community/talkbox/index.php?showtopic=77677; and the extended discussion of Habermas's *Diskursmodell* in Paul Gottfried's *The Strange Death of Marxism*, 94–105.

32. See Nolte, *Der europäische Bürgerkrieg*; and my comments on this subject on the German website *Blaue Narzisse*, http://www.blauenarzisse.de/index.php/gesichtet/item/3528-ernst-noltes-faschismus.

33. Michael Kelpanides, *Das Scheitern der Marxschen Theorie und der Aufstieg des westlichen Neomarxismus: Über die Ursachen der unzeitgemässen Renaissance* (Bern: Peter Lang, 1999), especially 380–474.

34. Ibid., 23–26, 475–78. See also Birgit Wellie, *Emanzipation in kritischer Theorie, Erziehungswissenschaft und Politikdidaktik: Studien zur Transformation einer sozialphilosophischen Kategorie* (Hamburg: P. Kramer, 1991).

35. See Niklas Luhmann, *Universität als Milieu* (Bielefeld: Haux, 1992); Jost Bauch, *Der Niedergang* (Graz: Ares Verlag, 2010); and Helmut Schelsky, *Die Arbeit tun die anderen: Klassenkampf und Priesterherrschaft der Intellektuellen*, 2nd ed. (Opladen: Westdeutscher Verlag, 1975).

36. See Stefan Scheil, *Transatlantische Wechselwirkungen: Der Elitenwechsel in Deutschland nach 1945* (Berlin: Duncker & Humblot, 2012), 85–89, 188–92.

37. Ibid., 72–81.

38. David Gordon, *Resurrecting Marx: The Analytical Marxists on Freedom, Exploitation, and Justice* (New Brunswick: Transaction Publishers, 1991).

39. See, for example, Immanuel Wallerstein, *After Liberalism* (New York: New Press, 1995); and Michael Hardt and Antonio Negri *Empire* (Cambridge: Harvard University Press, 2001). A discussion of non-German neo-Marxists can be found in my work *The Strange Death of Marxism*, 27–78.

40. See Bernd Rabehl's *Rudi Dutschke* (Dresden: Antaios, 2002); Rabehl's blog *Anschläge* http://rabehl.wordpress.com/2012/06/10/sozialismus-und-barbarei-zur-theorie-der-negativen-aufhebung/#more-1127; Manuel Seitenbecher, *Mahler, Maschke & Co.: Rechtes Denken in einer linken Bewegung?* (Submitted as dissertation in Modern History at University of Potsdam, 2012); and correspondence exchanged between Maschke and the author in 1989 and 1990, mostly in regard to our shared research on Carl Schmitt. Maschke's study *Der Tod des Carl Schmitt: Apologie und Polemik* (Wien: Karolinger Verlag, 1987) stands out from his other writings of the period by virtue of the absence of any anti-American passion.

41. See the perceptive essay on this subject in *Dissent* (Winter 2005), "The European and American Left Since 1945," by Andrei S. Markovits, http://www.discoverthenetworks.org/Articles/The%20European%20and%20American%20Left.htm; and Paul Gottfried, "Anti-War Anti-Americanism?" in *Telos* (Winter 1999), 176–78.

42. For an exhaustive study of Fritz Fischer's *Griff nach der Weltmacht. Die Kriegszielpolitik des kaiserlichen Deutschland 1914/1918* (Düsseldorf: Droste Verlag, 1961) and an examination of Fischer's conceptually ambitious but factually flawed work, see Gunter Spraul, *Der Fischer-Komplex* (Halle: Verlag Cornelius, 2011). The almost total neglect of Spraul's

work in the German press and academic journals may witness to its incompatibility with the emphasis of German elites on German "collective guilt" extending from the Third Reich back into the Second Empire and the outbreak of World War I. Also, little journalistic attention has been bestowed on Konrad Canis's minute, ponderous study of German foreign policy under the last Kaiser, *Der Weg in den Abgrund, Deutsche Aussenpolitik, 1902–1914* (Paderborn: Ferdinand Schöningh, 2011) A longtime distinguished diplomatic historian who prudently avoids attacking Fischer, Canis is unmistakably challenging the antinational school of German historians when he blames the breakdown of Anglo-German relations before the war primarily on the British government.

43. See Walter Andreas Hofer's study, which was published in the shadow of the Nuremberg Trials, *War Premeditated, 1939* (London: Thames, 1955).

44. For a critical view of "right-wing extremism" in Hungary and throughout eastern and central Europe, see *The Daily. HU*, http://www.thedaily.hu/right-wing-extremism-in-central-and-eastern-europe; Tony Judt, *Postwar: A History of Europe since 1945* (New York: Penguin Books, 2006), 732–45; and for a markedly different view, James Kurth, "The Strange Death of Postwar Europe," *Orbis* 52, no. 2 (Spring, 2008), 373–81.

45. On Le Pen's recent gaffes, see http://www.telegraph.co.uk/news/worldnews/europe/france/10885098/Fury-over-Jean-Marie-Le-Pens-anti-semitic-remark.html. The independent-minded editor of the French publication *Causeur*, Elisabeth Lévy, has engaged in an extended dialogue with Le Pen's daughter Marine, whom Lévy considers more teachable than her father. Marine is thought to be capable of creating a "new right" that would battle Islamicist theocrats while fighting for intellectual freedom against politically correct antifascists. See *Causeur*, January 13, 2013, page 1.

46. Angelica Fenner and Eric D. Weitz, eds., *Fascism and Neofascism: Critical Writings on the Radical Right in Europe* (New York: Palgrave MacMillan, 2004), 226.

47. Ibid., 227.

48. Ibid., 247–58; and Frank H. Adler, "Immigration, Insecurity, and the French Far Right," ibid., 229–46.

49. An angry but comprehensive and technically detailed account of the *Loi Gayssot* is Eric Delcroix's *La police de la pensée contre le révisionnisme* (Paris: Diffusion, 1994); see also the discussion of the advocates and critics of the law in my study *After Liberalism: Mass Democracy in the Managerial State* (Princeton, NJ: Princeton University Press, 1999), 102–7, 163–65; and Fenner and Weitz, eds., *Fascism and Neofascism*, 15 and 16.

50. According to NDP Chairman Holger Apfel and his party's organ, *Deutsche Stimme*, June 1, 2011, page 2, the National Democratic Party has two preeminent goals: restoring a "sound currency to Germany," and preventing it "from being overrun by Muslims who are bringing a foreign way of life." Both points were impressed on me by two party officials, Thorsten Thomsen and Arne Schimmer, with whom I corresponded in February and May 2012. Whether or not one agrees with these goals or with what the German press and other German parties attack as old-fashioned "German nationalism," it is hard to see how the NDP embodies "neo-Nazism." A now marginalized party, the NDP has no significant popular base, and the energy in German politics has been, for decades, with leftist parties, which are emphatically antinational and multicultural. See my essay "How European Nations End," *Orbis* 49, no. 3 (Summer 2005), 559–69. In *Europe since Hitler*, 477, Laqueur points out that in the 1970s the old NDP, while under a former Nazi party member, Adolf von Thadden, was a potent political force in Germany. Laqueur, whose own family was murdered by the Nazis, associates the NDP not with Hitler's party but with the

national conservative parties of the Weimar Republic. The current NDP does not enjoy even a fraction of the political acceptability of Thadden's party: it is routinely attacked, sometimes with physical violence, as a neo-Nazi danger. The party is also on the verge of being outlawed as a "threat to Germany's free democratic foundations."

51. See Nolte, *Der Faschismus: Von Mussolini zu Hitler*, 369.

52. See Maria Bucur's "Fascism and the New Radical Movement in Romania," in *Fascism and Neofascism*, 159–74; and for a Romanian nationalist perspective, Ovidiu Hurduzeu and Mircea Platon, eds., *A Treia Forta: Romania profunda* (Bucharest: Logos, 2008).

53. A critical, thoughtful study of Orban's regime is by Christopher Caldwell's "To Viktor Goes the Spoils," in *The Weekly Standard* (October 15, 2012), http://www.weeklystandard.com/articles/viktor-go-spoils_653822.html.

54. Orban has been excoriated in the *Wall Street Journal* for daring to say that "it is of paramount importance for Hungary to remain a nation state speaking the same language and having Christianity as its religious cornerstone," http://blogs.wsj.com/emergingeurope/2014/08/25/hungarys-orban-bashes-liberal-immigration-policy/. One could easily imagine Churchill, de Gaulle, or even FDR expressing such sentiments about their countries in an earlier time. On antifascism as a bludgeon in the hands of international organizations, see Alain Finkielkraut's comment in *Le Monde*, June 6, 2000, 6; François Darras, "L'épouvantail Haider," *Politis*, February 10, 2000, 4.

55. See "Greece's Golden Dawn Party Describes Hitler as a 'Great Personality,'" *The Guardian*, April 16, 2014.

56. Ibid.; and Fiona Govan, "Greece's Golden Dawn to Enter EU Parliament for First Time," *The Telegraph*, May 25, 2014.

57. For a detailed study of this era, see Sakmyster, *Hungary's Admiral on Horseback*; and, by the same author, *Hungary, the Great Powers, and the Danubian Crisis, 1936–1939* (Athens, GA: University of Georgia Press, 1980).

58. Characteristic of Atlanticists who were hated by the Sixty-Eighters as neo-Nazis was the Münster professor of history Heinz Gollwitzer (1917–1999), who was harassed by student radicals in the late 1960s. Nothing in Gollwitzer's discussions of German society would indicate that he wished to return to his country's recent political past. Moreover, his interpretation of World War I is written from a pro-Allied position. See Gollwitzer's *Weltpolitik und deutsche Geschichte*, edited by Hans-Christof Kraus (Göttingen: Vandenhoeck & Ruprecht, 2008), especially 115–36, 363–84. In *Transatlantische Wechselwirkung*, 100–104, Stefan Scheil documents how German historians during the Occupation became participants in formulating and applying "educational politics" that aimed explicitly at overcoming nationalist sentiments. Those who were included in these institutional arrangements, which were shaped by the Western powers, were Ritter on the Right and Ernst Nolte and Karl Bracher on the Left. Although the septuagenarian historian and ardent Atlanticist Michael Stürmer has deviated from the authorized interpretation of the outbreak of the Great War in German universities, he has taken the journalistically safe course of pointing to tsarist Russian rather than Anglo-French contributions to the outbreak of World War I: http://www.welt.de/debatte/kolumnen/Weltlage/article13831494/Die-oestlichen-Wurzeln-des-Ersten-Weltkriegs.html. For a particularly revealing study of the continuity and deepening of this characteristically pro-American, internationalist perspective among contemporary journalists, and particularly among those tied to the German Christian Democrats, see Uwe Krüger's *Meinungsmacht: Der Einfluss von Eliten auf Leitmedien und Alpha-Journalisten-eine kritische Netzwerkanalyse* (Cologne: Herbert von Halem Verlag, 2013), especially 115–264.

59. See Hans B. von Sothen's minutely detailed study of Zehrer, "Hans Zehrer als politischer Publizist nach 1945," in *Die Kupierte Alternative: Konservatismus in Deutschland nach 1945*, edited by Frank-Lothar Kroll (Berlin: Duncker & Humblot, 2005), 125–80; and Kroll's introduction to this anthology, 3–24.

60. A comprehensive collection of Schmitt's anti-American writings, which go back well before the end of World War II, is available in the Italian anthology *L'Unità del mondo*, ed. Alessandro Campi (Roma: Antonio Pellicani Editore, 1994). Anyone looking at Schmitt's anti-American grievances may find it hard to account for them entirely by means of two standard explanations: namely, Schmitt's desire to limit American power to the Western Hemisphere and his imprisonment by the American occupying forces for more than a year after the war. See, for example, Joseph W. Bendersky, "Schmitt at Nuremberg," *Telos*, 72 (Summer 1987), 91–129; and Paul Piccone and Gary L. Ulmen, "Introduction to Carl Schmitt," *Telos*, 72 (Summer 1987), 3–14. In his anti-American broadsides, Schmitt was expressing an ingrained cultural attitude that was perceptible on the European Right well into the second half of the twentieth century. An even more exhaustive treatment of Schmitt's post–World War II thinking is in Reinhard Mehring, *Carl Schmitt. Aufstieg und Fall* (Munich: C. H. Beck Verlag, 2009), 438–548.

61. See Helmut Schelsky, *Die Soziologen und das Recht: Abhandlungen und Vorträge zur Soziologie von Recht, Institutionen und Planung* (Opladen: Westdeutscher Verlag, 1980), especially 73–78; and Volker Kempf, *Wider die Wirklichkeitsverweigerung, Helmut Schelsky, Leben, Werk, Aktualität* (Munich: Olzog, 2012), 161–74.

62. Alexander and Margarete Mitscherlich, *Die Unfähigkeit zu trauern* (Munich: Piper Verlag, 2009); Martin Dehli, *Leben als Konflikt: Zur Biographie Alexander Mitscherlichs* (Göttingen: Wallenstein Verlag, 2007); and Kempf, *Wider die Wirklichkeitsverweigerung*, 144–47.

63. Mitscherlich, *Die Unfähigkeit zu trauern*, 362.

64. On the treatment of ethnic Germans in eastern Europe after World War II, see Alfred de Zayas, *A Terrible Revenge: The Ethnic Cleansing of Eastern European Germans, 1944–1950* (New York: St. Martin's Press, 1994); Ulrich Merten, *Forgotten Voices: The Expulsion of the Germans from Eastern Europe after World War II* (New Brunswick: Transaction Publishers, 2013); and R. M. Douglas, *Orderly and Humane: The Expulsion of the Germans after the Second World War* (New Haven: Yale University Press, 2012).

65. For an excruciatingly detailed study of the civilian casualties of Allied bombing in World War II, see Jörg Friedrich, *Der Brand: Deutschland im Bombenkrieg 1940–1945* (Berlin: Propyläen, 2002), especially 358–62 for Brand's casualty figures for the bombing of Dresden. Friedrich notes on page 358 that, by the beginning of 1945, Churchill and British military commanders were planning to wage chemical and bacterial warfare against Berlin, which they hoped would cause more than 100,000 civilian deaths.

66. Rainer Zitelmann, in *Wohin treibt unsere Republik* (Berlin and Frankfurt: Ullstein, 1994), offers another reason for the wielding of the Holocaust as an ideological symbol. It ensures and enhances the power of the antifascist media elite, which, according to Zitelmann, has acquired far more power since German unification than it had exercised before. See particularly the media attack on Stefan Heitmann's bid for the position of *Bundespräsident* in 1993 and the transformation of this politician's widely shared sentiments about valuing women's homemaking role and about seeing no reason "why Germans of future generations must spend their lives atoning for the onetime event of the Holocaust" into an attempt to whitewash Nazi crimes (ibid., 148–201). According

to Zitelmann, the overwhelming majority of Germans agreed with Heitmann's extremely tempered statements, but even self-described German patriots believed the politician was a right-wing extremist after the media reconstructed his personality. Zitelmann notes the stridently ideological factors that permeated this campaign of defamation.

67. See Peter Novick, *The Holocaust in American Life* (Boston: Houghton Mifflin, 1999), especially 206–63.

68. See Daniel J. Goldhagen, *Hitler's Willing Executioners: Ordinary Germans and the Holocaust* (New York: Alfred A. Knopf, 1996); and Daniel J. Goldhagen, A *Moral Reckoning: The Role of the Church in the Holocaust and Its Unfulfilled Duty of Repair* (New York: Vintage, 2003). For a devastating critique of the invented "facts" in *Hitler's Willing Executioners* by two Jewish scholars whose families had suffered in the Holocaust, see Norman G. Finkelstein and Ruth Bettina Birn, A *Nation on Trial: The Goldhagen Thesis and Historical Truth* (New York: Henry Holt & Co., 1998); and my comment "Counterfeit Courage" in *The American Conservative*, September 16, 2002, 21–23.

69. For documents pertaining to the German Evangelical Church's original confession of guilt and its later restatements, see *Im Zeichen der Schuld: 40 Jahre Stuttgarter Schuldbekenntnis* (Neukirchener Verlag, 1985).

70. A work that deals critically and provocatively with the French antifascist cult of victims is Eric Zemmour's *livre de scandale, Le Suicide Français* (Paris: Albin Michel, 2014). Although a deliciously irreverent attack on the French version of political correctness, Zemmour's work would have benefited from a more detailed treatment of certain subjects, such as the complicity of the French people in the deportation of Jews under the Vichy government and the extent of the criminalization of hate speech in France since 1972. According to Zemmour, an entire work should be devoted to reassessing what has become the authoritative study of Vichy anti-Semitism by Robert O. Paxton, written and translated in the 1970s (ibid., 87–95). See Paxton, *Vichy France: Old Guard and New Order,* and Robert O. Paxton and Michael Marrus, *Vichy France and the Jews* (New York: Basic Books, 1981). The notion of "functional collaboration" introduced by Paxton has allowed French antifascists and antiracists to assign collective guilt to any French inhabitant who failed to resist the German authorities. This stigma has now been passed on in *perpetuo* to the entire French nation.

71. Quoted in Zemmour, *Le Suicide Français*, 384–85.

72. See Alain Besançon, *Le malheur du siècle sur le communisme, le nazisme, et l'unicité de la Shoah* (Paris: Fayard, 1998).

73. For an in-depth study of Weiszäcker's speech in the context of German politics and the Federal President's own controversial family history, see Thorsten Hinz, Die Weizsäcker-Komplex: Eine politische Archäologie (Berlin: Junge Freiheit Verlag, 2012).

74. See Michael Kleeberg's citation of Fischer's remark in *Die Welt*, May 22, 1999.

75. See *Le Monde*, June 21, 2000, for the storm of protest generated by the plan to transfer Berlioz's remains; and ibid., February 29, 2000, for the commentary by Joël-Marie Fauquet, "Une fausse note."

Notes to Chapter Four

1. See Erik von Kuehnelt-Leddihn, *The Left from de Sade and Marx to Hitler and Marcuse* (New Rochelle: Arlington House, 1974); its revised edition, *Leftism Revisited:*

From de Sade and Marx to Hitler and Pol Pot (Washington, DC: Regnery, 1991); and *Liberty or Equality: The Challenge of Our Times* (Auburn, Alabama: Ludwig von Mises Institute, 2007). The work that states most fully the author's case against democracy is *Demokratie: Eine Analyse* (Graz: Leopold Stocker Verlag, 1996).

2. See De Felice, *Interpretations of Fascism*, 191–92.

3. See Schivelbusch, *Entfernte Verwandtschaft*, especially 31–36, 73–76, and 143–47.

4. See Diggins, *Mussolini and Fascism*.

5. See Bertrand de Jouvenel, *On Power*, trans. by J. F. Huntington (New York: Viking, 1949), 268.

6. Ibid., 236–79. Jouvenel's critical observations about the natural tendency of modern democracy to become imperialistic and exalt a collectivistic will is made to apply to fascist states as well as other contemporary forms of popular government. Jouvenel prefaces his work with the line from Juvenal warning every good Roman to bolt his gates and stand firm against the multitudes: *"Pone seram, cohibe."* A recent published anthology of my essays, *War and Democracy* (London: Arktos, 2012), offers similar thoughts on the militaristic tendencies of human rights-based democracies.

7. See Augusto del Noce, *L'epoca della secolarizzazione* (Milano: A. Giuffré, 1970).

8. Augusto del Noce, *Fascismo e antifascismo* (Milan: Leopardi, 1995) accentuates the shared assumptions of the fascists and antifascists as seen from a traditional Catholic perspective.

9. Not surprisingly, del Noce's last major work, which he died before completing in 1989, was an intellectual biography of Italian fascism's leading thinker. See *Giovanni Gentile: Per une interpretazione filosofica della storia contemporanea*.

10. Gregor, *The Fascist Persuasion in Radical Politics*, 139–322.

11. Ibid., 86–138; and A. James Gregor, *Contemporary Radical Ideologies: Totalitarian Thought in the Twentieth Century* (New York: Random House, 1968).

12. See Carl Schmitt, *The Concept of the Political*, trans. and intro by George Schwab (New Brunswick, NJ: Rutgers University Press, 1976); and Ernst Wolfgang Böckenförde's "Der Begriff des Politischen als Schlüssel zum staatsrechtlichen Werk Carl Schmitt," in *Complexio Oppositorum: Über Carl Schmitt*, ed. Helmut Quaritsch (Berlin: Duncker & Humblot, 1988), 283–300.

13. Payne, *Fascism, Comparison and Definition*, 20.

14. Ibid., 20, 21.

15. See Karl Mannheim, *Konservatismus: Ein Beitrag zur Soziologie des Wissens*, ed. David Kettler, Volker Meja, and Nico Stehr (Frankfurt am Main: Suhrkamp, 1984), especially 49–136.

16. See Philip Morgan, *Fascism in Europe, 1919-1945* (London and New York: Routledge, 2003), 169–71.

17. See John Lukacs, *The Hitler of History* (New York: Vintage Books, 1997), 118. Lukacs's attempt to refute the concept of generic fascism by mentioning the obvious dissimilarities between Hitler and Mussolini is problematic. Whether or not this contrast is valid does not disprove the existence of generic fascism. Neither German Nazism nor its foreign imitations, it may be argued, were typical fascist movements.

18. See Flynn, *The Roosevelt Myth*, 140.

19. Ibid., 140–41.

20. See Friedrich A. Hayek, *The Road to Serfdom*, expanded edition (Chicago: University of Chicago Press, 1956); and John T. Flynn, *As We Go Marching*, paperback edition (Auburn, AL: Ludwig von Mises Institute, 2007).

21. For a defense of this libertarian position as the American old Right, see Justin Raimondo, *Reclaiming the American Right: The Lost Legacy of the Conservative Movement*, 2nd ed. (Wilmington: ISI Books, 2008); and George H. Nash, *The Conservative Intellectual Movement in America since 1945*, 2nd ed. (Wilmington: ISI Books, 1996), 1–30.

22. See Justin Raimondo's biography of his mentor, *An Enemy of the State: The Life of Murray N. Rothbard* (Amherst, NY: Prometheus Books, 2000), especially 105–9; and Buckley's embittered comment on the occasion of Rothbard's death "Murray Rothbard, RIP," *National Review*, February 6, 1995.

23. Frank S. Meyer, *In Defense of Freedom: A Conservative Credo* (Chicago: Henry Regnery Company, 1962), 122–23; and Meyer's essay "Freedom, Tradition, Conservatism," in *Modern Age* 4 (Fall 1960), 355–63.

24. Goldberg, *Liberal Fascism*, particularly 78–242.

25. Ibid., 317–57.

26. Ibid., 243–78.

27. See my commentary on these inconsistencies in "Jonah Goldberg: A Comfortable "Conservative" in the Belly of the Beast" on the Takimag website, http://takimag.com/article/jonah_goldberg_a_comfortable_conservative_in_the_belly_of_the_beast/print#axzz2IXfT0j2W. Perhaps the best dissection of Goldberg's polemic comes from his close friend, Michael Ledeen, who has written knowledgeably on Italian fascism. See Ledeen's online review of Goldberg's *Liberal Fascism* on History News Network, http://historynewsnetwork.org/article/122592.

28. Ibid., 404.

29. Ibid.

30. Republican publications and think tanks naturally saw in Goldberg's work a retaliatory tool against the Left for depicting their side as fascistic. See the report in *Accuracy in Media*, "Liberal Fascism Explained," http://www.aim.org/briefing/liberal-fascism-explained/. For a penetrating critique of the partisan intent of Goldberg's work, although one not entirely free of its own bias, see Alex Koppelman, "We're all fascists now," in *Salon*, January 11, 2008, http://www.salon.com/2008/01/11/goldberg_2/. It would have been interesting if Goldberg evaluated his interpretation in light of Mussolini's *Dottrina del Fascismo*, which was published in 1931 and was largely the work of Gentile. It is unimaginable that, like Mussolini, the Clintons would be praising the "spiritual unity" of the historic nation or recommending "life as struggle" aimed at enhancing "virility." In any case one could not imagine these Nietzschean tropes issuing from an American liberal Democratic administration. See *The Social and Political Doctrines of Contemporary Europe*, ed. by Michael Oakeshott (Cambridge, England: Cambridge University Press, 1939), 164–79.

31. Keller, Emma G., "Whole Food CEO John Mackey calling Obamacare fascist is tip of the iceberg," *The Guardian*, Jan. 18, 2013, http://www.guardian.co.uk/business/us-news-blog/2013/jan/18/whole-foods-john-mackey-fascist.

32. Herbert I. London, "Fascism in America," *herblondon.org*, January 9, 2013, http://www.herblondon.org/12800/fascism-in-america.

33. Ibid.

34. "A Student's Guide to Hosting Islamo-Fascism Awareness Week," *terrorismawareness.org*, http://media0.terrorismawareness.org/files/Islamo-Fascmism-Awareness-Week-Guide.html.

35. Don Feder, "Left-Fascism Awareness Week," *FrontPageMag.com*, November 07, 2007, http://archive.frontpagemag.com/readArticle.aspx?ARTID=28791.

36. George Will, "Vladimir Putin's Hitlerian Mind," September 4, 2014, http://www.kyivpost.com/opinion/op-ed/george-will-vladimir-putins-hitlerian-mind-363313.html.

37. George Will, "NATO's Moment of Truth," *National Review*, September 6, 2014, http://www.nationalreview.com/article/387274/natos-moment-truth-george-will.

38. A similar argument is offered by John Gray in the London *Times Literary Supplement* (January 2, 2013), namely, that many intellectuals continue to deny that the "radical evil that comes from the pursuit of progress" can in any way be associated with the Left. This denial also takes place when a reprehensible act is ascribed to the failure of the Left to be on guard against rightist ideas.

39. William Gairdner, "Getting Used to the F-Word," in *The New Criterion* (October 2011), 18.

40. Ibid., 18, 19.

41. Ibid., 20, 21.

42. Ibid., 22.

43. Ibid., 24.

44. See Panajotis Kondylis, *Machtfragen: Ausgewählte Beiträge zur Politik und Gesellschaft* (Darmstadt: Wissenschaftliche Gesellschaft, 2006), especially 28–118; and Panajotis Kondylis, "Alte und neue Gottheit," *Deutsche Zeitschrift für Philosophie* 60.3 (2012), 351–64.

Notes to Chapter Five

1. Among the multiple biographical studies of Drieu la Rochelle worth consulting are Pierre Andreu Drieu, *témoin et visionnaire* (Paris: Grasset, 1952); Frédéric Grover, *Drieu la Rochelle* (Paris: Gallimard, 1979); Marie Balvet, *Itinéraire d'un intellectuel vers le fascisme: Drieu la Rochelle* (Paris: PUF, 1984); Jean Bastier, *Pierre Drieu la Rochelle, Soldat de la Grande Guerre, 1914–1918* (Paris: Albatros, 1989); Julien Hervier, *Deux individus contre l'histoire : Drieu la Rochelle et Ernst Jünger* (Paris: Klincksieck, 1978); and Arnaud Guyot-Jeannin, *Drieu la Rochelle, antimoderne et européen* (Paris: Remi Perrin, 1999).

2. Drieu, *Gilles*, 660–69.

3. Ibid., 672.

4. Ibid.

5. Ibid., 673.

6. Ibid.

7. Ibid., 674.

8. Ibid.

9. Ibid., 675.

10. Ibid.

11. Drieu's frustrations in dealing with the German Occupation authorities are recounted in the concluding sections of his *Chroniques politiques (1934–1943)* (Paris: Gallimard, 1943). A similar attitude, although one expressed with more cynicism by another literary collaborator of the Vichy regime, is in Lucien Rebatet's wartime reflections *Les Décombres* (Paris: Les éditions denoel, 1942), especially 422–49.

12. Drieu, *Gilles*, 491.

13. Ibid., 266–67.

14. *Ibid*, 569. For an exhaustive and reflective study of Gilles's Provençal mentor, see Stéphane Giocanti, *Maurras: Le chaos et l'ordre* (Paris: Flammarion, 2006). Like Sternhell in

La Droite Révolutionnaire, 399, Giocanti (394–396) notes the AF's declining fortunes in the face of the rising tide of French fascism in the 1930s, as exemplified by Doriot's movement. For a learned attempt to explain the political theories of Maurras against the background of a corrupt, widely scorned Third Republic, see Domenico Fisichella, *La democrazia contro la realtà. Il pensiero politico di Charles Maurras* (Rome: Carocci, 2006); and Danilo Breschi's thoughtful review of this work on his website: http://www.danilobreschi.com/2014/10/10/charles-maurras-e-le-destre-di-francia/.

15. Drieu, *Gilles*, 553.
16. Ibid., 520.
17. Ibid., 521–22.
18. Ibid., 512.
19. For a factually detailed study of the Stavisky Affair, see Paul Jankowski, *Stavisky: A Confidence Man in the Republic of Virtue* (Ithaca: Cornell University Press, 2002).
20. Drieu, *Gilles*, 597.
21. Ibid., 599.
22. Ibid.
23. Ibid., 604 and 605; see also Drieu's germinal essay on the need for a European-wide revolutionary right, *L'Europe contre les patries* (Paris: Gallimard, 1931). On page 537 of *Gilles*, Drieu puts into the mouth of Gilles Gambier his own advocacy of "a party that is national but not nationalist, which would break with all the prejudices and routines of the classical right, a party that will be social without being socialist and which will reform boldly without following the beaten path of any doctrine."
24. Drieu, *Gilles*, 605.
25. Ibid., 679.
26. Ibid., 680.
27. See Maurice Barrès, "La grande pitié des églises en France," (Paris: Émilie Paul, 1914); Sternhell, *Maurice Barrès et le nationalisme français*; and Albert Thibaudet, *La Vie de Maurice Barrès* (Paris: Nouvelle Revue Française, 1924).
28. Two lucid treatments of this mystifying Italian neo-pagan mystic are Antimo Negri, *Evola e la filosofia* (Milan: Spirali, 1988); and Paul Furlong, *Social and Political Thought of Julius Evola* (London: Routledge, 2011).
29. In Drieu, *Gilles*, 542–43, the protagonist, presumably speaking for Drieu, announces that "pagans were already Christians to their very marrow, and Christians, by which I mean Catholics with their rites, are reasonably pagan, and thank Heaven for that." Giles then concludes his statement by reminding his listeners that "all roads lead to Rome."
30. See the editorial "Neuheidnische Strömungen im italienischen Faschismus," in *Schönere Zukunft* 5, no. 50 (1930), 1214.
31. Giuseppe Attilio Fanelli, "Mussolini contra Lutero," *Antieuropa* 1, no. 7 (1929), 520–28.
32. Drieu, *Gilles*, 686. At least some of the autobiographical material in *Gilles* is already present in Drieu's other popular novel of the late 1930s, *Reveuse bourgeoisie* (Paris: Gallimard, 1937). But Drieu's turning toward fascism is not as apparent in the earlier novel as it is in his later, more revealing one. By 1936 Drieu had joined the Parti Populaire Français and penned a pamphlet, "Doriot ou la vie d'un ouvrier français," on behalf of the party's leader. Two radically different views of continuities in Drieu can be found in Robert Soucy's *Fascist Intellectual: Drieu la Rochelle* (Berkely and London: University of California Press, 1979) and Benedikt Kaiser's *Eurofaschismus und Bürgerliche Dekadenz. Europakonzeption und Gesellschaftskritik* (Kiel: Regin

Verlag, 2011). While Soucy dwells on the authoritarian personality behind Drieu's fascist views, Kaiser treats his subject as a misguided idealist in search of a nonleftist path to European unity.

33. Beate Scholz, *Italienischer Faschismus als "Export"-Artikel (1927–1935)*. *Ideologische und organisatorische Ansätze zur Verbreitung des Faschismus im Ausland*, online revised dissertation (Trier, 2001), 1–26.

34. See Emilio Gentile, "Fascism as Political Religion," *Journal of Contemporary History* 25, nos. 2–3 (1990), 179–208; and *Il culto del littorio. La sacralizzazione della politica nell'Italia fascista* (Rome and Bari: Laterza, 1993).

35. Scholz, *Italienischer Faschismus als "Export"-Artikel (1927–1935)*, 13–68; and Michael Ledeen, *Universal Fascism: The Theory and Practice of the Fascist International, 1928–1936* (New York: H. Fertig, 1972), 39–45.

36. Gregor, *The Ideology of Fascism*, 227.

37. Quoted in Scholz, *Italienischer Faschismus*, 162.

38. James Strachey Barnes, *The Universal Aspects of Fascism* (London: Williams and Norgate, 1929), 104 and 105.

39. Ibid., 137; and the glowing praise in *Critica Fascista* 9, no. 15 (1931), 289 of the English writer "il quale è anche un valoroso militare, ad accorgersene non solo, ma a proclamarlo con voce alta è certo un segno dei tempi nuovi che son tempi di predominio, per l'Italia, nel mondo."

40. For a sympathetic overview of Coudenhove-Kalergi's life and work, see Stefan Solle, *Die Paneuropa-Konzeption des Grafen Richard Nikolaus Coudenhove-Kalergi und ihre ideengeschichtlichen Wurzeln* (Verlag Müller, 2008).

41. Asvero Gravelli, *Verso l'internazionale fascista* (Rome: Nuova Europa, 1932), 35; and Asvero Gravelli, *Panfascismo* (Rome: Nuova Europa, 1935), 223; Scholz, *Italienischer Faschismus*, 160.

42. Ibid., 160–61.

43. Ibid., Roberto Suster, "L'Italia fascista e i destini dell'Europa," *Antieuropa* 1, no. 4 (1929), 261–273; and the essay by the historian Gennaro Magieri on the close ties between Gravelli and the Paneuropa movement extending into the mid-1930s: http://segnavi.blogspot.com/2013/04/richard-coudenhove-kalergi-profeta.html.

44. Asvero Gravelli's roller-coaster relations with *Il Duce* are evident from two of his postwar (partly anecdotal) biographies, *Le Mani di Mussolini* (Rome: Latinita, 1950) and *Mussolini aneddottico* (Rome: Latinita, 1951).

45. Robert J. Soucy, *Fascist Intellectual: Drieu la Rochelle*, 152–74, 240–78; and Robert J. Soucy, *French Fascism: the Second Wave, 1933–1939* (New Haven and London: Yale University Press, 1995).

46. Asvero Gravelli, *Verso l'internazionale fascista* (Rome: Nuova Europa, 1932), 10–12.

47. Scholz, *Italienischer Faschismus*, 163; the theme of a continuing European revolution starting with the March on Rome dominates Gravelli's tract *La marche de Rome et l'Europe* (Rome: Antieuropa, 1931); see also Roberto Suster, "Della rivoluzione permanente nella vita degli uomini e dei popoli," *Antieuropa* 2, no. 3 (1930), 915–923.

48. *Verso l'internazionale fascista*, 208–210.

49. Henry Ashby Turner, "Fascism and Modernization," in *World Politics* 24, no. 4 (June, 1972), 547–564; A. James Gregor, "Fascism and Modernization: Some Addenda," in *World Politics* 26, no. 3 (April 1974), 370–84; and Robert Skidelsky, *Oswald Mosley* (New York: Holt Rinehart, and Winston, 1975), 14–17. Skidelsky's exhaustive biography of Mosley is a model of professionalism and a treasure trove of factual information. Another extensive

biography of Mosley that is worth reading, despite the author's blatant political agenda, is Stephen Dorril's *Black Shirt: Sir Oswald Mosley and British Fascism* (New York: Penguin, 2008).

50. Skidelsky, *Oswald Mosley*, 93–107; Nicholas Mosley, *Rules of the Game/Beyond the Pale: Memoirs of Sir Oswald Mosley and Family*, originally in 2 vols. (Dalkey Archive Press, 1991), 45–64.

51. Nicholas Mosley, *Rules*, 108–132; Skidelsky, *Oswald Mosley*, 77–246.

52. Oswald Mosley, *My Life*, 4th ed. (London: Black House Publishing, 2012), 214–19.

53. Nicholas Mosley, *Rules*, 12–45.

54. Skidelsky, *Oswald Mosley*, 248–262; see also Mosley's account of the split with Strachey in his autobiographical *My Life*, 284, 285.

55. Oswald Mosely's *The Greater Britain* (London: Black House Publishing, 2012) is now available in paperback. See also Skidelsky, *Oswald Mosley*, 283–315.

56. Ibid., 240.

57. Ibid., 352–90.

58. Nicholas Mosley, *Rules*, 132–33; *My Life*, 326. Oswald has little to say about his association with William Joyce, and what he does relate dwells on his former assistant's vanity.

59. Ibid., 342; Skidelsky, *Oswald Mosley*, 342–92; and Colin Cross, *The Fascists in Britain* (New York, St. Martin's Press, 1963), 74–76.

60. Nicholas Mosley, *Rules*, 346.

61. Ibid., 347–49.

62. Skidelsky, *Oswald Mosley*, 457–64. Mosley received subsidies from the Italian Foreign Office, through Dino Grandi, the Italian ambassador to Great Britain. A copy of the order to transmit a monthly subsidy of 5,000 sterling (sterling pounds) to Mosley is reproduced in Nicholas Mosley's biography, 298. Between 1933 and 1935 the Italian government made available to the BUF subsidies amounting to 165,000 pounds.

63. See David Littlejohn, *Patriotic Traitors* (New York: Doubleday, 1972) for an investigation of the charge that Mosley and other high-ranking members of the BUF were in the pay of Nazi Germany. Littlejohn shows this accusation had no substance.

64. Oswald Mosley, *The Alternative* (London: Black House Publishing, 2012). Many of Mosley's writings, including his autobiography, were reissued by Black House Publishing in 2012.

65. Skidelsky, *Oswald Mosley*, 507–13.

66. Ibid., 486–88.

67. In Eric Fröhlich and Benedikt Kaiser's *Phänomen Inselfaschismus. Blackshirts, Blueshirts und weitere autoritäre Bewegungen in Großbritannien und Irland 1918-1945* (Auflage: Regin Verlag, 2013), Mosley emerges as an admirable visionary who offered a nonleftist vision of a unified Europe after the Second World War. See also Mosley's *My Life*, 457–73.

68. Skidelsky, *Oswald Mosley*, 492–94.

69. Oswald Mosley, *My Life*.

70. Quoted in Nicholas Mosley, *Rules*, 9.

71. Ibid., 225–34.

72. Oswald Mosley, *My Life*, 383.

73. Ibid., 383.

74. See Camillo Pellizi, "la penetrazione della lingua e della cultura italiana in Inghilterra," *Lavoro Fascista* (December 11, 1931); and "Il Fascismo in Inghilterra," in *Il Legionario* (October 3, 1925).

75. Scholz, *Italienischer Faschismus*, 114–17.

76. Skidelsky, *Oswald Mosley*, 333, explicitly denies that it was "political culture" that "killed off British fascism" and attributes this development entirely to an "antifascist war." He thereby overlooks the fact that fascism never became a critical political force in England. The BUF generated newspaper headlines mostly because its meetings attracted embattled opponents and often ended in violence.

77. See Eugen Weber, "The Men of the Archangel," *Journal of Contemporary History* 1, no. 1 (1966), 101-26; and Weber, *Varieties of Fascism*, 522-25.

78. See Ledeen, *Universal Fascism*; and Gregor, *The Ideology of Fascism*, especially 130-37.

79. Gregor, *The Ideology of Fascism*, 357.

80. For the key points in the now widely forgotten Declaration of Venice by nationalist parties seeking to form a European national party, see the online entry in Metapedia, http://en.metapedia.org/wiki/Declaration_of_Venice. For an explanation of the points, see Mosley's *My Life*, 459-63.

81. *Verso l'internazionale fascista*, 223.

82. Bruno Spampanato, "Universalità di ottobre. Ottobre principio del secolo," *Critica Fascista*, 10/3 (1932), 54.

Notes to Chapter Six

1. See Karl Mannheim, *Ideologie und Utopie*, eighth edition (Frankfurt am Main: Vittorio Klostermann, 1995), 169-77.

2. Ibid., 184-213.

3. Ibid., 199-203.

4. See Mannheim, *Konservatismus: Ein Beitrag zur Soziologie des Wissens*, 137-180.

5. See Mannheim, *Ideologie und Utopie*, 203.

6. Ibid. On the world views of Stahl and Savigny, see two of my articles, "German Romanticism and Natural Law," *Studies in Romanticism* 7, no. 4 (Summer 1968), 231-42; and "The Historical and Communal Roots of Legal Rights and the Erosion of the State," in *Rethinking Rights*, edited by Bruce P. Frohnen and Kenneth L. Grasso (Columbia, MO: University of Missouri Press, 2009), 153-76.

7. See my monograph, *Conservative Millenarians: The Romantic Experience in Bavaria* (New York: Fordham University Press, 1979); Hans Grassl, *Aufbruch zur Romantik: Bayerns Beitrag zur deutschen Geistesgeschichte 1765-1785* (Munich: Beck'sche Buchverhandlung, 1968); Jacques Droz, *Le romantisme politique en Allemagne* (Paris: Colin, 1963); and my essay "Utopianism of the Right," *Modern Age* (Spring 1980), 150-60.

8. Mannheim, *Ideologie und Utopie*, 214-18; the unmentioned work by Alfred Weber to which Mannheim is alluding that deals with the utopian imagination is *Ideen zur Staats-und Kultursoziologie* (Karlsruhe: G. Braun, 1927). Mannheim's view of his utopian subjects as precursors of his own self-designated group is amply confirmed by his flattering discussion of the *Intelligenz* as free-floating, classless thinkers in Mannheim's *Ideologie und Utopie*, 134-42. There he praises a distinctly conservative world view that he sees as arising among his fellow intellectuals.

9. See Georg Lukacs, *The Destruction of Reason*, trans. Peter R. Palmer, transcribed edition (Merlin Press, 2005); and Marcuse, *Reason and Revolution*, 340-88.

10. Mannheim, *Ideologie und Utopie*, 204.

11. See Panajotis Kondylis, *Konservativismus: Geschichtlicher Gehalt und Untergang* (Stuttgart: Klett, 1988), especially 387-441.

12. Unlike generic fascists or more traditional conservatives, the American Right has developed a *sui generis* character that distinguishes it from any historic Right as well as from the European liberalism of the nineteenth century. In recent decades this *soi-disant* Right has merged with the Republican Party, for want of a better patron. It has also largely divested itself of its traditionalist elements or pushed them into the background. See the postscript to the French translation of my *Le conservatisme en Amérique: Comprendre la droite américaine* (Paris: L'œuvre, 2012), 289–97; and Paul Gottfried, *Conservatism in America: Making Sense of the American Right* (New York: Macmillan, 2007), 1–30.

13. See Joseph de Maistre's *Considerations on France*, translated and edited by Richard A. Lebrun (Cambridge, England: Cambridge University Press, 1994), 36–37. In an otherwise informative introduction, Isaiah Berlin announces that Maistre "is a kind of protagonist of the militant anti-rational Fascism of modern times" (ibid., xxxii). But it is inconceivable that any fascist would have shared Maistre's contempt for "national sovereignty," an invention that he traced to Rousseau and the French Revolution.

14. Quoted in Weissmann, *Alles was rechts ist*, 15.

15. Ibid., 18. Also, Bodo Scheurig, *Ein Konservativer gegen Hitler*, new edition (Berlin: Propyläen, 1994).

16. Quoted in Weissmann, *Alles was rechts ist*, 18. Significantly, Kleist-Schmenzin held a very different view of Hitler from that of his fellow anti-Nazi and personal friend Ernst Niekisch, who was a self-styled "National Bolshevik." Unlike Kleist-Schmenzin, Niekisch depicted Hitler as the "henchman of reactionary bourgeois forces," in *Hitler-Ein deutsches Verhängnis*, (Schnellbach: Bublies Verlag, 1932).

17. Weissmann, *Alles was rechts ist*, 18.

18. Ibid., 15.

19. Del Noce, *Giovanni Gentile*, 288–90; Norberto Bobbio, *Profilo ideologico del Novecento italiano* (Turin: Einaudi, 1986); and Danilo Breschi's examination of the Gentilian transformation of Mazzini into a precursor of Italian authoritarian nationalism in "Fascism, Liberalism and Revolution," *European Journal of Political Theory*, 410–25.

20. A. James Gregor, *Giovanni Gentile: Philosopher of Fascism* (New Brunswick and London: Transaction Publishers, 2001), 101.

21. Ibid., 101–2.

22. Ibid., 83–87. Gregor mentions Gentile's frequent contacts with Jewish scholars and students and his support for Jewish intellectuals who were fleeing Nazi Germany after 1933. The decision by Mussolini to introduce anti-Semitic legislation into Italy in 1938, while drawing close to Nazi Germany politically, "created moral problems of unimaginable magnitude" for Gentile, who registered strong objections to *Il Duce*'s anti-Semitic course (ibid., 87). Undoubtedly a man of conscience, Gentile also pleaded with the leaders of the Salò Republic to release their prisoners, albeit to no avail. Significantly, however, he stayed (more or less) loyal to the fascist regime, or to what the Germans put in its place after Mussolini's fall from power, up until his assassination in 1944.

23. Ibid., 1 and 2; and Giovanni Gentile, *Rosmini e Gioberti* (Florence: Sansoni, 1943).

24. An informative study of the effects of Latin Catholic feudal culture, including Catholic social theory, on South America is Howard Wiarda's *The Soul of Latin America* (New Haven: Yale University Press, 2003).

25. Arnaud Imatz, *José Antonio et la Phalange Espagnole* (Paris: Editions Albatros, 1981), 254–57; and Payne, *Falange: A History of Spanish Fascism*, 69–115. For an apprecia-

tion of José Antonio as a social thinker by a later Spanish parliamentary leader, see Manuel Fraga Iribarne, *José Antonio: actualidad de su doctrina* (Madrid: Delegación nacional del Movimento, 1961). There is an at least implicit disagreement between Payne and Imatz, both of whom have produced solid studies of the Falange, about the movement and personality of José Antonio. Imatz depicts José Antonio as a devoted, almost otherworldly Christian while Payne treats him as an impulsive advocate of violence. One gathers equally from both monographs that there was heavy borrowing, particularly from the Italian template, that went into Spanish fascism.

26. See Charles Maurras, *Action Française*, April 1, 1912, 1; and *Mes idées politiques* (Paris: Fayard, 1968).

27. Del Noce offers an overview and critical analysis of this interpretation of fascism from Croce through Bobbio in *Giovanni Gentile*, 283–417. For another view from a socialist perspective, see Max Gallo, *L'Italie de Mussolini* (Paris: Libraire Académique Perin, 1964). One reason Del Noce dismisses the notion of fascism as a reactionary movement was its periodic overlap with the Italian Left, which was equally intent on promoting national reeducation and secularization. But the presence of this partially shared agenda does not mean that the fascists were not on the Right in terms of the political sides taken in the interwar era. Beyond rejection of a Catholic educational agenda, Del Noce cites fascism's dependence on Gentilian modernism as proof of its leftist character.

28. See Ludwig Gumplowicz, *Grundriss der Soziologie* (Vienna: Manzsche k.und k. Hof-Verlags und Universitäts-Buchhandlung, 1905), especially 202–64; Harry Elmer Barnes's entry on Gumplowicz in the *International Encyclopedia of the Social Sciences* (1968) Encyclopedia.com; and my essay "Rassenkampf als Triebfeder der Geschichte," in *Neue Ordnung* 3 (Fall 2014), 13–16.

29. See Arthur de Gobineau, *The Inequality of Human Races* (Ulan Press, 2012).

30. Giovanni Gentile, *I Fondamenti della filosofia del diritto* (Florence: Sansoni, 1961); and Giovanni Gentile, *Teoria generale dello spirito come atto puro* (Florence: Sansoni, [1916] 1959).

31. See Giovanni Gentile, *I Fondamenti*, 70 and 114–17.

32. Del Noce, quoted in *Giovanni Gentile*, 340.

33. See H. S. Harris, *The Social Philosophy of Giovanni Gentile* (Urbana: University of Illinois Press, 1960), especially 291–334. Although this text cites Del Noce far more often than Harris for illustrative purposes, Harris has produced (certainly in English) the most comprehensive, nonpolemical examination of Gentile's thought.

34. Zeev Sternhell cites spiritualism as a characteristic of French fascism and deals with this orientation not only as a body of ideas but through such once widespread fads as necromancy. Sternhell's key insight is indispensable for understanding the cultural background of Latin fascism. See "Sur le fascisme et sa variante française," *Le Débat*, November, 1984; and "Emmanuel Mounier et la contestation de la démocratie libérale dans la France," *Revue française de science politique*, December, 1984.

35. Giovanni Gentile, *I Fondamenti*, 74–76.

36. Del Noce, *Giovanni Gentile*, 355.

37. See G. W. F. Hegel, *Enzyklopädie der philosophischen Wissenschaften im Grundrisse (1830). Werke in zwanzig Bänden* 8 (Frankfurt: Suhrkamp, 1970), 502.

38. Ibid., 503.

39. See Georges Sorel, *Reflections on Violence*, Jeremy Jennings, ed. (Cambridge: Cambridge University Press, 1999).

40. See Georges Sorel, *Les Illusions du Progrès* (Paris: Ulan Press, 1908); and Michael Curtis, *Three Against the Third Republic: Sorel, Barrès and, Maurras* (Princeton, NJ: Princeton University Press, 1959); and Zeev Sternhell, Maia Asheri, and Mario Sznajder, *The Birth of Fascist Ideology: From Cultural Rebellion to Political Revolution*, David Maisel, trans. (Princeton, NJ: Princeton University Press, 1994).

41. Perhaps the definitive work in English on the effects of Sorel's thought on the French and Italian revolutionary rights is J. J. Roth's *The Cult of Violence: Sorel and the Sorelians* (Berkeley: University of California Press, 1980).

42. Nolte, *Späte Reflexionen*, 156–57.

43. The most gruesome example known to me of the continued obsession with fascist evils was in the *New York Post*, March 10, 2013. Below a picture of the dangling body of Mussolini riddled with bullets was mention of how the "fascist Italian strongman's . . . body was beaten and passed around." This ghoulish description followed a verbal attack on the "dictator" Hugo Chavez, who was accused of "anti-Semitism" and other qualities that were intended to remind us of interwar fascists.

44. See Ernst Jünger, *Der Arbeiter: Herrschaft und Gestalt*, reprint from 1932 (Stuttgart: Kletta-Cotta Verlag, 2007); and Oswald Spengler, *Preussentum und Sozialismus*, reprint from 1919 (London: Arktos Media Limited, 2012), especially 26–67.

45. Robert Nisbet, *The Quest for Community: A Study in the Ethics and Order of Freedom*, new edition (San Francisco: ICS Press, 1990), 204.

46. Robert Nisbet, *The Sociology of Emile Durkheim* (New York: Oxford University Press, 1974), 16.

47. Robert Nisbet, *The Social Philosophers: Community and Conflict in Western Thought* (New York: Crowell, 1973), especially 407–49 for Nisbet's favorable assessment of the European conservative tradition.

48. See Meyer, *In Defense of Freedom: A Conservative Credo*, 129. An essay of mine, "Robert Nisbet and the Present Age," in *Society* 52, no. 5, August 2015, 335–343, advances the argument that American traditionalists could not defend the "state" in the same way as Mannheim's counterrevolutionary subjects because they could not imagine a nonleftist state or one that was not highly centralized and committed to egalitarian ends. Fascism as conceived by the revolutionary Right held absolutely no appeal for these Americans, particularly in view of its associations with the Nazis in the Second World War. See also my entry on Robert Nisbet in the *International Encyclopedia of the Social and Behavioral Sciences*, 2nd ed.

49. See Harris, *The Social Philosophy of Giovanni Gentile*, 82–98.

50. Payne, *Fascism in Spain, 1923–1977*, 28–48.

Notes to Chapter Seven

1. For a dispassionate analysis of what is at stake in this altercation, see Robert Golan-Vilella "The Meaning of the Hagel Fight," *The National Interest*, February 26, 2013, http://nationalinterest.org/commentary/the-meaning-the-hagel-fight-8155.

2. This confused and confusing taking of sides in the fight over Hagel's confirmation as secretary of defense was the theme of my featured commentary on the *American Conservative* website on December 28, 2012: http://www.theamericanconservative.com/2012/12/28/hagel-gets-a-sensitivity-litmus-test-from-the-neocon-press/.

3. See Gottfried, *After Liberalism*, especially 72–109.

4. This argument runs through what may be Lasch's best-known work, *The True and Only Heaven*.

5. See the relevant statements in the *Hamburger Abendblatt*: http://www.abendblatt.de/politik/article1400242/Kauder-Die-CDU-ist-keine-konservative-Partei.html.

6. See Niklas Luhmann, *Soziologische Aufklärung 3: Soziales System, Gesellschaft, Organisation* (Opladen: Westdeutscher Verlag, 1981); and the still unpublished essay by his student Jost Bauch earmarked for the bound proceedings of the Weikersheimer Stiftung, "Das Reglement des Politischen. Politischen Leitunterscheidungen bei Carl Schmitt, Otto von Bismarck und Niklas Luhmann."

7. See Giovanni Sartori, "The Essence of the Political in Carl Schmitt," *Journal of Theoretical Politics* 1, no. 1 (January 1989), 63.

8. A variation on Luhmann's plan, which minimizes ideological differences even further, can be found in the editorial essay in *La Stampa* on October 29, 2014, "resta la destra." The editorialist calls for a "moderate Right" that would operate mostly in opposition to a more dynamic Left and help "create a mature bipolarism between two liberal blocs that are politically close to each other." The opposition advocated is almost too minimal to be distinguished from the "liberal bloc."

9. See Zeev Sternhell, *Les anti-Lumières du XVIII siècle à la guerre froide* (Paris: Fayard, 2007).

10. Ibid., especially 492–580.

11. See Joseph de Maistre, *Considérations sur la France* (Paris: Garnier, 1980), 64; Sternhell, *Les anti-Lumières*, 237–64; and Isaiah Berlin, "Joseph de Maistre and the Origins of Fascism," *The Crooked Timber of Humanity*, ed. Henry Hardy (London: John Murray, 1990). It may behoove us to examine the context of this strangely controversial statement to understand its meaning. Maistre was commenting on whether the French constitution of 1795 was congruent with the political traditions of the French people. He is making the point that no single constitution can fit all nations, and, therefore, those who support a French constitution should make sure that it truly reflects the customs and mentality of the French people.

12. Although Sternhell in *The Founding Myths of Israel: Nationalism, Socialism, and the Jewish State*, trans. David Maisel, (Princeton, NJ: Princeton University Press, 1997) criticizes Israel's Labor Zionist founders for being insufficiently socialist, even in that critical work he never challenges the Zionist claim to a Jewish national homeland.

13. See David Hume, *Essays Moral, Political, Literary*, edited and introduced by Eugene F. Miller (Indianapolis: Liberty Classics, 1987), 465–87. In his essay "Of the Original Contract," Hume provides historical and empirical evidence that government by consent never existed. Indeed, "reason, history and experience shew us, that all political societies have had an origin much less accurate and regular; and were one to choose a period of time, when the people's consent was the least regarded in public transactions, it would be precisely on the establishment of new government. In a settled constitution, their inclinations are often consulted; but during the fury of revolution, conquests, and public convulsions, military force or political craft usually decides the controversy" (ibid., 474). Sternhell seems particularly fascinated by Hume, whom he regards as someone who had one foot in the good Enlightenment but the other planted in the less agreeable "other modernity." See Sternhell, *Les anti-Lumières*, especially 141–67 and 371–76.

14. Sternhell (ibid., 60) defends without reservations Kant's utopian side, which he also finds in Habermas, someone who teaches that the abandonment of utopian dreams "is only another way of sapping the foundations of modernity." The Israeli historian anchors

his "vision" of steady human moral and political improvement in what he calls "the dream of Reason." Unfortunately, this mythic invention is no more of a rational argument than Sternhell's insistence that we should all believe in "linear" progress.

15. German historian Karlheinz Weissmann (*Alles was rechts ist*, 180) mentions that he was present at a lecture delivered by Sternhell at the Carl von Siemens Stiftung in 1997. Although this lecture was mostly about the French origins of fascism, the speaker also dwelled on the need for accepting the "ideals of 1789." Habermas, who was on hand, began to applaud loudly at this point. A question that might have been addressed to the speaker is "which revolutionary ideals are you privileging?" During the first phase of the Revolution, distinctions were drawn between active citizens, who were allowed to vote, and less wealthy or passive citizens, who were not. The Revolution also produced the *Loi Le Chapelier* in 1790, which declared workers' unions to be illegal because they violated the sanctity of contract. One might guess that these classical liberal stands that also came out of the Revolution are not the ones that Sternhell and Habermas would like to legislate universally.

16. Payne, *Fascism in Spain*, 59–65, 165–75.

Notes to Appendix: Fascism and Modernization

1. Roger Griffin, *Modernism and Fascism: The Sense of a Beginning under Mussolini and Hitler* (NY: Palgrave Macmillan, 2010), 51.
2. Ibid.
3. Theodor Adorno, *Minima Moralia* (Frankfurt: Suhrkamp, 1951), vol. 3, aphorism 140.
4. Griffin, *Modernism and Fascism*, 116–17.
5. Ibid., 117.
6. Ibid.
7. For relevant studies of the German essayist and novelist, see Walter Lennig, *Gottfried Benn in Selbstzeugnissen und Bilddokumentation*, 18th ed. (Hamburg: Rowohlt, 1994); Werner Rübe, *Provoziertes Leben: Gottfried Benn* (Stuttgart: Klett Verlag, 1993); and for Céline, Patrick McCarthy, *Céline: A Portait* (NY: Viking, 1974). One could not imagine a more cynical autobiographical novelist than Céline, whose credo may be found most clearly stated in his 700-page account of his flight through Germany at the end of the war, avoiding both Allied bombing and arrest by the SS, *Nord* (Paris: Gallimard, 1960): *"le monde nouveau, commune-bourgeois, sermonneux, tartufe infini, automobiliste, alcoolique, bâfreur, cancéreux, connaît que deux angoisses: son cul, son compte? Le reste s'il en fout! Prolos Plutos réunis! Parfaitement d'accord!"* One would be hard put to find here or elsewhere in Céline's misanthropic and very modernist prose any sense of "futurity" or "canopy of meanings."
8. See Griffin, *Modernism and Fascism*, 41 and 358. For an easily accessible account of Jünger's unfriendly relations with the Nazis and his connection and his son's to the German resistance, see http://www.ask.com/wiki/Ernst_J%C3%BCnger?o=2801&qsrc=999. Griffin's contention that Jünger's glorification of work in his novel *Der Arbeiter* (1932) is "philo-Nazi" is entirely unsubstantiated.
9. Griffin, *Modernism and Fascism*, 53.
10. On Eliot's relation to Maurras, see *Eliot in Perspective: A Symposium*, Martin Graham, ed (New York and London: Macmillan, 1970), 16–17, 202–29; and Stéphane Giocanti, *Maurras: Le chaos et l'ordre* (Paris: Flammarion, 2006), 286–88, 314, 317. A disci-

ple and friend of Eliot, Russell Kirk, in a sadly underappreciated biography, *Eliot and His Age* (New York: Random House, 1971), 256, supplies a context for Eliot's controversial statement about "the bogey of fascism" on the European "ultra-left." Eliot was criticizing the Popular Front's overblown attacks on generic fascism, which contributed to diverting attention from the major threat to western and central Europe that was then coming from Nazi Germany. The poet was ridiculing the Left's untimely war against fascist counterrevolutionaries in the face of a menacing Nazi challenge.

11. Ibid., 55; see also, Zygmunt Bauman, *Modernity and Ambivalence* (Ithaca, NY: Cornell University Press, 1991); and Griffin, *The Nature of Fascism*.

12. Griffin, *Modernism and Fascism*, 265–90.

13. See Volker Kempf, *Wider die Wirklichkeitsverweigerung*, 23–54, 95–114.

Notes to Appendix: A Final Loose End

1. Among the numerous Anglophone exemplifications of this now established view of the German past are: Fritz Stern, *The Failure of Illiberalism* (New York: Knopf, 1972); Ian Kershaw, *Weimar: Why Did German Democracy Fail?* (London: Weidenfeld and Nicolson, 1990); Ian Kershaw, *The Nazi Dictatorship: Problems and Perspectives of Interpretation* (London: Arnold, 2000); and Richard J. Evans, *The Coming of the Third Reich* (New York and London: Penguin, 2004). Most current, academically respectable treatments of German history have been built around the idea of a dangerous German *Sonderweg*, or growing deviation of the Germans from an ideal Western model, and this argument has been given currency by such groundbreaking German historians as Hans Ulrich Wehler and Jürgen Kocka. Not all historians of Germany emphasize this idea equally, and it might be unfair to place Evans or Kershaw in the same category as Stern and Wehler in their stress on the almost uninterrupted badness of German history from the period of unification until the end of the Second World War. Still neither British historian would deny association with those who highlight the Sonderweg theory. The same reading of the German past dovetails with the now conventional picture of German history that is conveyed by the media and popular culture. The German deviation from the Western liberal democratic path supposedly had cumulative effects resulting in the political disaster that overwhelmed Europe with Hitler's accession to power.

2. The view of Hitler as a radical modernizer is most fully developed in Rainer Zitelmann's massive dissertation, which was subsequently published as a book, *Hitler: Selbstverständnis eines Revolutionärs* (Hamburg, Oxford and New York: Berg Publishers, 1987), especially 414–65.

3. See *Nationalsozialismus und Modernisierung*, edited by Michael Prinz and Rainer Zitelmann (Darmstadt: Wissenschaftliche Buchgesellschaft, 1994), 7–10 and 1–20; and Zitelmann, *Hitler: Selbstverständnis eines Revolutionärs*, 195–271.

4. Ralf Dahrendorf, *Gesellschaft und Demokratie in Deutschland* (Munich: Piper, 1965), 432.

5. Ibid., 434.

6. Prinz and Zitelmann, *Nationalsozialismus und Modernisierung*, 13.

7. Wehler, *Modernisierungstheorie und Geschichte*, 198.

8. Zitelmann, *Hitler: Selbstverständnis eines Revolutionärs*, 20 and 21.

9. Jürgen W. Falter, "War die NSDAP die ersts deutsche Volkspartei?," in *Nationalsozialismus und Modernisierung*, 21–47; and Jürgen W. Falter, "Mythen über die Wähler der

NSDAP," in *Die Schatten der Vergangenheit: Impulse zur Historisierung des Nationalsozialismus*, 2nd ed., edited by Uwe Backes, Eckhard Jesse, and Rainer Zitelmann (Frankfurt and Berlin, 1992), 265–90.

10. Zitelmann, *Hitler: Selbstverständnis eines Revolutionärs*, 85–90.

11. See Rainer Zitelmann, "Zur Begründung des 'Lebensraum' Motivs in Hitlers Weltanschauung," in *Der Zweite Weltkrieg: Analysen, Grundzüge, Forschungsbilanz*, edited by Wolfgang Michalka (Munich and Zürich: Seehamer, 1989), 551–56; and Zitelmann, *Hitler: Selbstverständnis eines Revolutionärs*, 316–36.

12. Rainer Zitelmann et al., eds., *Die Schatten der Vergangenheit*, 2nd ed. (Frankfurt and Berlin, 1992), 218–42.

13. Ronald Smelser, *Robert Ley: Hitler's Labor Front Leader* (New York, Oxford, Hamburg: Berg Publishers Limited, 1988), 117–49.

14. Ibid., 149–80.

15. Ibid., 302.

16. Ibid., 170.

17. Ibid., 300.

18. It has been known for some time that the rapid rate of social mobility in the first six years of the Nazi regime vastly exceeded that of the Weimar Republic. See, for example, Richard Grunberger, *The 12-Year Reich: A Social History of Germany, 1933–1945* (London: Weidenfeld and Nicholson, 1971), 55–57; and Zitelmann, *Hitler: Selbstverständnis eines Revolutionärs*, 460–62.

19. See Sean McMeekin, *The Russian Origins of the First World War* (Cambridge: Harvard University Press, 2011); and Christopher Clark, *The Sleepwalkers: How Europe Went to War in 1914* (New York: Harper and Collins, 2013). A general German history for the period that seems far better balanced than the conventional expositions of the German *Sonderweg* and carefully examines Germany's position vis-à-vis its neighbors is Thomas Nipperdey's *Deutsche Geschichte 2* (Munich: C. H. Beck, 1991). Gunter Spraul, in *Der Fischer-Komplex* (Halle: Projekte Verlag, 1911), demonstrates to what extent the assault on Nipperdey's scholarship and other historiography that is not seen as sufficiently critical of the national past is ideologically motivated. Spraul further challenges the Fischer thesis by documenting how its creator misquoted or quoted in an elliptical fashion such key political figures as the Kaiser, Helmuth von Moltke, and the German Chancellor.

20. See Henry Ashby Turner, *Reappraisals of Fascism* (New York: New Viewpoints, 1975), 117–39; and David Schoenbaum, *Hitler's Social Revolution: Class and Status in Nazi Germany, 1933–1945* (New York: Norton, 1997). Although Zitelmann makes a cogent case (*Hitler: Selbstverständnis eines Revolutionärs*, 6, 7, 304, 321) that Hitler did not view himself as a reactionary German, Nazi propaganda nonetheless often emphasized Germany's agrarian or mythological past.

21. See Spengler, *Preussentum und Sozialismus*, 1–25. Spengler denounced bogus or ineffective revolutionaries. Hitler did in the same time period: "*Ein Französe würde den Vergleich mit 1789 als eine Beleidigung seiner Nation mit Recht ablehnen.*" See also Carl Schmitt, *Die Diktatur: Von den Anfängen des modernen Souveränitätsgedanken bis zum proletarischen Klassenkampf*, 3rd ed. (Berlin: Duncker & Humblot, 1964), especially 25–40; and Zitelmann, *Hitler: Selbstverständnis eines Revolutionärs*, 401–12.

22. Zitelmann, *Hitler: Selbstverständnis eines Revolutionärs*, 60–78.

23. Prinz and Zitelmann, *Nationalsozialismus und Modernisierung*, 17.

24. Henry Ashby Turner, in *Hitler's Thirty Days to Power: January 1933* (Reading, MA: Addison-Wesley, 1996), stresses the element of contingency that enabled Hitler to seize control of the German state, starting with his appointment as chancellor. Although Turner does not frontally controvert the "continuity thesis," a critique of this view is at least implicit in his interpretation.

25. Ibid., 15–16.

26. See Zitelmann, *Wohin treibt unsere Republik*, 186–90; and *Westbindung: Chancen und Risiken für Deutschland*, edited by Karlheinz Weissmann, M. Grossheim, and Rainer Zitelmann (Frankfurt and Berlin: Propyläen, 1993).

INDEX

A

aberrant historical path, 163
abortion, 102–3
accelerazione totalitaria, 114
Action Française, 18, 161
Action Française (Maurras), 108
Adler, Les K.
 "Red Fascism," 47–48
Adorno (Wiggershaus), 187n29
Adorno, Theodor
 Authoritarian Personality, The, 7, 66
 and California Test, 66
 on Cold War, 66
 and Communist Party members, 66
 Dialectic of the Enlightenment, The, 65, 187n29
 and Frankfurt School, 59, 60
 and F-scale, 66
 at Goethe University, 62
 and House Un-American Activities Committee, 66
 Minima Moralia, 60
 on modernity, 159
 and music, 60
 Negative Dialektik, 60
 on poetry, 83
 religion of, 62
 and TAP, 61
"Adorno's Failed Aesthetic of Myth" (Pan), 187–88n29
Aeneid (Virgil), 86
Age of Reason, 129
AJC (American Jewish Committee)
 discussed, 62, 66
 Studies in Prejudice, 61, 69, 76
Alleanza Nazionale, 128
Allende, Salvador, 178n30
Allgemeiner Deutscher Gewerkschaftsbund, 168
Allied High Commission, 68, 73
Altemeyer, Bob, 67
Alternative, The (O. Mosley), 121

ambienti industriali, 40
American Jewish Committee (AJC)
 discussed, 62, 66
 Studies in Prejudice, 61, 69, 76
Analytic Marxists, 74
anti-Americanism, 81, 82, 191n60
Anti-Comintern Pact, 25
Antieuropa, 112, 115, 116, 117, 128
antifascism
 and *The Black Book of Communism*, 55
 and Croce, 137
 discussed, 58, 72, 76, 82, 152
 and G. Wagner, 86
 and Gayssot, 78
 in Germany, 82, 85
 in *Gilles*, 107
 and Habermas, 64
 and Habermas/Jens, 69–70
 and Holocaust, 85, 191–92n66
 and *Homage to Catalonia*, 183n15
 and Niekisch/Paetel, 181n70
 and *Studies in Prejudice*, 76
 and TAP, 66, 67
antimodern modernism, 23
anti-Semitism. *See also* Final Solution; Holocaust; Jews
 and American Jewish Committee, 66
 in *Blackshirt*, 121
 discussed, 32, 34
 at Fascist International Congress, 95
 and Final Solution, 84
 and Frankfurt School, 62
 of French nationalists, 77
 and Fromm, 62
 of Gombos, 80
 of Hitler, 24, 120, 166
 in Hungary, 79
 and Institute for Social Research, 62
 in Italy, 200n22
 of Ley, 168
 in literature, 125
 of Mussolini, 26, 200n22
 of Nazi collaborators, 32

in Nazi electoral propaganda, 166
in Romania, 34, 95
and Romanian fascists, 95
in Soviet bloc, 51
and *Studies in Prejudice*, 61
in Vichy France, 192n70
of von Schönerer, 37
Antonescu, Ion, 14, 33–35, 126
Antonio, José, 140–41, 157, 201n25
Anything Goes (Porter), 96
Apfel, Holger, 189n50
architect of fascist internationalism, 115, 117
Arendt, Hannah
   compared to Brzezinski, 51
   discussed, 15, 43–44, 50, 53, 54, 170
   Origins of Totalitarianism, The, 7, 43, 52, 103
   on totalitarianism, 51, 52
Aristotle
   Politics, 116
Arlington House, 123
arretratezza, 141
Arrow Cross Party, 32–33
As We Go Marching (Flynn), 96
assassinations, 74
Atlanticists, 190n58
Auschwitz, 85
Austrian Freedom Party, 76, 77, 79
Austrofaschismus, 179n48
authoritarian personality, 60, 62, 66, 70, 196n32
Authoritarian Personality, The (Adorno/Horkheimer), 7, 66
Authoritarian Society, The (Institute for Social Research), 61
authoritarianism, 32–33, 34, 56

B

Baathists, 93
Babbitt, Irving, 103
Bachofen, Johann Jakob
   Mutterrecht, 63
Back to Africa, 18
backwardness, 141
Balilla, 8

Barnes, James Strachey, 115, 116
Barrès, Maurice, 20, 111
Basic Law, 78
Battle against the Right, 67
Bauch, Jost, 73
   "Das Reglement des Politischen," 203n6
Bauman, Zygmunt, 170
Being and Time (Heidegger), 131
Benn, Gottfried, 160
Bergengruen, Werner, 50
Berlin, Isaiah, 155, 200n13
Berlioz, Hector
   discussed, 85–86
   Les Troyens, 86
Besancon, Alain, 84
Betar, 18
Beyond the Pale (N. Mosley), 123
Big Brother, 48–49
Black Book of Communism, The (Courtois), 55, 78
Black Front, 39, 123
Black House Publishing, 198n64
Blackshirt, 120–121
Blue Division, 33
Blueshirts, 18, 95
Blum, Léon, 29
Bobbio, Norberto, 5, 137
Bolshevik Revolution, 59, 90, 140
Bolsheviks/bolshevism
   discussed, 18, 21, 91, 105, 127
   German National Bolsheviks, 40
   and Hitler, 175n3
   and Iron Guard, 34
   and Niekisch/Paetel, 181n70
   von Kleist-Schmenzin on, 134
Bonaparte, Napoleon, 71
borghesia vigliarda, 92
Borkenau, Franz, 5, 48
Bottai, Giovanni, 91
Bottai, Giuseppe, 28, 39
Bourne, Randolph, 97
Bracher, Karl, 190n58
Braque, Georges, 160
Breschi, Danilo
   "Fascism, Liberalism, and Revolution," 180n61
Briand, Aristide, 116

Brickner, Richard, 68
bricolage, 40
British Union of Fascists (BUF)
    discussed, 119, 120–21, 126, 199n76
    founding of, 18, 29, 124
    and *Giovinezza*, 124
    and *Patriotic Traitors*, 198n63
    subsidies to, 198n62
brown revolution, 168
Brzezinski, Zbigniew, 44, 51, 52, 53, 56
Buchheim, Hans
    discussed, 50
    Totalitarian Rule, 43
Buckley, William F., Jr., 97, 100, 123
BUF (British Union of Fascists)
    discussed, 119, 120–21, 126, 199n76
    founding of, 18, 29, 124
    and *Giovinezza*, 124
    and *Patriotic Traitors*, 198n63
    subsidies to, 198n62
bureaucratic centralization, 50
Burke, Edmund, 159
Burleigh, Michael, 47
Burnham, James
    Managerial Revolution, The, 26, 49
Bush, George W., 46, 182n9
Butterfield, Herbert, 49, 184–85n40

C

California Test, 66–67
Calvinism, 63
Campbell, Roy, 123
Campi, Alessandro
    L'Unità del mondo, 191n60
Canis, Konrad
    Der Weg in den Abgrund, Deutsche Aussenpolitik, 1902–1914, 189n42
    discussed, 170
Carentan (character in *Gilles*), 108, 111
Carl von Siemens Stiftung, 204n15
Carol II (king), 34
Carta del Lavoro, 7, 27–28, 181n71
Catholic Center Party, 165
Caudillo, 33
CDU-CSU, 67

Céline, Louis-Ferdinand, 160
Cercle-Proudhon, 20
Chamberlain, Joseph, 122
Chase, Stuart, 96
Chavez, Hugo, 202n43
Chiappe, Jean, 110
"Chile" (Hobsbawm), 178n30
Chodorov, Frank, 97
Christian Democratic-Christian Social Union, 67
Christian Democrats
    discussed, 45, 81, 149
    in Hessen, 69
    Kauder on, 154
    and Pershing missiles, 75
Christianity, 84, 145, 149, 164, 190n54
Churchill, Winston, 116, 119, 122, 190n54, 191n65
CIA, 61, 183n14
Cicero, 187n29
Civil Rights Act of 1964, 99
Clark, Christopher, 170
Clinton, Bill, 98–99, 194n30
Clinton, Hillary, 98–99, 194n30
Codreanu, Corneliu Zelea, 34, 125
Cold War
    and Adorno, 66
    discussed, 4, 48, 74, 81
    and military dictatorships, 22
    and totalitarianism, 47
Comitati d'Azione per l'Universalità di Roma, 114
Communist Party, 53, 78, 79, 98
concentration camps, 5, 34
Confindustria, 40
Congdon, Lee
    George Kennan, 181n63
Conservatism (Kondylis), 133
"Conservatism" (Mannheim), 94
Conservative Party, 94, 119
conservative utopia, 131, 133
Considerations on France (de Maistre), 131, 155, 200n13
continuity thesis, 169, 207n24
Corriere degli Italiani, 30
Coughlin, Charles Edward, 29, 178n38
Counter-Reformation, 115

Courrier International, 14
Courtois, Stéphane
  Black Book of Communism, The, 55, 78
cowardly burghers, 92
crisis of bourgeois society, 63
Critica Fascista, 28, 115, 116, 128
critical theory, 59, 60, 69, 70
Croce, Benedetto, 137, 141
Croix de Feu, 109
crony capitalism, 100
Cubists, 160
cult of personality, 6, 53
cultural imperialism, 115
culture of remembering, 85
Curzon, George Nathaniel, 119
Cuza, Alexander, 125

D

Dahrendorf, Ralf
  discussed, 163–64
  Gesellschaft und Demokratie in Deutschland, 164
Daily Mail, 120
Daladier, Édouard, 110
D'Annunzio, Gabriele, 11
Das Kapital (Marx), 72
"Das Reglement des Politischen" (Bauch), 203n6
datori del lavoro, 28, 40
days of reconciliation, 84
De Felice, Renzo
  on *Carta del Lavoro*, 181n71
  discussed, 40, 57, 87–88, 95
  Interpretations of Fascism, 42, 45
  Mussolini il duce, 43
de Gaulle, Charles, 77, 116, 122, 146, 190n54
de Gobineau, Arthur, 142
de Jouvenel, Bertrand
  discussed, 28
  Du Pouvoir, 88–89
  Of Power, 88–89
de Maistre, Joseph
  Considerations on France, 131, 155, 200n13
  discussed, 134, 159, 203n11
de Man, Hendrik, 29–30
de Mun, Albert, 38, 141
de Rivera, José Antonio Primo, 29, 80, 103, 136
de Spinoza, Benedict, 138, 143
Déat, Marcel, 29, 33
Dégrelle, Leon, 32, 33, 35
Del Noce, Augusto
  discussed, 10, 47, 49
  on G. Gentile, 137–38, 143–44
  Giovanni Gentile: Per una interpretazione filosofica della storia contemporanea, 176n19, 193n9, 201n27
  L'epoca della secolarizzazione, 90–91
Democratic National Convention, 100
Democratic Party, 98, 152
Department of Education, 99
Der Brand (Friedrich), 191n65
Der europäische Bürgerkrieg (Nolte), 18
Der Faschismus in seiner Epoche (Nolte), 3, 18
Der Fischer-Komplex (Spraul), 188–89n42, 206n19
Der Fragebogen (von Salomon), 187n23
Der lange Schatten des Staates (Hanisch), 179n48
Der Weg in den Abgrund, Deutsche Aussenpolitik, 1902–1914 (Canis), 189n42
Descartes, René, 138
Destruction of Reason, The (G. Lukacs), 132
detotalitarization process, 52
Deutsche Arbeitsfront, 167
Deutsche Stimme, 189n50
Deutschnationale, 37
Dialectic of the Enlightenment, The (Adorno/Horkheimer), 65, 187n29
"Dictatorships and Double Standards" (Kirkpatrick), 184n36
Die deutsche Universitätsphilosophie in der Weimarer Republik und im Dritten Reich (Tilitzki), 183n27
Die Diktatur (Schmitt), 171
Die Entwicklung des Christusdogma (Fromm), 63
Die Frankfurter Schule (Wiggershaus), 187n29

Die Unfähigkeit zu trauern (Mitscherlich/Mitscherlich), 82–83
Die Welt, 82
Diggins, John P.
   discussed, 88
   Mussolini and Fascism, 30
Disraeli, Benjamin, 38
Doctrine of Fascism, The (G. Gentile), 143
Dollfuss, Engelbert
   discussed, 14, 31, 35, 146, 179n48
   Gombos on, 80
   Kennan on, 37
Doriot, Jacques, 28–29, 33
"Doriot ou la vie d'un ouvrier français" (La Rochelle), 196n32
Dottrina del Fascismo (Mussolini), 194n30
dream of Reason, 203n14
Dreyfus Affair, 51
du Pin, François René de la Tour, 141
Du Pouvoir (de Jouvenel), 88–89
"*Due Anni Dopo*" (G. Gentile), 138
Durkheim, Emile, 148–49

E

Eatwell, Roger, 23
"Economia programmatica" (Spirito), 178n36
economy
   discussed, 39, 44
   in France, 77
   and Frankfurt School, 60
   in Germany, 53
   in Greece, 79–80
   and Hitler, 40, 181–82n72
   and O. Mosley, 121–122
   and Mussolini, 30
   and Obama, 100
   and Spirito, 28
Edelmarxisten, 64
Edinburgh Review, 115
educational politics, 190n58
Eighteenth Brumaire of Louis Bonaparte, The (Marx), 71–72
Einstein, Albert, 116
El Fascio, 157
Eliade, Mircea, 55, 160

Eliot, T. S., 160, 161, 205n10
Eliot and His Age (Kirk), 205n10
Elster, Jon, 74
Empire (Hardt/Negri), 74
Encyclopedia of the Social Sciences, 46
Engels, Friedrich, 63
English Speaking Union, 120
Enlightenment
   discussed, 10, 140, 145, 159
   G. Gentile on, 143
   and Sternhell, 156–157
enterprise association, 50
Entfernte Verwandtschaft (Schivelbusch), 30, 88
epochal character, 22, 26–27
Erinnerungskultur, 85
Escape from Freedom (Fromm), 103
escape from transcendence, 10, 11, 17, 132, 141
Ethiopia, 9, 86, 88, 114, 117
ethnic cleansing, 58
Europe of nations, 122
Europe since Hitler (Laqueur), 189–90n50
European, 122–23
European Civil War, The (Nolte), 18
Evans, Richard J., 168
Evola, Giulio, 111, 112
exile, 60–61

F

factualness, 52
Falanga, 18
Falange
   discussed, 29, 33, 141, 149
   El Fascio, 157
   in *Gilles*, 106
   Imatz on, 140–141, 200–201n25
   Payne on, 20, 140–141, 200–201n25
Falter, Jürgen M., 165–66
Fanelli, Giuseppe Attlio
   "Mussolini contra Luterò," 112
Faschismus, von Mussolini zu Hitler (Nolte), 21
Fasci all'estero, 124
fascism

abuse of term, 3
and Democratic Party, 98
in England, 124–125, 126
examinations of, 3
Gairdner on, 102–4
Latin Catholic character of, 9
as movement of the Left, 87–88
in Romania, 125–26
TAP's interpretation of, 65
vision of the future, 127
Fascism (Payne), 20
"Fascism, Liberalism, and Revolution" (Breschi), 180n61
fascist ferment, 115
Fascist Grand Council, 26
fascist ideology, 18–19
Fascist International Congress, 17, 95. See *also* Montreux conferences
fascist minimum, 35, 36
fascist Pan-Europeanism, 116
fascist revival, 69, 101
fascist visions, 142–44
Fascist Week, 120
Fauquet, Joël-Marie, 86
FDR (Franklin Delano Roosevelt), 7, 30, 88, 119, 190n54
Feder, Don, 101
Federal Reserve, 29
Fenner, Angelica, 77
Final Solution, 84. See *also* anti-Semitism; Holocaust; Jews
Finer, Herman, 45, 51
Fini, Gianfranco, 128
Finzi, Aldo, 26
Firing Line (television series), 123
Fischer, Fritz, 187n29, 188–89n42, 206n19
Fischer, Joschka, 85
Flynn, John T.
discussed, 7, 96–97
As We Go Marching, 96
Founding Myths of Israel, The (Sternhell), 203n12
Fragebogen, 68
Franco, Francisco
discussed, 14, 33, 36, 146
Kennan on, 37
Franco-Prussian War, 177n9

Frank, Walter
Nationalismus und Demokratie im Frankreich der dritten Republik (1871 bis 1918), 177n9
Frankfurt School. See *also* Institute for Social Research
and anti-Semitism, 62
becomes Institute for Social Research, 61
discussed, 6–7, 59–61, 64, 72
and *TAP*, 66
Franz Josef, Emperor, 37
Frederick the Great, 169
freedom from alienation, 59
French Revolution, 90, 118, 134, 135, 137
Freud, Sigmund, 59–60, 116
Freudianism, 62
Freyer, Hans, 74
Friedrich, Carl, 44, 52
Friedrich, Jörg
Der Brand, 191n65
Frölich, Eric
Phänomen Inselfaschismus, 198n67
Fromm, Erich
Die Entwicklung des Christusdogma, 63
discussed, 59, 60, 62
Escape from Freedom, 103
Front National, 15, 77
F-scale, 66–67, 186n19
functional collaboration, 192n70
Furet, François, 10, 17

G

Gadamer, Hans-Georg, 54
Gairdner, William, 102–4
Gamble, Richard
War for Righteousness, The, 182n9
Garibaldi, Giuseppe, 36
Garrett, Garet, 97
Garvey, Marcus, 18
Gayssot, Guy, 78
generic fascism, 36, 95, 123, 151–52, 193n17
genocide, 77
Gentile, Emilio, 40, 43, 45, 46–47, 114

Gentile, Giovanni
    death, 139
    Del Noce on, 137–38
    discussed, 25, 91, 136–37, 149, 200n22
    Doctrine of Fascism, The, 143
    "*Due Anni Dopo*," 138
    fascist vision, 142–44
    I fondamenti della filosofia del diritto, 142–43
    La Dottrina politica del fascismo, 139
    La Filosofia di Marx, 137
    on League of Nations, 144
    on *Risorgimento*, 137
    Rosmini e Gioberti, 139
    Teoria generale dello spirito come atto puro, 142
    What Is Fascism?, 162
George Kennan (Congdon), 181n63
German Communist Party, 59
German Democratic Party, 182n72
German Evangelical Church, 84
German Federal Republic, 4, 6, 22, 85
German ideology, 137
German Labor Front, 167
German National Bolsheviks, 40
German National People's Party, 135
German National Socialism, 1, 29, 30, 143
German Nationalists, 37
German Second Republic, 69
German Social Democrats, 67
Gesellschaft und Demokratie in Deutschland (Dahrendorf), 164
Gewerbetreibende, 37
Gilles (La Rochelle), 105–06, 196n23, 196n29, 196n32
Gilles Gambier (character in *Gilles*), 106, 108–11, 113, 196n23, 196n29
Giolitti, Giovanni, 180n61
Giovanni Gentile: Per una interpretazione filosofica della storia contemporanea (Del Noce), 176n19, 193n9, 201n27
Giovanni Gentile: Philosopher of Fascism (Gregor), 138–39
Giovinezza (song), 124
Gnosticism, 47
Goebbels, Paul Joseph, 167
Goldberg, Jonah
    discussed, 194n27
    Liberal Fascism, 8–9, 98–100, 194n27, 194n30
Golden Dawn, 79–80
Goldhagen, Daniel, 84
Goldstein (character in *1984*), 49
Gollwitzer, Heinz
    discussed, 81
    Weltpolitik und deutsche Geschichte, 190n58
Golsan, Richard, 78
Gombos, Julius, 80
Gordon, David, 74
Gran Consiglio, 114
Grand Council of Fascism, 46
Grandi, Dino, 198n62
Gravelli, Asvero
    Antieuropa, 112
    discussed, 9, 117, 126, 128
    "*Verso l'internazionale fascista*," 115, 116
Gray, John, 195n38
Greater Britain, The (O. Mosley), 120
Greater Romania Party, 76, 79
Gregor, A. James
    on *Carta del Lavoro*, 27
    compared to J. Lukacs, 19
    compared to Nolte, 13, 18–19, 22, 27
    compares fascists to Marxist-Leninists, 40
    on *Critica Fascista*, 115
    discussed, 3, 23, 24, 87, 126–27
    and *European*, 123
    on fascism as a movement of the Left, 92–93
    on fascism in the Third World, 22–23
    on fascist ideology, 19
    on G. Gentile, 136
    Giovanni Gentile: Philosopher of Fascism, 138–39
Griffin, Roger
    discussed, 3, 13–14
    on modernism, 159–60, 162
    Modernism and Fascism, 159
    on reactionary modernism, 161
Gropius, Walter, 160
groupthink, 50

Guérin, Daniel, 25
guillotine, 135
Gumplowicz, Heinrich, 142

H

Habermas, Jürgen
    discussed, 64, 69–70, 82, 163
    dispute with Nolte, 70–71
    at lecture, 204n15
    Sternhell on, 203n14
    and Third Reich, 187n29
Habsburg monarchy, 90
Hagel, Chuck, 152–53
Haider, Jörg, 76, 77, 79
Hanisch, Ernst
    Der lange Schatten des Staates, 179n48
Hardt, Michael
    Empire, 74
Harris, H. S.
    discussed, 201n33
    Social Philosophy of Giovanni Gentile, The, 143
Havers, Grant, 47
Hayek, Friedrich, 7
    Road to Serfdom, 96
Hegel, Georg Wilhelm Friedrich
    discussed, 60, 132, 138, 144, 152
    Mannheim on, 130
    Marx on, 71
Heidegger, Martin
    Being and Time, 131
Heitmann, Stefan, 191–92n66
Herbert Butterfield (McIntyre), 185n40
Herf, Jeffrey, 23
Herrschaftsformen, 62
Hilferding, Rudolf, 26
Himmelfarb, Gertrude
    discussed, 185n40
    "Whigged Out," 184n40
Himmler, Heinrich, 166
historical science, 173
Hitler, Adolf
    Arendt on, 51
    and Austria, 31
    and class system, 51
    compared to Stalin, 5, 51, 54, 55
    on dictatorship, 171
    discussed, 1, 162, 165
    and economy, 100
    and Eliot, 161
    and fascist movements, 36
    Final Solution, 84
    government of, 53
    and Hungary, 33
    influences, 170
    and Jews, 1
    and Jünger, 160
    Linz on, 5
    Mein Kampf, 120
    and Mitford, 119
    and Mussolini, 8
    Nolte on, 175n3
    Panagiotaros on, 79
    Payne on, 32
    and Planned Capitalist State, 96
    and Reichswehr, 171
    as revolutionary, 163, 166
    and Schacht, 40
    and science, 166–67
    scientific racism, 24
    and Seyss-Inquart, 33
    and Slavs, 1
    and social radicals, 39–40
    von Kleist-Schmenzin on, 135
    and Work Order Act, 168
Hitler: The Politics of Seduction (Zitelmann), 23–24
Hitler: Selbstverständnis eines Revolutionärs (Zitelmann), 166
Hitlerjugend, 8, 70
Hitler's Thirty Days to Power (Turner), 207n24
Hjalmar Schacht: Confessions of the "Old Wizard" (Schacht), 181n72
Hjalmar Schacht: For and Against Hitler (Peterson), 181n72
Hobsbawm, Eric
    "Chile," 178n30
    discussed, 27
Hollande, François, 84
Hollander, Paul
    Political Pilgrims, 54

Holmes, Stephen, 155
Holocaust, 58, 78, 82, 85, 191–92n66. *See also* anti-Semitism; Final Solution; Jews
Holocaust in American Life, The (Novick), 83–84
Homage to Catalonia (Orwell), 183n15
Horkheimer, Max
  and American Jewish Committee conference, 69
  Authoritarian Personality, The, 7, 66
  Dialectic of the Enlightenment, The, 65, 187n29
  discussed, 62, 70
  and Frankfurt School, 59, 60
  on Schopenhauer, 65
  and *Studien über Autorität und Familie*, 63
  and *Studies in Prejudice*, 61
  and *TAP*, 61
Horowitz, David, 101
Horthy, Miklós, 33, 80, 146
hot politics, 154
House Un-American Activities Committee, 66
Hume, David
  discussed, 156
  "Of the Original Contract," 203n13
  Sternhell on, 203n13
Hungary, 32, 80, 190n54

I

I fondamenti della filosofia del diritto (G. Gentile), 142–43
Ideen zur Staats-und Kultursoziologie (A. Weber), 199n8
Ideengestalt, 76
Ideology and Utopia (Mannheim), 129, 130, 131
Il Duce, 28, 123. *See also* Mussolini, Benito
Iliescu, Ion, 55
Illusions of Progress, The (Sorel), 145
Imatz, Arnaud, 140, 201n25
In Defense of Freedom (Meyer), 98
Independent Labour, 29
Institute for Social Research. *See also* Frankfurt School
  and anti-Semitism, 62
  Authoritarian Society, The, 61
  reestablished in Frankfurt, 73
  Studien über Autoritmät und Familie, 63
  TAP, 61, 63, 64, 65–66, 67
integral nationalism, 20
internazionale rossa, 117
Interpretations of Fascism (De Felice), 42, 45
Iron Guard, 18, 34, 79, 125–26, 180n56
Islamofascist Awareness Week, 101
"It Just Happened," 187n23
Italienischer Faschismus als "Export"-Artikel (1927–1935) (Scholz), 113–14

J

Jabotinsky, Vladimir, 18
Jacobins, 125
Jaspers, Karl, 54
Jens, Walter, 69, 70
Jewish quotas, 80
Jews. *see also* anti-Semitism; Final Solution; Holocaust
  in Communist Party, 79
  exclusion from German professional and political life, 99
  in France, 77, 84, 192n70
  in Germany, 53
  and Gilles, 109, 110
  and Giovanni Gentile, 200n22
  and La Rochelle, 106
  in Romania, 34–35
Jobbik Magyarorzagert Mozgalom, 76
Jobbik Party, 76, 79, 80
Jospin, Lionel, 55, 77
Journal of Abnormal and Social Psychology, 67
Joyce, William, 120–21, 198n58
Jünger, Ernst, 54, 147, 160, 177n9

K

Kahn, Jean, 86
Kaiser, Benedikt
  Phänomen Inselfaschismus, 198n67

Kallen, Horace, 96
Kant, Immanuel, 203n14
Kauder, Volker, 154
Kelpanides, Michael, 72, 73, 75
Kennan, George F., 37, 140
Kennedy, John F., 46
Kershaw, Ian, 168
Khrushchev, Nikita, 52–53
Kirchheimer, Otto, 59
Kirk, Russell
   discussed, 97, 103, 149
   Eliot and His Age, 205n10
Kirkpatrick, Jeane
   "Dictatorships and Double Standards," 184n36
Kocka, Jürgen, 205n1
Kondylis, Panajotis
   Conservatism, 133
   discussed, 104, 157
Krüger, Uwe
   Meinungsmacht, 190n58
Kultur, 71

L

La Dottrina politica del fascismo (G. Gentile), 139
La droite révolutionnaire (Sternhell), 20
La Filosofia di Marx (G. Gentile), 137
La Rochelle, Pierre Drieu
   discussed, 106
   "Doriot ou la vie d'un ouvrier français," 196n32
   Gilles, 105, 196n23, 196n29, 196n32
   Reveuse bourgeoisie, 196n32
Labour Party, 29, 119
l'Apocalypse, 109
Laqueur, Walter
   Europe since Hitler, 189–90n50
Lasch, Christopher, 66, 154
Last European War, The (J. Lukacs), 18
Lateran Pact, 25, 28, 114, 138
Latin authoritarianism, 125–26
Latin heritage, 125
Le Journal du Dimanche, 55
Le Pen, Jean-Marie, 77

Le Pen, Marine, 14–15, 77, 189n45
le Play, Frédéric, 141
Le Suicide Français (Zemmour), 192n70
League for Christian Defense, 125
League of Nations, 107, 111, 117, 144
Lebensraum, 166
Ledeen, Michael, 126, 194n27
Left, 152, 154
Lega Nord, 76
Legion of the Archangel Michael, 34, 79, 125
Leninism, 127
Leo XIII (pope), 31, 38
L'epoca della secolarizzazione (Del Noce), 90–91
LeRoy, Roland, 55
Les anti-Lumières du XVIIIe siècle à la guerre froide (Sternhell), 155
Les Troyens (Berlioz), 86
Levinson, Maria Herz, 64
Lévy, Elisabeth, 189n45
Lewin, Kurt, 68
Lewis, Wyndham, 160
Ley, Robert, 24, 167–68, 169
liberal antifascism, 100
Liberal Fascism (Goldberg), 8–9, 98–100, 194n27, 194n30
"L'iniziativa individuale" (Spirito), 178n36
l'Internazionale fascista, 127
Linz, Juan L.
   discussed, 5, 12, 48
   Totalitarian and Authoritarian Regimes, 5
Lipset, S. M., 66
Littlejohn, David
   Patriotic Traitors, 198n63
Loi Gayssot, 78
Loi Le Chapelier, 204n15
Lombard separatists, 76
London, Herb, 100
Lorin (character in *Gilles*), 109
Louis Ferdinand, Prince, 135
Louis-Napoléon, Emperor, 38
Louis-Philippe, King, 86
Löwenthal, Leo, 59
Luhmann, Niklas, 73, 154–55
Lukacs, Georg

Destruction of Reason, The, 132
    discussed, 155
Lukacs, John
    compared to Gregor, 19
    discussed, 95
    Last European War, The, 18
Lukes, Steven, 74
L'Unità del mondo (Campi), 191n60

M

MacDonald, Ramsay, 119
Machtfrage, 104
Mackey, John, 100
MacLeish, Archibald, 68
macrofascism, 102, 103
makeweights, 89
managerial control, 49
Managerial Revolution, The (Burnham), 26, 49
Manchestrian economics, 38
"Manifesto of the Members of the Belgian Labor Party," 30
Mann, Thomas, 116
Mannheim, Karl
    "Conservatism," 94
    discussed, 132, 133, 140, 157
    Ideology and Utopia, 129, 130, 131
Manoilescu, Mihail, 34
March on Rome, 10, 12, 17, 80, 138
Marcuse, Herbert
    discussed, 59, 60, 61–62
    Reason and Revolution, 60, 132
Marinetti, Filippo, 160, 162
Marrus, Michael, 33
Marx, Karl
    Das Kapital, 72
    discussed, 27, 131, 137–38, 138
    Eighteenth Brumaire of Louis Bonaparte, The, 71–72
Maschke, Günter, 75
mass democracy, 50
mass murders, 53, 55, 58, 77, 78
Matteoti, Giacomo, 31
Maurice Morel (character in *Gilles*), 108
Maurras, Charles

Action Française, 108
    discussed, 109, 111–12, 141, 161
Mazzini, Giuseppe, 36
McIntyre, Kenneth B.
    Herbert Butterfield, 185n40
Mead, Margaret, 68
Meiji Restoration, 93
Mein Kampf (Hitler), 120
Meinecke, Friedrich, 53–54
Meinungsmacht (Krüger), 190n58
men of the Archangel, 125
Merkel, Angela, 6, 67, 154
Meyer, Frank S.
    In Defense of Freedom, 98
Michaloliakas, Nikos, 79
microfascism, 102, 103
military dictatorships, 22
Minima Moralia (Adorno), 60
Mitford, Diana, 119, 121, 124
Mitscherlich, Alexander
    Die Unfähigkeit zu trauern, 82–83
Mitscherlich, Margarete
    Die Unfähigkeit zu trauern, 82–83
Moa, Pio, 3–4
Modernism and Fascism (Griffin), 159
modernization, 164–65, 170
Montesquieu
    Persian Letters, 155
Montreux conferences, 114. See also Fascist International Congress
Mosley, Cynthia, 119
Mosley, Nicholas
    Beyond the Pale, 123
    discussed, 120, 121
Mosley, Oswald Ernald
    Alternative, The, 121
    as authoritarian modernizer, 119
    and BUF, 119, 120, 121
    and Churchill, 119
    discussed, 9, 18, 29, 105, 118
    European, 122–23
    and FDR, 119
    on *Firing Line*, 123
    Greater Britain, The, 120
    incarceration/house arrest, 121
    and Joyce, 120–21
    lectures by, 123

My Life, 123
and Nicolson, 119
"Philosophy of Fascism, The," 120
and phlebitis, 121
and Rothermere, 120
and Sieff, 120
Skidelsky on, 118, 119, 121, 122
and Strachey, 119
and Union Movement, 121
visits Germany, 124
visits Italy, 123
Motza, Ion, 34, 125
Movimento Sociale Italiano, 128
Müller, Adam, 38, 130
Murdoch Media Empire, 8
Mussert, Anton Adriaan, 32, 33
Mussolini, Benito. *See also Il Duce*
and *Aeneid*, 86
and *ambienti industriali*, 40
and *Anything Goes*, 96
and *Carta del Lavoro*, 28
and *datori del lavoro*, 28, 40
discussed, 114, 133
Dottrina del Fascismo, 194n30
and economy, 100
and experiment, 30
and Fascist International Congress, 17
Gombos on, 80
and Gravelli, 117
Gregor on, 27
and Hitler, 8, 30, 151
introduces anti-Semitic legislation, 200n22
invades Ethiopia, 9, 86, 88, 114, 117
and Lateran Pact, 25, 28, 114, 138
and *Les Troyens*, 86
and March on Rome, 10, 12, 16, 80, 138
and O. Mosley, 120
and Nazi Germany, 88, 114
1930 address by, 128
and Olivetti, 40
picture in *New York Post*, 202n43
and proposal for missionary international fascist organization, 118
and Protestant Reformation, 112
and Scholz, 114

and Spanish Civil War, 8
tracts and speeches by, 136
Mussolini and Fascism (Diggins), 30
"Mussolini contra Lutero" (Fanelli), 112
Mussolini il duce (De Felice), 43
Mutterrecht (Bachofen), 63
My Life (O. Mosley), 123
mystical revolution, 115
myth of Progress, 154

N

Nasjonal Samling, 32
Nationaal Socialistische Bewiging, 32
National Democratic Party (NDP), 21–22, 78, 189–90n50
National Front, 76, 77
National German People's Party, 165
National Review, 97, 98, 101, 123
National Socialist Industrial Cell Organization, 168
National Socialists, 39
national syndicalism, 141
National Trade Union Club, 121
National Union for Social Justice, 29
Nationaldemokratische Partei Deutschlands, 77
Nationalismus und Demokratie im Frankreich der dritten Republik (1871 bis 1918) (Frank), 177n9
Nationalsozialistische Betriebszellenorganisation, 168
Nazi Left, 171
Nazi Party Platform, 99
Nazi propaganda, 166, 206n20
Nazi race policies, 99
Nazi speeches, 170
Nazism/Nazis, 18, 58, 60–61, 166
NDP (National Democratic Party), 21–22, 78, 189–90n50
negative dialectic, 60
Negative Dialektik (Adorno), 60
Negri, Antonio
Empire, 74
Nenni, Pietro, 30
neofascism, 74, 75, 76, 77, 78

neo-Marxists, 72, 74, 75
Nera, Camicia, 124
Neuheidnische Strömungen im italienischen Faschismus, 112
Neumann, Franz, 25
New Criterion, The, 102–3
New Deal Democratic Party, 29
New Deal/New Dealers, 7, 96
New Left, 27, 47, 58, 100
New Order, 14
New Party, 105, 119, 120, 124
New Republic, The, 7, 88, 96
new right, 189n45
New Statesman, 123
Ni droite ni gauche (Sternhell), 20
Nicolson, Harold, 119
Niekisch, Ernst, 40, 181n70, 200n16
Niemeyer, Gerhart, 49
Nietzsche, Friedrich, 20, 144, 152
Night of the Long Knives, 39, 171
1984 (Orwell), 49
Nisbet, Robert
    discussed, 49, 148–49
    Quest for Community, The, 148
    Sociology of Emile Durkheim, The, 148–49
Nkrumah, Kwame, 22
Nock, Albert J., 7, 97
Nolte, Ernst
    compared to Del Noce, 10–11
    compared to Gregor, 12–13, 18–19, 22, 27
    Der europäische Bürgerkreig, 18
    Der Faschismus in seiner Epoche, 3, 18
    discussed, 16
    dispute with Habermas, 70–71
    and epochal character, 26–27
    and escape from transcendence, 10, 17, 132, 141
    European Civil War, The, 18
    and European civil war, 72
    Faschismus, von Mussolini zu Hitler, 21
    on fascism, 1–2, 21, 151
    and fascist ideology, 18–19
    and fascist vision, 142
    and Furet, 10–11, 17
    on German National Socialism, 143
    on Hitler, 175n3
    influences, 26
    on Nazism, 1
    on NDP, 21–22, 78–79
    on practical transcendence, 140
    and radical fascists, 32
    Späte Reflexionen, 175n3
    and Zitelmann, 167
November Revolution, 171
Novemberverbrecher, 171
Novick, Peter
    Holocaust in American Life, The, 83
Nuremberg Court/Trials, 68, 75, 78, 83

O

Oakeshott, Michael, 49, 50
Obama, Barack, 9, 99, 100
ochlocracy, 180n62
O'Connor (character in *Gilles*), 106, 107
Of Power (de Jouvenel), 88–89
"Of the Original Contract" (Hume), 203n13
Office of Strategic Services, 61
Olivetti, Gino, 40
Olivier, Philippe, 86
ontololgical negation, 49
Orban, Victor, 79, 190n54
Order of Creation, 134
Organization of Strategic Services, 68
Origins of Totalitarianism, The (Arendt), 7, 43, 52, 103
Ortega, Onésimo Redondo, 157
Orwell, George
    discussed, 48
    Homage to Catalonia, 183n15
    1984, 49

P

Paetel, Karl Otto, 181n70
Pan, David
    "Adorno's Failed Aesthetic of Myth," 187–88n29
Panagiotaros, Ilias, 79

Pan-Europa (von Coudenhove-Kalergi), 116
Paneuropean Movement, 116
Parti Ouvrier et Paysan Français, 29
Parti Populaire Français (PPF), 28, 196n32
Parti Rexiste, 32, 35
Parti Socialiste de France, 29
partido único, 33
Partidu Romania Mare, 76
Paterson, T. G.
  "Red Fascism," 47–48
Patriotic Traitors (Littlejohn), 198n63
Paul, Rand, 99
Paul, Ron, 29
Pavelitsch, Ante, 32
Paxton, Robert O.
  discussed, 33, 41
  Vichy France, 192n70
  Vichy France and the Jews, 192n70
Payne, Stanley
  compared to Imatz, 201n25
  and definition of fascism, 35, 36
  discussed, 19–20, 94, 146
  on *El Fascio*, 157–58
  Fascism, 20
  on Hitler, 32
  on Vichy France, 33
Peasant Party, 32
Pellizzi, Camillo, 124, 126
permanent revolution, 9, 118
Peron, Juan, 14
Pershing missiles, 75
Persian Letters (Montesquieu), 155
Peterson, Edward Norman
  Hjalmar Schacht: For and Against Hitler, 181n72
Phänomen Inselfaschismus (Frölich/Kaiser), 198n67
Philosophiefakultäten, 183n27
"Philosophy of Fascism, The" (O. Mosley), 120
phlebitis, 121
Picasso, Pablo, 160
Pirandello, Luigi, 160
Pius XI (pope), 31, 38
planisme, 30
Planned Capitalist State, 96
Planned Economy, 96

Platon, Mircea
  discussed, 180n56
  "Iron Guard and the Modern State, The," 177n6
poetry, 83
Pole (character in *Gilles*), 106, 107
political exotica, 178n30
Political Pilgrims (Hollander), 54
political religion, 45, 46–47, 48
Politics (Aristotle), 116
Pollock, Friedrich, 59
Popular Front, 29, 147, 205n10
Porter, Cole
  Anything Goes, 96
postfascism, 128
Pound, Ezra, 123, 160
PPF (Parti Populaire Français), 28, 196n32
practical transcendence, 140
prehistory, 27
prejudice
  conference, 69
  discussed, 66, 186–87n19
  and F-scale testing, 67
  Studies in Prejudice, 61
  TAP, 61
Preussentum und Sozialismus (Spengler), 171
Prinz, Michael, 163
private initiative, 28
private self-affirmation, 178n36
Progressive Era, 98
Protestant Reformation, 90, 112
Protocols of the Elders of Zion, The, 34
Putin, Vladimir, 14–15, 101

Q

Quest for Community, The (Nisbet), 148
question of power, 104
questionnaires, 68
Quisling, Abraham Vidkun, 32, 95

R

Rabehl, Bernd, 75
radical fascism, 1, 2, 139, 142

radical politics, 93–94
Radical Socialists, 110
Ramos, Ramiro Ledesma, 29, 140, 157
Randgruppen, 62
Rassemblement National Populaire, 29
Rassengegensätzlichkeit, 142
reactionary modernism, 57, 161
Reason and Revolution (Marcuse), 60, 132
Red Brigades, 74
Red fascism, 48
"Red Fascism" (Adler/Paterson), 47–48
redemptive myths, 145
reeducation/reeducators, 67–68, 69, 73, 74, 75
Reflections on Violence (Sorel), 145
Reichswehr, 171
Republican Party, 152
Restoration Era, 131
Reveuse bourgeoisie (La Rochelle), 196n32
Revolutionary Right, 125
Right, 152, 154
Risorgimento, 137, 149, 180n61
Ritter, Gerhard, 81
Ritter, Joachim, 81
Road to Serfdom (von Hayek), 96
Rocco, Alfredo, 25, 28, 36
Röhm, Ernst, 171
Rohrmoser, Günter, 81
romantic-conservative counterutopia, 130
Roosevelt, Franklin Delano (FDR), 7, 30, 88, 119, 190n54
Rosenberg, Alfred, 166
Rosmini e Gioberti (G. Gentile), 139
Rothbard, Murray N., 97
Rothermere, Lord, 120
Rousseau, Jean-Jacques, 134

S

Salazar, Antonio de Oliviera, 14, 31, 37
Salò Republic, 32, 39, 91, 200n22
Salvatorelli, Luigi, 45
Salvemini, Gaetano, 45
Sarfatti, Margherita, 26
Sartori, Giovanni, 154
Schacht, Hjalmar
  discussed, 40, 181–82n72
  Hjalmar Schacht: Confessions of the "Old Wizard," 181n72
Schatten der Vergangenheit, 167
Scheil, Stefan
  discussed, 73
  Transatlantische Wechselwirkung, 190n58
Schelsky, Helmut, 49, 73, 81, 82, 162
Schimmer, Arne, 189n50
Schivelbusch, Wolfgang
  Entfernte Verwandtschaft, 30, 88
Schmitt, Carl
  Die Diktatur, 171
  discussed, 38–39, 81, 82, 169, 191n60
Schoenbaum, David, 170
Scholz, Beate
  discussed, 127
  Italienischer Faschismus als "Export"-Artikel (1927–1935), 113–14
Schönere Zukunft, 112
Schopenhauer, Arthur, 65
Schröder, Gerhard, 67
science, 52, 166–67
scientific racism, 24
Second Empire, 75, 81, 172
secret police, 44, 53
selective identitarianism, 156
Senghor, Leopold, 22
Seyss-Inquart, Arthur, 33
Shapiro, J. Salwyn, 155
Shapiro, Leonard
  Totalitarianism, 55–56
Sidelsky, Robert, 118–19, 121–22
Sieff, Israel, 120
six point syndrome, 56
Sixty-Eighters, 75, 190n58
Smelser, Ronald, 167–68
social engineering, 50, 67
Social Justice, 29
social mobility, 206n18
Social Philosophy of Giovanni Gentile, The (Harris), 143
social sciences, 162
social statistics, 162, 173
Sociology of Emile Durkheim, The (Nisbet), 148–49

soft despotism, 50
Solzhenitsyn, Aleksandr, 49
Sonderweg, 163
Sorel, Georges
    discussed, 20, 144–45, 161, 162
    Illusions of Progress, The, 145
    Reflections on Violence, 145
Soucy, Robert, 117
Soule, George, 96
Soviet-Nazi Non-Aggression Pact, 146
Spampanato, Bruno, 128
Spanish Civil War
    discussed, 25, 33, 106, 141
    and Mussolini, 8
Spanish Republicans, 29
Spann, Othmar, 74
Späte Reflexionen (Nolte), 175n3
Spengler, Oswald
    discussed, 146, 152, 162
    Preussentum und Sozialismus, 171
Spirito, Ugo
    discussed, 28, 39, 137
    "Economia programmatica," 178n36
    "L'iniziativa individuale," 178n36
Spraul, Gunter
    Der Fischer-Komplex, 188–89n42, 206n19
Springer, Axel, 82
Stahl, Friedrich, 130, 134, 148
Stalin, Joseph
    Arendt on, 51
    and class system, 51
    and collectivization of agriculture, 54
    compared to Hitler, 54
    compared to Khrushchev, 53
    and cult of personality, 53
    death of, 52
    discussed, 186n13
    Jospin on, 77
Ständestaat, 133
Stavisky, Serge Alexandre, 109–10
Stavisky Affair, 109
Stern, Fritz, 165
Sternberger, Dolf, 163
Sternhell, Zeev
    and definition of fascism, 35
    discussed, 156–57, 177n9, 203–4n14

    and fascist minimum, 35
    Founding Myths of Israel, The, 203n12
    on Habermas, 203n14
    on Hume, 203n13
    on Kant, 203n14
    La droite révolutionnaire, 20
    lecture by, 204n15
    Les anti-Lumières du XVIIIe siècle à la guerre froide, 155
    Ni droite ni gauche, 20
    on spiritualism, 201n34
    as super-Zionist, 155–56
Strachey, John, 119
Strasser, Gregor, 39
Strasser, Otto, 39, 123
Strauss, Leo, 140
Stresa Front, 31
Studien über Autoritmät und Familie (Institute for Social Research), 63
Studies in Prejudice (American Jewish Committee), 61, 69, 76
Stürmer, Michael, 81, 190n58
Stuttgart Confession of Guilt, 84
subversives, 37
Suster, Roberto, 116–17
Syriza Party, 79–80
Szálasi, Ferenc, 32

T

TAP (Institute for Social Research), 61, 63, 64, 65–66, 67
Teoria generale dello spirito come atto puro (G. Gentile), 142
terror, 5, 44
tessere del partito, 26
"Theme of Indivisibility in the Post-War Struggle against Prejudice in the United States, The" (Whitfield), 186–87n19
Third Reich
    discussed, 53, 78
    J. Lukacs on, 18
    and modernization, 164–65
    and social sciences, 162
    and social statistics, 173
Third Republic, 20, 106, 108

Third World dictatorships, 92–93, 151
Thomism, 31
Thomsen, Thorsten, 189n50
Tilitzki, Christian
  Die deutsche Universitätsphilosophie in der Weimarer Republik und im Dritten Reich, 183n27
Tismaneanu, Vladimir, 55
Tory Democrats, 136
Totalitarian and Authoritarian Regimes (Linz), 5
Totalitarian Rule (Buchheim), 43
totalitarianism
  Arendt on, 51
  Brezezinski on, 53
  and the Cold War, 47
  discussed, 43, 44, 48, 50, 170
  and managerial control, 49
Totalitarianism (Shapiro), 55–56
Touré, Ahmed Sékou, 22
tradesmen, 37
Transatlantische Wechselwirkung (Scheil), 190n58
transfuges, 28
trauern, 83
Treuhänder der Arbeit, 168
Trittin, Jürgen, 67
Tudor, Corneliu Vadim, 76
Tugwell, Rexford, 7, 30, 96
Turner, Henry Ashby
  discussed, 170
  Hitler's Thirty Days to Power, 207n24
Twentieth Party Congress, 53

U

Umerzieher, 75
Union Movement, 121
Ustashi, 32, 33
utopia, 130–31

V

Venice Declaration, 127
Vergangenheitsbewältigung, 68

Versailles Treaty, 173
Verso l'internazionale fascista (Gravelli), 115, 116
Vichy France, 30, 33, 84, 192n70
Vidal, Gore, 100
Virgil
  Aeneid, 86
Voegelin, Eric, 45, 47, 103, 170
volkspädagogische, 165
Vollblutmarxisten, 64
von Baader, Franz, 38
von Beckerath, Erwin, 46
von Bismarck, Otto, 38, 169
von Coudenhove-Kalergi, Richard Nikolaus
  discussed, 117
  Pan-Europa, 116
von Habsburg, Otto, 90, 116
von Hassell, Ulrich, 50
von Hayek, Friedrich
  Road to Serfdom, 96
von Hindenburg, Paul, 134
von Ketteler, Wilhelm Emmanuel, 141
von Kuehnelt-Leddihn, Erik
  discussed, 37, 89–90, 97
  Left, The, 87, 90
von Kleist-Schmenzin, Ewald, 134–35
von Moltke, Helmuth, 206n19
von Papen, Franz, 134
von Salomon, Ernst
  Der Fragebogen, 187n23
von Savigny, Karl, 130
von Schleicher, Kurt, 134
von Schönerer, Georg Ritter, 37–38
von Thadden, Adolf, 189–90n50
von Vogelsang, Karl, 38
von Weizsäcker, Ernst, 85
von Weizsäcker, Richard, 85

W

Wagner, Gottfried, 86
Wagner, Richard, 86
Wallerstein, Immanuel, 74
Walter (character in *Gilles*), 106–8
War for Righteousness, The (Gamble), 182n9

Weber, Alfred
   discussed, 132
   Ideen zur Staats-und Kultursoziologie, 199n8
Weber, Eugen, 3, 125, 180n56
Weber, Max, 36, 63
Wehler, Hans-Ulrich, 164, 205n1
Weil, Felix, 59
Weimar Republic, 172–173, 206n18
Weissmann, Karlheinz
   Die Konservative Revolution in Deutschland 1918-1932, 184n28
   discussed, 204n15
Weitz, Eric D., 77
welfare state
   discussed, 8, 88, 91, 126, 148
   expansion of, 99, 100
   and FDR, 7
Weltanschauung, 152
Weltpolitik und deutsche Geschichte (Gollwitzer), 190n58
"We're all fascists now" (Koppelman), 194n30
Westbindung, 173
What Is Fascism? (G. Gentile), 162
"Whigged Out" (Himmelfarb), 184n40
Whitfield, Stephen J.
   "Theme of Indivisibility in the Post-War Struggle against Prejudice in the United States, The," 186–87n19
Whole Foods, 100
Wieviorka, Michel, 77
Wiggershaus, Rolf
   Adorno, 187n29
   Die Frankfurter Schule, 187n29
   discussed, 66
Wilhelm I (emperor), 38
Wilhelm II (kaiser), 169
Will, George F., 101
Wissenssoziologie, 132
Wodehouse, P. G., 96
Wohin treibt unsere Republik (Zitelmann), 191–92n66
Work Order Act, 168
Wühler, 37

Y

Yeats, William Butler, 160

Z

Zehrer, Hans, 81–82
Zemmour, Eric
   Le Suicide Français, 192n70
Zhukov, Georgy, 52–53
Zitelmann, Rainer
   discussed, 13, 169, 170–73
   on Hitler, 40, 165
   Hitler: The Politics of Seduction, 23–24
   Hitler: Selbstverständnis eines Revolutionärs, 166
   on Nazis, 163–64
   on Nolte, 167
   Wohin treibt unsere Republik, 191–